The African American Woman's Health Book

D1073265

The African American Woman's Health Book

A Guide to the Prevention and Cure of Illness

Valiere Alcena M.D., F.A.C.P.

Published by Barricade Books Inc.
185 Bridge Plaza North, Suite 308-A
Fort Lee, NJ 07024

Library of Congress Cataloging-in-Publication Data
Alcena, Valiere.
    The African American woman's health book / Valiere Alcena.
        p.cm.
    Includes bibliographic references.
    1. Afro-American women--Health and hygiene. I. Title.

RA778.4.A36 A38 2001
613'04244'08996073--dc21

                                                00-063034

Printed in the United States of America.

First Printing

Contents

I would like to thank my friend Alison Berry for all the help that she provided in preparing and organizing the manuscript for this book.

Preface

This book is written in memory of my mother, Florisane Lacoste, who died while giving birth to her seventh child at age thirty-seven, and also to honor the memories of my brothers and sisters who died without medical care.

While being attended by a midwife, it became obvious that my mother's baby was a breech. The midwife called for a physician, who showed up twelve hours later—my mother hemorrhaged; she and the baby died.

My mother was a caring, loving, extremely beautiful woman of African heritage. Her untimely death devastated her entire family.

My older sister, Lisamaine, died of an undiagnosed abdominal disease that caused her constant pain. My sisters, Esperanta and Vierge, also died of easily preventable diseases—malnutrition and parasitic infestations among them—due to grossly neglectful medical care. My oldest brother simply collapsed in the road in Carrefour Laville in the early eighties and died. He'd never received medical treatment.

My youngest brother, Grecet, was the genius of the family. He attended the village school faithfully, barefooted, and earned a perfect score on the Certificat d'Etude Primaire. Grecet died of a perforated appendix a few months after graduating high school.

I remember his swollen abdomen and cries of pain, teeth rattling, drenched in feverish sweat as he lay on a mat at my grandfather's house in Carrefour Laville. He was to have started college in a few weeks.

The village of Carrefour Laville had no hospital, public or private, and my elderly grandfather did not have the money to take him to the hospital in St. Marc, many miles away. He received no medical care.

My sisters and brothers died like paupers and vagrants under the most miserable human conditions imaginable. The family my mother worked so hard to create with love, grace, and an intense desire for success disintegrated because of Third World medical conditions within which the impoverished must live. This is an injustice that must be rectified. It is in that spirit that I have written this book.

It took five years for me to assemble these essential instructions for maintaining health. It is written in their memory, especially that of my mother, whom I love with the most intense love a son can have for a mother. What I could not do for them, I hope to do here for all of you.

Introduction

There exists a health crisis in the black communities of the United States of America. There are about forty-five million individuals with no health insurance coverage, most of whom simply cannot afford its cost.

The majority of blacks reside at the bottom of the American financial ladder. Being black and poor places men and women in the precarious position of skimping on the necessities of life. Health insurance is often the most neglected of these necessities.[1]

The percentage of uninsured working black women is several times higher than their white counterparts. *Most of these black women don't seek medical care until a crisis because they have no health insurance.* If they have a medical problem, they either go to the emergency room or simply ignore it. Thus, the emergency room becomes the healthcare provider.

Black women who are unemployed and on welfare are usually on Medicaid and visit Medicaid clinics or the offices of the few physicians who accept Medicaid insurance.

The list of black women's medical problems when they are forced, in agony, to seek help is longer than that of white women. Often very high blood pressure exists that was never diagnosed before, or if diagnosed was not properly treated. The same can be said for diabetes, glaucoma, anemia, blood in the stool, a mass in the breast, a lesion in the skin, a lump in the groin, a lump under the arm, an unrepaired hernia, cataracts, coughing blood, recurring headache, prolonged vaginal bleeding, vaginal pain, abdominal pain, back pain, shortness of breath, chest pain, recurrent diarrhea or constipation...the list goes on and on. All of these conditions have dire consequences.

Medicaid, the system for welfare, is ineffective. It pays the least amount of money to physicians to provide medical care for Medicaid recipients. A physician in New York who sees a medicaid patient for a physical examination in his or her office is paid more than if the patient were seen as an in-patient at the hospital. However, doctors receive the largest fees for treating medicaid patients at a hospital-run clinic. A bill is being proposed by the New York State Legislature to increase the office fee for Medicaid patients from the present rate of *seven* dollars to *thirty dollars!*

It's easy to see why the care given to Medicaid patients is marginal. Competent physicians are not likely to see patients for such low pay. The reality is that health care providers who provide medical care to Medicaid patients must, by necessity, see seventy-five to one hundred patients per day in order to barely make a living.

No physician, no matter how competent and committed, can provide proper care for so many patients, whose medical problems have become acute. The irony is that the worst medical care is given to groups with the most serious and complicated health problems.

Health Maintenance Organizations (HMOs) have not helped the health care problems of poor black men, women, and children.

The health care industry is an eight-hundred-billion-dollar-industry, one of the biggest in the United States. HMOs got involved in the health care business because there was money to be made. They and their shareholders remain involved for the same reason.

They have a piece of Medicare and Medicaid, as well as commercial insurance. Some HMO companies have gotten out of Medicare because they have lost money, but their involvement in Medicaid continues to be financially viable.

Ninety percent of the providers that care for minorities are themselves minority professionals. But HMOs seem to have eliminate many black and Hispanic physicians as medical providers for Medicaid recipients, most of whom live in the inner cities and frequent clinics for medical care. They require that a physician be Board certified in order to be allowed to join HMO Medicaid plans as a provider; many fine minority doctors don't fall into this category.

Some HMOs are better than others. The better ones are less controlling. Medical care should be a right and not a privilege for a select few. A Patients' and Physicians' Bill of Rights is sorely needed to restore fairness to the health care system in the United States.

Congress should take responsibility and pass a law that allows Medicare to pay for prescription drugs. It is not only the elderly who are unable to afford expensive medications. Black female Medicare recipients who aren't elderly are also unable to pay for prescription drugs because of their financial status.

TURNING IT AROUND

Black women and other minorities can change their lives for the better by being disciplined, organized, purposeful, goal oriented, and especially by pursuing good health, in order to achieve meaningful goals. Most important of all, African Americans must pool their knowledge and resources to improve their collective health. In this way they will attain a better quality of life.

This book defines the major health problems that target black and other minority women. It outlines their source and provides solutions. It also seeks to outline roles that government and other health agencies can play in solving black women's health problems. Black women must be proactive to prevent the diseases to which they are particularly prone. It can be done through self-discipline and awareness. It is hoped that this book will serve as a resource not only for black women and the public at large but also for those in policy-making positions and academia.

Hypertension in African American Women

A note to the reader: the health issues discussed in this guide are interconnected. In the same way that the complex workings of our bodies function in cooperation with one another, illnesses and body functions overlap. Repetition of facts is occasionally necessary to provide a clear picture of the workings of the body. The frequency of certain explanations should help to clarify and reinforce what has already been learned.

Hypertension is one of the most common diseases in black women. It is associated with other diseases such as **obesity, diabetes and high lipids in the blood**.

What is hypertension?

Hypertension occurs when the **systolic** blood pressure is higher than normal and the **diastolic** blood pressure is higher than normal.

What is systolic blood pressure?

The **systolic** part of the blood pressure is the upper part of the number in the blood pressure reading machine. It's the amount of pressure exerted against the walls of the vessels.

What is a normal systolic blood pressure?
Normal systolic blood pressure ranges from 100 to an upper limit of 139.

What is diastolic blood pressure?
Diastolic blood pressure is the bottom part of the number on the blood pressure reading. It's the rate at which blood pulses through the vessels, in terms of beats per minute.

What is normal diastolic blood pressure?
A normal diastolic blood pressure ranges from 60 to an upper limit of 89.

CLASSIFICATION OF BLOOD PRESSURE IN ADULTS AGE 18 YEARS AND OLDER

CATEGORY	SYSTOLIC MM/HG	DIASTOLIC MM/HG
Normal	100-130	60-85
High Normal	130-139	85-89
Hypertension		
Stage I	140-159	90-99
Stage II	160-170	100-109
Stage III	180-209	110-119
Stage IV	210 or greater	120 or greater

(*Archives of Internal Medicine*, Volume 153, January 1993)

Taking Blood Pressure
The instruments needed to take blood pressure are:

1. A blood pressure cuff, attached to a manometer on which is listed numbers from 20 to 300 mm/Hg.

2. A stethoscope, placed on a pulsating artery, most often the artery at the bend on the inside part of the arm.

What to Watch in the Taking of Blood Pressure

Make sure the blood pressure cuff is neither too large or too small. If the cuff is too small, the blood pressure reads too high. If the cuff is too large, the reverse can happen; namely blood pressure will be read as too low.

Both errors can seriously impact the care of a patient being treated for hypertension. The patient can receive either too much or too little medication. Make sure that the blood pressure cuff is functioning properly before using it. In particular check to be sure that the blood pressure cuff is not leaking. If it's leaking air then it is sure to give a false reading.

Use a cuff that is appropriate for the size of the person. There are cuffs made to suit the needs of very large individuals. Using an undersized cuff to take the blood pressure of a person with a large arm can cause a false reading. For example, a person with a large arm whose blood pressure reading is 140/90 when using an undersized cuff, may in fact have a pressure of 130/80 when the proper cuff is used. This type of error must be avoided because the person's emotional state can be quite seriously affected when told erroneously that his or her pressure is high. An erroneously high blood pressure reading can adversely affect life insurance premiums, or sometimes prevent them from being insured at all.

The stethoscope being used to take the blood pressure should be in good working order, as it can also cause improper blood pressure readings as well. Be certain there are no holes in the diaphragm (the bottom part) of the stethoscope. Check the rubber tubing for holes and cracks. If these problems are found do not use it, because if air escapes while the doctor is trying to listen false readings may occur.

Automatic blood pressure machines are helpful, if you know

how to use them. Always take the blood pressure in three positions:

1. When the person is lying down.
2. When the person is sitting.
3. When the person has been standing up for at least 3 to 5 minutes.

Why is it important to take blood pressure in this way? Because most active individuals are either sitting up or standing up most of the time, and when they lie down, it's to sleep at night or nap during the day. Several antihypertensive medications work best when the patient is standing. Therefore, it's important to know what their blood pressure readings are in all three positions—standing, sitting, and lying.

If a person is bleeding or dehydrated, their blood pressure will drop when sitting or standing as compared to lying still. The pulse rate of somebody who has lost a lot of blood or fluid is likely to climb. This is the cause of **orthostatic hypotension**. (Orthostatic means caused by erect posture. Hypotension means abnormally low blood pressure.) That is, the pulse goes up and the blood pressure goes down. The pulse rate going up is a much stronger sign of orthostatic hypotension than the blood pressure dropping by itself.

Of course, the older the individual, the weaker the tone within the wall of their vessels. Standing the patient up can in itself cause the blood pressure to drop. These individuals have what is called a **wide pulse pressure**.

It takes a minimum of 1200 to 1800 cc of fluid or blood loss for orthostatic hypotension to occur. Again, it depends on the age and the size of the individual, because an older individual who has lost between 800 to 1000 cc may have his or her blood pressure drop significantly. This is because of their intravascular (inside the blood vessel) volume. The vessels become contracted with age. A younger person is more likely to tolerate the loss of 1800 cc of blood/fluid with only slight evidence of orthostasis as opposed to an older individual who might develop cardiovascular collapse on the same loss.

Other conditions that can cause an acute drop in blood pressure include:

1. too many antihypertension medications
2. heart attack
3. abnormal rhythms of the heart; too fast or too slow heart rate
4. severe infection in the blood, such as sepsis
5. oversensitivity of the carotid bodies, located in both sides of the neck

Vasovagal reaction can also cause blood pressure to drop. In fact, it can bring on collapse during emotional crisis. Vasovagal reaction in an older person with underlying cardiac disease can actually drop his or her blood pressure during a bowel movement. Straining activates the vasovagal reaction mechanism that brings blood pressure down. Severe vomiting with retching can cause an older individual to collapse as well.

It is necessary to take blood pressure in the elderly in both arms and, when feasible, lying down, sitting, and standing up as outlined above.

REVIEW:

As a person gets older he or she loses muscle elasticity within the blood vessels, resulting in what is called wide pulse pressure (a large difference between the systolic and diastolic blood pressure). A drop in blood pressure can occur in the standing position naturally in the elderly person and should not be automatically treated as a problem.

The Elderly

Although it is important to treat their hypertension, it is prudent to make all efforts not to be too aggressive with antihypertensive medications as they could cause too great a drop in the systolic blood pressure. The systolic blood pressure of an elderly person must remain in the range of 130 to 140 for proper **perfusion** to take place in the brain: in other words, for blood to flow properly into it. As the blood vessels of the veins become stiff and narrowed due to the accumulation of plaques, a higher systolic pressure is needed to push blood to the brain to deliver the necessary oxygen for proper brain function.

If medication forces the systolic blood pressure down too low in the elderly, stroke can occur. On the other hand, if the systolic blood pressure is allowed to remain too high, 170 to 180, for example, for too long a period of time the end result will also be stroke, heart attack, or congestive heart failure and possibly death.

HYPERTENSION'S ROOT CAUSES

The root causes of hypertension in black women are many. Chief among them are:
    1. Salt sensitivity
    2. Salt rich diet
    3. Obesity
    4. Stress
    5. Genetic salt sensitivity transferred from black women in Africa to the African American generations

Salt sensitivity is most responsible for hypertension in black women. The gene for salt sensitivity in blacks originated in Africa hundreds of years ago, in the bodies of blacks living under severe conditions.

The gene was necessary for survival. Working in the hot sun in the fields of Africa caused massive salt loss due to extreme perspiration. (Incidentally, the conditions that existed then persist for those who have to work the land in Africa and other tropical countries of the world.) Massive salt loss leads to water loss, resulting in dehydration and death if the dehydration goes unchecked. To prevent death the body developed a gene, located in the kidneys of black people, to retain salt and water in the body to preserve life.

This lifesaving gene was a necessity in old world Africa but is a detriment to health in America. It is responsible for **hypertension**. The salt sensitive gene is extremely strong. When it combines with the diet many black people enjoy, it contributes to the most common diseases that afflict black men and women. The interplay of 1. hypertension, 2. diabetes, 3. obesity, and 4. high cholesterol, referred to as **metabolic hypertension**, or **Syndrome X**, is quite common in black women.

All four components of this disease are genetically transmitted.

In this country 48.6 percent of African women are classified as obese. A female African American baby begins with this genetic package and grows up in a world where she endures all the psychosocial and racial stress of being a black woman in America. It's not surprising that if she is unaware of her health risks, then she is without defenses against the adverse effects of metabolic hypertension.

Salt sensitivity and secondary fluid retention results in elevated blood pressure today, but it did not start out as a disease: it came about as a positive mutation that maintained life.

Once the intravascular system is depleted of fluid, the body risks collapse. It takes between 1800 cc and 2500 cc of fluid lost to cause blood pressure to fall in an average size adult. Once the kidneys sense that the blood pressure is falling, they prevent salt from leaving the body during urination by retaining water in the system. This maintains blood pressure in the normal range. As far as the kidney gene is concerned, a black person is a black person whether he or she lives in Africa, the U.S. or anywhere else in the world.

Many people have ancestry that can be traced to the African continent. They suffer the same salt sensitivity as do those who are clearly African in appearance. The African gene is quite penetrating regardless of the degree to which one is associated.

Actually, blacks have the syndrome of salt sensitivity to thank for their survival. When slaves were being transported in the holds of the ships, chained and shackled, they survived unspeakable conditions in extreme heat because their kidneys were able to hold enough salt, which held water, in their bodies.

Those of us alive today are the result of forebears who survived not only the voyage, but the grueling life that followed. Slaves were forced to work from the very early hours of the morning under the hot sun until nightfall, day in and day out. Unfortunately, now the salt sensitive gene that formed is causing hypertension and it has brought on more death than any other disease in black people in the United States and the world. So let's try to understand it in order to fight it.[1]

COMPLICATIONS OF HYPERTENSION

Hypertension causes problems for black women because it affects the heart, the brain, the kidneys, and the eyes. These four organs are referred to as **end organs**.

The Heart

The damage done to the heart by hypertension causes arteriosclerotic plaques to be deposited within coronary arteries, resulting in heart attacks and death.

Hypertension also causes the heart to become enlarged because it has to pump against a higher load. Over time, the muscles around the heart become atrophied, the ventricle in particular. Once atrophy sets in the muscle only has a finite length to which it can be stretched. And once it reaches that point, it loses effectiveness.

The condition of an ineffective heart muscle is referred to as **cardiomyopathy** with secondary (a problem caused by the first condition) congestive heart failure. This is when the pressure within the ventricles (heart chambers) rises. The heart is unable to push the blood away from the ventricles and it backs up into the lungs where it accumulates as fluid. Shortness of breath develops and congestive heart failure sets in.

If not treated quickly it can result in **pulmonary edema** (fluid in lung tissues). Untreated, it sometimes results in immediate death. If not the heart becomes enlarged and the sufferer develops lassitude, inability to walk without resting, inability to sleep flat, and constant night coughing.

All of these are signs that the heart is failing. If the person gets to a physician quickly, it can be discovered and treated.

The Kidney

Another organ that suffers immensely from hypertension is the kidney, when pressure rises within the vessels that run through it. Hypertension unchecked results in kidney failure.

The many tissues of the kidney require blood vessels of different sizes to carry blood and oxygen to them. There are clusters of capillaries, referred to as glomeruli, which need blood and oxygen. As the blood pressure rises these very delicate blood vessels begin to rupture from the force of high blood pressure without the person even realizing it.

After a while, the vessels die out and the kidney tissues they are responsible for are starved of blood and oxygen and die. Eventually, the person loses so many glomeruli that the kidneys can no longer function properly. When all of the glomeruli die, the kidneys fail. As the patient has been unaware of their deterioration, this failure is frighteningly sudden.

Uremia

Once the kidneys fail, waste material accumulates within the body, resulting in swollen legs, strong smelling breath, and salty skin. A condition referred to as **chronic renal failure with uremia** develops. From that point on, a person will have to undergo peritoneal dialysis or hemodialysis to clean the blood of toxic materials in order to maintain life. If a person is fortunate enough to get a successful kidney transplant that succeeds he or she can return to a normal life. This is a lucky break; it doesn't happen as often as we'd like.

So high blood pressure that goes untreated can damage the kidney to the point of kidney failure. Typically, the kidneys fail gradually, the problem can really sneak up on you, and suddenly you're dependent upon a dialysis machine. Was the neglect worth it? Hardly.

The Eye

Another organ sensitive to the effects of hypertension is the eye. When the blood pressure rises in the body, pressure rises within the vessels in the eyes. These vessels are quite fragile and easily damaged. Damage to the vessels causes leakage, and if left untreated ends in blindness.

The Brain

Hypertension causes different degrees of damage in the brain. Over time, elevated pressure causes plaques to develop within the small vessels and large vessels inside of it. The damage that occurs within the small vessels results in multiple small vessel **infarctions** (obstructions).

This condition inevitably leads to a more serious one known as **multi-infarct syndrome**. Multi-infarct syndrome is the most common cause of senility in the world. It affects hundred of millions of individuals. It can all be traced directly back to hypertension.

Of the millions who suffer, only about 40 percent seek medical attention. Sadly, only about 20 percent get their blood pressure controlled to about 140/90; and this is not good blood pressure control. Because the incidence of hypertension is the highest among blacks, it is blacks that are more prone to the development of early senility due to untreated or poorly treated hypertension.

Elevated blood pressure can cause three types of major strokes (referred to as cerebrovascular accident) to occur. The first is **ischemic stroke**, the second is **hemorrhagic stroke** and the third is **embolic stroke**.

Ischemic stroke occurs because of chronic narrowing of the affected vessel with plaques and/or the rupture of plaques within the affected vessels. Bleeding from the ruptures with clot formation closes the vessel, cutting off blood flow. The result is a stroke.

Hemorrhagic stroke is brought on by elevated blood pressure, which causes chronic damage to the blood vessels. From damage can come rupture, and then hemorrhage inside the brain.

Embolic stroke is related to hypertension. It occurs as a result of hypertensive heart disease with enlargement of the heart. **Atrial fibrillation** (irregular contraction of muscle fibers) develops. If the atrial fibrillation is not treated with **anticoagulants** such as Heparin or Coumadin to prevent clot formation, then a clot can get dislodged from the atrium to the brain, causing stroke.

FYI

The eyes, kidneys, heart, and the brain are the four organs most affected by hypertension. It is the number one disease in black women the world over and certainly the number one disease in African American women. Hypertension is combined with obesity, diabetes, and elevated lipids in black women. All are preventable with a healthy diet and healthy mindset.

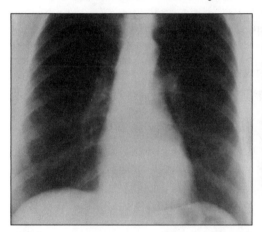

Figure 1.1: A Normal Black Female Chest X-ray

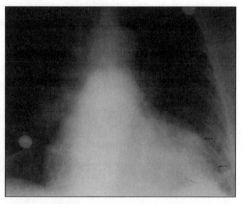

Figure 1.2: An abnormal chest x-ray in a female patient with hypertensive cardiovascular disease, showing heart failure, as a result of chronic hypertension with secondary coronary artery disease, leading to an enlarged heart and heart failure, with arrow showing enlarged border of the right heart and arrows showing enlarged border of the left heart with pleural effusion. (Fluid in lower left lung)

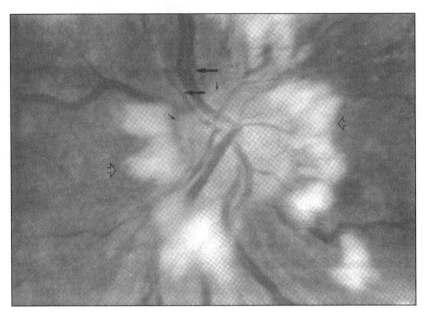

Figure 1.3: Showing different degrees of abnormalities in the eye of a hypertensive patient (hypertensive retinopathy). Small arrow showing silver wiring; Big arrow showing hard yellow exudates, open arrow head showing hemorrhage; arrow head showing A-V nicking.

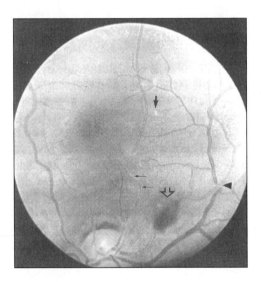

Figure 1.4: Showing different types of abnormalities in the eye of a hypertensive patient (hypertensive retinopathy). Small arrows showing early papilledema, one big arrow pointing to engorgement (larger vessel). The other big arrow pointing to arterial attenuation (smaller vessel): open arrowheads showing cotton wool exudates.

TREATMENT OF HYPERTENSION IN AFRICAN AMERICAN WOMEN

If a black woman's blood pressure is 138/88, she is overweight, and has a family history of hypertension, then this upper normal limit of blood pressure should be checked at an office visit scheduled one month after her initial visit.

If the blood pressure at the second visit is still 138/88, then the treatment is a 4 g sodium, 90 g protein, 160 g carbohydrate, 31 g fat per day diet, along with an exercise regimen to reduce weight and prevent the blood pressure from creeping up even higher.

The daily American diet contains an average of 7 grams of sodium. That of an African American woman is likely to contain an average of 10 grams of sodium. This is because of the so-called "soul food" or other foods many African American women enjoy. Salt has a lot to do with taste. If a person is accustomed to eating food that is salty, no matter what kind of food it is, they tend to add more salt to it.

The vast majority of African American women live in substandard economic conditions, surrounded by fast food. It is of such poor quality that a lot of fat and seasoning is added to improve its taste. So fast foods end up containing tons of salt.

The poorer the individual, the more likely they are to eat a diet of poor quality. It is not my intent to insult black women; this is a commentary on society. In fact, so-called "soul food" is a legacy from slave days, when Africans were forced to eat foods of poor quality. They devised all sorts of ingenious ways of preparing meats so they could be kept without spoiling.

Meat was cured with sour juice. Sour is a wild orange that has a very bitter juice in it. Curing also involved a lot of crushed hot pepper, citrus juice, and, again, *a lot of salt*. Meat would be hung on a rope in the sun to dry so it wouldn't get rotten. This way it could be eaten gradually. It tasted very good, but unfortunately was unhealthy due to the salt content in particular.

The worst part is that virtually nothing has changed. Today the poorer people are, the poorer the quality of their foods. Foods that are of higher quality cost more than these people are able to afford because they are living on a severely restricted budget. With children to support and other bills to pay, they can only eat what they can afford to buy. Many Americans cannot even imagine what it's like to have a limited amount of food to eat.

There is an answer. Repairing our culture will not happen tomorrow, but African American women can learn to control their own health today. Controlling blood pressure is a good place to begin.

Medication

Treatment of high blood pressure should be started right away. Once blood pressure reaches 140/90 in a black woman, medication should be dispensed, particularly if the woman is obese. The best and most effective medication for hypertension in a black woman or man is a water pill, known as a diuretic. Water pills control high blood pressure by preventing salt from being reabsorbed by the kidneys from the bloodstream, instead of passed out through the urine. The trapped salt results in a rise in blood pressure.

Some of the common diuretics available in the United States are hydrochlorothiazide, Dyazide, Moduretic, Lozol, Maxzide, Lasix, and Bumex. All of these are effective in removing salt and water from the body. The cost of hydrochlorothiazide is about $5.00 for a month's supply. Take heed, some more expensive medications actually treat blood pressure much less effectively. One could spend four to six times more for medications that are inappropriate for blood pressure in a black person.

Because of the intrinsic nature of the kidneys of blacks, certain medications do not work to decrease blood pressure for them. The mechanism of hypertension in blacks is different than it is in whites. The most effective medication for the treatment of hypertension in black men or women is a diuretic (known as a water pill).

REVIEW:

Water pills work to control high blood pressure by preventing salt from being reabsorbed by the kidneys. Some of the common diuretics available in the Unites States for treatment of hypertension are:

1. Hydrochlorothiazide
2. Dyazide
3. Modiuretic
4. Lozol
5. Maxzide
6. Microzide

Lasix and Bumex are loop diuretics and not really appropriate for treatment of hypertension.

There is a substance made by the human kidney called **renin** (an enzyme released by the kidney that raises pressure). Once made, renin enters into a biochemical reaction producing another substance called **aldosterone**, which causes salt/water retention. This in turn causes expansion of water within the intravascular compartment. The result is elevated blood pressure. This system is called the renin angiotensin system.

However, blacks have low renin in the blood, so prescribing medications that work to attack the renin angiotensin system are useless to decrease blood pressure. Furthermore, these medications have a lot of side effects and are very expensive. Some such medications are beta-blockers, like Inderal, Lopressor, and Tenormin. They are excellent for angina, migraine headaches, and cardiac arrhythmias in all people and work very well under those circumstances. However, they don't work in blacks to decrease blood pressure and should not be prescribed for this purpose.

Another example of medications that do not work well in blacks to decrease blood pressure are the angiotensin converting enzyme inhibitors (ACE inhibitors). One example is Capoten, another is Zestril. These ACE inhibitors work very slightly to decrease hypertension in blacks. Again, they are very good medications to control hypertension in caucasians and to control congestive heart failure in everyone, including blacks.

The only situation in which a beta-blocker might control hypertension in a black person is if the person is under extreme pressure and is secreting a lot of adrenaline. A beta-blocker might transiently shut off the sympathetic system (a branch of the involuntary nervous system that controls body function) to decrease blood pressure. However, when a black person's kidneys fail and the person develops what is called chronic renal failure, their renin level increases.

At this point, beta-blockers will decrease the blood pressure because the renin level is elevated; however, they are dangerous if the person has renal failure and severe congestive heart failure.

Another situation in which the beta-blocker might work to decrease blood pressure even though the person is black is in renovascular hypertension. When plaque or a fibrous substance within the vessels obstructs the circulation of the kidneys, renin levels are elevated. In this circumstance, beta-blockers work to decrease the blood pressure. But these are rare instances.

Renovascular hypertension is the second most common form of hypertension in African American people. With age, plaques develop within the blood vessels carrying blood to the kidneys. This results in elevation of renin, which is found in blocked kidneys. It is referred to as **hyperanemia**. The end result is high renin hypertension. Frequently, in renovascular hypertension, a sound referred to as a **bruit** can be heard in the abdomen with a stethoscope.

In a certain percentage of patients with renovascular hypertension a bruit is not heard. In this situation either the Capoten test or renal angiography has to be done to determine whether renovascular obstruction exists or not.

Medications such as Procardia, Adalat, Verapamil, Cardizem, Norvasc, and so on, are called calcium channel blockers. They work to decrease blood pressure by relaxing the smooth muscles inside blood vessels. They are expensive but excellent medications for treating hypertension even in blacks when used in combination with water pills.

They should not be used without water pills to treat hypertension in blacks or anyone with the slightest trace of African blood running through their veins. Several billion people represent this segment of the population. Alpha-blockers such as Hytrin or Cardura are also good medications must be used in conjunction with water pills in blacks. Clonidine, Aldomet, or Hydralazine in either pill or patch form are effective with water pills as well. There are many other medications that can be used in combination with water pills to treat hypertension in blacks.

It is wrong to treat any person of African ancestry with beta-blockers such as Lopressor, Inderal, Corgard, Tenormin. They are good medications, but not for hypertension in blacks, who require a water pill with any antihypertensive medication.

Let's say for the sake of argument a physician were to prescribe a non-water pill containing medication for a person of African ancestry, and the dose was high enough to send the blood pressure down. The kidneys will sense the decrease and retain salt to counter the effect of the lowering blood pressure almost immediately. This is so because it is the kidney's job to hold salt and maintain the blood pressure regardless of why the blood pressure is being decreased.

Blacks may suffer from low renin (an enzyme released by the kidney that raises blood pressure) hypertension. It is also called **high volume hypertension**. "Volume" refers to the amount of water retained in the intravascular system of the body as a result of salt retention. If an individual is both hypertensive and diabetic then it is appropriate to prescribe an ACE inhibitor along with any other combination of antihypertensive medications, to prevent the development of a condition called microalbuminemia.

Microalbuminemia can cause damage to kidney tubules, which leads to kidney failure. Care must be taken not to give an ACE inhibitor to a patient who has renal insufficiency or renal failure because one of the side effects of ACE inhibitors is elevation of serum potassium—lethal to the patient. In addition,

21

patients with renal insufficiency already have a propensity toward elevated serum potassium as part of the kidney failure.

Often, opponents of the water pill argue that they cause potassium loss (it's secreted in the urine), thereby decreasing the serum potassium level, which can be dangerous. The truth is that a middle-aged or young adult takes in roughly 80 mg of potassium a day by eating fruits, drinking juice, and so on. This is clearly enough to remain in potassium balance. Further, medications such as Modiuretic, Dyazide, Maxzide, and so on, contain triamterene, which prevents potassium loss. Potassium chloride by mouth can be prescribed along with the water pills if blood tests show the potassium to be low.

Conversely, it is standard practice to prescribe a potassium supplement for an elderly patient on water pills to prevent low serum potassium levels. The elderly frequently eat a diet that contains less than 80 mg of potassium per day and lose potassium when taking water pills. So when an elderly person is on water pills, particularly digitalis, close attention must be paid to prevent potassium loss, which can cause severe cardiac dysrhythmias.

There is also an argument that water pills cause blood sugar to rise. It is in fact a false argument, because replacing potassium restores insulin receptor sensitivity, which holds the blood sugar at a normal level. The benefit of having well-controlled blood pressure far outweighs the slight increase in cholesterol rarely seen in those taking water pills. All that is required is a low fat diet, and responsible monitoring of the serum cholesterol. It should be done as often as possible.

High blood pressure is on the decrease in white females but on the *increase* in black females and continuing steadily!

Tests—Start Simply

Because ninety-five percent of high blood pressure is due to hypertension, it is more cost effective to do a complete physical examination followed by a few simple tests, then start treatment for high blood pressure if hypertension is revealed by those tests. It is inappropriate in most cases to do extensive tests before trying antihypertensive medications. The tests necessary to evaluate hypertension are:

1. Complete blood count
2. Blood chemistries—blood sugar, blood urea nitrogen, serum electrolytes, serum creatinine; lipid profiles such as cholesterol, triglycerides, high-density and low-density lipoprotein
3. Urinalysis
4. EKG
5. Chest x-ray

REVIEW:

These are all the tests to determine how much damage the hypertensive individual has *already* suffered to his or her end organs. They are not only reasonably inexpensive, but prevent further damage from the maladies that are the most likely to be causing pain.

The end organs are the brain, the eyes, the heart, and the kidneys.

Further Tests

There is a rare tumor of the adrenal gland called **pheochromocytoma** that secretes substances that cause an elevation in blood pressure. The test for pheochromocytoma is extensive, tedious, and costly. It requires a blood test, twenty four hour urine test and a specific diet. It is simpler to do an abdominal CT scan to check adrenal glands for abnormality rather than embarking on extensive tests right away. Again, the above tests are the most effective diagnostic tool in ninety-five percent of patients.

A CBC (complete blood count) tells whether a person is anemic or not. In renal failure associated with long time hypertension, the red blood cell count is low because the kidneys are damaged and unable to make erythropoetin. **Erythropoetin** stimulates the production of red cells by the bone marrow. When high blood pressure damages the kidneys, the urine specific gravity is low, the urine is likely to have protein in it, and the urine sediment contains substances called casts which indicate intrinsic kidney damage.

If the blood sugar is elevated in addition to positive blood chemistry tests it means the patient may have hypertension *and* diabetes. A person who suffers elevated serum lipids (cholesterol, triglycerides, or LDH), plus hypertension, and elevated blood sugar combined with obesity has **syndrome X** or **metabolic hypertension**.

This is a very serious condition. The interplay of obesity, hypertension, hyperlipidemia, and diabetes is a very deadly combination. It must be treated carefully by an expert. The chest x-ray is important to determine whether the heart is enlarged or the lungs have fluid in them (congestive heart failure). If the heart is enlarged, it gives the physician a very good idea as to how long the person has been hypertensive. The electrocardiogram (EKG) is very important in that it allows the physician to see the sort of damage high blood pressure may have caused to the heart muscle over time.

It is the responsibility of the physician to organize a sensible, rational, safe, and cost-effective treatment plan for the hypertensive patient.

For black women to keep their blood pressure normal, in addition to appropriate medications such as diuretics, they must eat a diet that is low in salt, fat, and carbohydrates and high in fiber, protein, vitamins, iron, and minerals.

Another hypertension-associated problem in black women is preeclampsia, and eclampsia, which occurs during pregnancy. When a woman is pregnant, the function of the kidney changes. The rate of glomular filtration and renal plasma flow are increased by 30 to 50 percent. Similarly, the diastolic blood pressure goes up to 80 in the second trimester and above 85 in the third trimester. Corrective measures are necessary at this point to prevent the patient from going into toxemia. Also, if the blood urea nitrogen (BUN) and the serum levels increase it must be investigated.

Toxemia of pregnancy usually starts in the third trimester.

Different components of this syndrome include hypertension, protein in the urine, elevated serum uric acid, edema (swollen ankles), salt retention, consumptive coagulopathy, seizure, and hyperreflexia (reflexes are increased). This is called preeclampsia.

Preeclampsia exists when the blood pressure remains 140/85 or greater for several hours. If the patient has had high blood pressure before becoming pregnant, preeclampsia can accelerate quickly into eclampsia. Treatment of toxemia includes bed rest and magnesium sulfate to treat neurological abnormalities. Medications such as methyldopa and hydralazine will decrease the blood pressure by dilating the blood vessels. Diuretics should not be used.

REVIEW:

Hypertension is the leading cause of mortality in black women, but education and an understanding of this serious disease can delay its onset by many years or prevent it completely. Understanding that hypertension is a different disease in black women than in white women and adding a diuretic to the medication regimen will properly control this dreaded disease.

Stroke in African American Women

2

One of the leading diseases that kill women is stroke. Every year in America 750,000 people suffer a stroke. Of those who died over a one-year period, 97,467 were females.

According to recent literature, African Americans have a higher prevalence of small vessel strokes, (19% blacks vs. 6% whites), intracranial stenoses, (19% blacks vs. 6% whites), and lacunar strokes, (10% blacks vs. 2.7% whites). Small vessel strokes are associated with dementia.

The prevalence of hypertension in blacks is 68% vs. 30% in whites. In the U.S. 49% of blacks, as compared to 19% of whites have two or more risk factors for strokes, such as, cigarette smoking, hypertension, diabetes, or coronary artery disease.

What is a stroke?

A stroke occurs when an obstruction within the blood vessel prevents blood flow to an area of the brain. This area of the brain becomes damaged. It results in a stroke. Another term for stroke is **cerebrovascular accident**. An obstruction of blood flow can be caused by either plaques within a vessel or by a clot from the heart brought into the vessel by the blood stream. Another type of stroke is when a vessel inside the brain ruptures and leaks blood.

The rupture of a vessel in the brain is either due to a vessel filled with atherosclorotic plaques or the elevation of blood pressure within the vessel.

Elevated pressure in the vessel causes the membrane to rupture and leaks blood into the brain. Brain aneurysms, which are a meshwork of vessel malformations due to genetic defects, can rupture and leak blood into the brain when pressure is too high. Ruptured aneurysms cause a hemorrhagic stroke whether the blood pressure is elevated or not.

Another cause of bleeding into the brain is **hemangioma**, or **arteriovenous malformations**. These are a meshed group of small arteries and veins that form an abnormal network of vessels. They bleed easily, and lead to hemorrhagic stroke. There is a condition called **transient ischemic attacks (TIA)**. In TIA, there exists an obstruction of a vessel by a clot or a clump of platelet trapped within the vessel, preventing the flow of the blood that delivers oxygen to that part of the brain.

This temporary lack of oxygen to the brain causes a condition which can temporarily lead to loss of consciousness, seizures, weakness, lassitude, and nausea that lasts for several hours called **presyncope**. The most common types of stroke or cerebrovascular accident are:

1. Arteriosclerotic or ischemic stroke
2. Lacunae stroke
3. Embolic stroke
4. Hemorrhagic stroke associated with high blood pressure
5. Ruptured aneurysms
6. Bleeding arteriovenous malformations

In black women, arterioslcerotic–type strokes and hypertension-associated strokes are the two most common types seen. It is one of the leading causes of death. The combination of salt sensitivity, salt and water retention, and the resulting high blood pressure is largely responsible for such a high incidence of stroke.

Arteriosclerotic disease of the brain occurs in a large percentage of black women. The reasons for this high percentage of brain

arteriosclerotic disease are:
1. Hypertension
2. Obesity
3. Diabetes mellitus
4. Hyperlipidemia
5. Frequent use of birth control pills
6. Racial discrimination and the stress associated with it; poverty and all the bad conditions associated with it; including a poor diet with too much fat, too much salt, and too much carbohydrate

Hypertension causes strokes in two ways: 1) Increased blood pressure in the vessels within the brain damages the inside part of these vessels over time. The damaged areas trap platelets and other material from blood as it passes through 2) A nidus (cavity where bacterium develops) forms within these vessels and the end result is plaque formation. The formation of plaques narrows vessels impeding blood flow.

When a clot is superimposed on the plaque it can close off a vessel, resulting in a cerebrovascular stroke. Plaque causes myriad complications within vessels. It narrows them or creates seats inside the vessel can break off causing either an embolus or a clot to form. Remember: plaques come from hypertension; hypertension causes stroke.

Bleeding inside the brain from ruptured vessels can result in coma because of edema (swelling). If the coma lasts too long it ends in death. Another stroke that occurs from long term hypertension and neglected blood pressure is **multiple small vessel infarction** (death of tissue) of the brain.

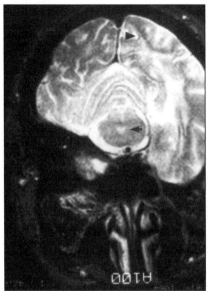

Figure 2.1: MRI of the brain in the patient with hypertension: small infarct in the pon (arrow) and right occipital white matter (arrow head).

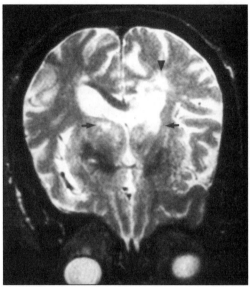

Figure 2.2: MRI of the brain in patient with hypertension: infarction of thalamus (arrows) and right parietal white matter (arrow head)

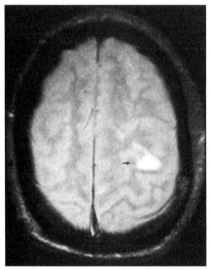

Figure 2.3: MRI of the brain in a patient with hypertension: left parietal small infarction. (arrow)

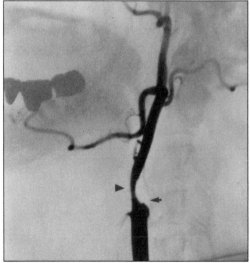

Figure 2.4: Arteriosclerotic disease of carotid arteries in patients with hypertension causing transient ischemic attacks. (pre-stroke syndrome), Carotid angiogram: occlusion of internal carotid artery at its origin. (arrow); narrowing of proximal internal carotid artery. (arrow)

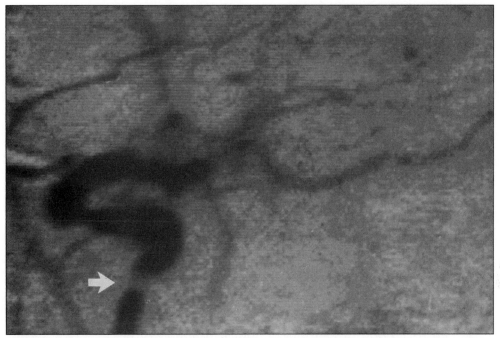

Figure 2.5: Cerebral angiogram 95% occlusion of internal carotid artery in a patient with hypertension. (arrow)

MEMORY LOSS AND BRAIN MALFUNCTION

Small vessels are located deep inside the brain and supply blood to very vital structures within it. Lack of blood is associated with early memory loss resulting in organic brain syndrome. Multiple small vessel infarctions are second only to Alzheimer's disease as a cause of senility.

In fact, it is probably more common than Alzheimer's in terms of senility because there are so many more hypertensive patients than people who have Alzheimer's. It is not uncommon to see 40-year-old black women that have been hypertensive since their 20's or 30's, with difficulty remembering simple things because of multiple small vessel infarctions of the brain. Infarctions can be seen on an MRI. This syndrome does not show up well on a CT scan.

In evaluating poor memory loss in 40 to 60-year-old hypertensive black women, the following should be done:

31

1. A complete history and physical examination by a competent internist or primary care physician or neurologist
2. CBC (Complete Blood Count) with differential
3. Blood chemistry
4. Urinalysis
5. Thyroid tests such as T4, TSH, T3
6. B_{12} level
7. VDRL
8. HIV test
9. Chest x-ray
10. EKG
11. Brain CAT scan and if normal, an MRI of the brain
12. A thorough neurological examination by—as stated above—a neurologist

The complete blood count tells the physician if the white blood cell count is too low or high. Either count may be associated with conditions that account for memory loss.

There is an important difference in white blood cell counts between whites and blacks. The normal white blood cell count in whites is 4,500 to 10,000. In blacks it's from 3,500 to 10,000. If the white blood cell count is found to be 3,500 in a black person, it should be repeated two to three times. If it is still in that range it should be kept under close observation.

The red blood cell count tells the physician if poor memory is due to low red cell count (anemia), or to high red blood cell count (polycythemia). When the red blood cell count is too low, oxygen cannot be delivered easily to the body's vital organs. When the red blood cell count is too high, stasis results within the vessels, making it difficult for oxygen to get to vital organs. The thicker the blood the more difficult it is for oxygen to get to the memory center in the brain.

The platelet count, which is part of the CBC, is also very important. If the platelets drop to less than 20,000 (normal platelet count is 150,000 to 400,000), spontaneous bleeding can occur anywhere in the body, including the brain. Bleeding in the brain results in serious malfunction.

If the platelet count is too high—750,000 to 1,000,000 or greater—both stroke and bleeding can occur within the brain. (This occurs only if the high platelet count is associated with a myelo proliferative disorder.)

Abnormalities in the differential blood count may indicate leukemia or lymphoma, both of which can be diagnosed by poor brain function. The blood chemistry and its component parts are very important in determining whether a person's poor memory is due to abnormalities in the body's chemistry.

Abnormalities in the **electrolytes** can bring on brain malfunction. The electrolytes are sodium, potassium, chloride, and bicarbonate. Severe acidosis (too low bicarbonate) or severe alkalosis (too high bicarbonate) can lead to abnormalities that can cause brain abnormalities and brain malfunction.

High blood sodium, a condition called **hypernatremia**, can cause confusion. Normal sodium is 135 to 140. Low blood sodium, 110 to 120, can cause confusion, poor memory, and seizures.

A frequently seen abnormality in blood chemistry that causes brain malfunction is low blood sugar, known as **hypoglycemia**. Normal blood sugar is between 60 and 112 mg/dc. When the blood sugar falls to less than 60 it can lead to confusion, poor memory, or seizure. Starvation is a common cause of low blood sugar.

When blood sugar is 400 or greater, it can lead to **diabetic ketoacidosis**, which causes confusion and seizures. In diabetic ketoacidosis a person is unable to use sugar as fuel due to lack of insulin. The body uses fat instead. The byproducts of fat are ketone bodies, which are toxic.

There is another condition involving high blood sugar called **non-ketotic hyperglycemia**, which can lead to coma if left untreated for too long. In this condition, there is no high level of ketones but the blood sugar rises, sometimes by more than 2,000, and usually in someone who never had trouble with high blood sugar. High blood sugar acts as a diuretic. The affected person passes a large quantity of urine daily and experiences extreme thirst. After a while, the volume of urine that the person passes is far in excess of the fluid intake, resulting in severe dehydration, including dehydration of the brain.

Blood chemistry evaluates the function of the kidneys, as reflected by high blood urea nitrogen, high serum creatinine, high serum potassium, and high serum phosphate. When the kidneys are malfunctioning, many abnormalities can be detected in the blood and urine. But some of the earliest and most important abnormalities seen when the kidneys start to fail are:

1. High BUN
2. High creatinine
3. High potassium
4. High phosphate
5. Abnormalities in urine electrolytes
6. Anemia

When the kidneys fail, toxic waste products cannot be removed from the blood. Their effect on the brain is seen in confusion and seizures.

Another important series of blood chemistry tests used by physicians to detect disease are the liver function tests such as serum calcium, serum phosphate, serum LDH, serum SGOT, serum SGPT, GGTP, serum uric acid, alkaline phosphatase, and prothrombin time. Abnormalities seen in these tests may indicate hepatitis, liver cancer, and more.

Complete liver failure causes mental confusion and, at times, seizures. If the urinalysis is abnormal, it may indicate infection in the bladder or kidneys. If sugar is found in the urine, it may indicate diabetes. If a substance called acetone is found in the urine, it indicates dehydration or diabetic ketoacidosis.

Sediment in the urine containing crystals indicates kidney stones. Materials called casts seen in sediments can indicate kidney disease. If blood is seen in the urine of a male, it always indicates disease. Possible diseases include urinary tract infection, kidney stone, sickle cell disease, cancer of the bladder, cancer of the kidney, cancer of the prostate or prostatitis, to name a few. In the female, the same diseases *might* be present if blood is seen in the urine.

When the kidneys fail, urination ceases. Mental confusion results if dialysis is not performed to cleanse the blood of toxins.

Low Vitamin B₁₂ Levels

Memory loss and neurological damage can result from low Vitamin B_{12}. If the B_{12} level remains low for five years or more, permanent brain and neurological damage are unavoidable. There are many conditions that cause low Vitamin 12. Among them are: anemia; tapeworm; gastritis, blind loop syndrome, and the recently studied low B_{12} syndrome as it occurs in the elderly population.

Therefore, it's crucial to do a B_{12} level when evaluating a person for memory loss. If the B_{12} level comes back normal, one should have a urine test for methylmalonic acid. It also can be done using the blood. If someone has B_{12} deficiency the methylmalonic acid will be elevated.

A test for syphilis, using the VDRL (Venereal Disease Research Laboratories), is very important because syphilis can cause severe brain damage. When a VDRL test is positive, it is very important to do the confirmatory blood test called FTA-ABS (Fluorescent Treponoma Antibody-Absorption Test).

In true syphilitic infection, this test stays positive for life. When neurosyphilis is suspected, then a CT scan should be done; if it appears normal, then a spinal tap to examine the cerebrospinal fluid should follow it.

In the evaluation of poor memory (organic brain syndrome) the HIV Type I or Type II test is very important. An early symptom of AIDS is loss of memory, due either to HIV infection of the brain tissue or infections of the brain such as toxoplasmosis, cryptococcus, or herpes.

In evaluating poor memory or organic brain syndrome, the chest X ray is very important. It may contain evidence of cancer in the lungs. There are many infectious processes that can be seen in the lungs on chest X rays that affect the function of the brain, resulting in poor memory, confusion, and sometimes coma.

Sometimes confusion and memory loss are due to a **syncopal episode** (loss of consciousness). The episode can be caused by a number of things, among them heart malfunction. It can be seen on an EKG or 24-hour holter. Other causes of syncope are TIA (transient ischemic attack), seizures, hypoglycemia, and carotid artery stenosis.

After a stroke, a CT scan of the brain is done immediately to look for blood or swelling within the brain, ventricles that are pushed to one side, or a brain tumor. Any of these findings can cause symptoms consistent with a stroke. Sometimes evidence of old strokes can be seen on the same scan. When contrast material is injected into the patient's blood stream more can be seen within the brain, such as metastatic brain tumor or a fungal infection like toxoplasmosis, as sometimes seen in AIDS patients.

It takes one to two weeks to see evidence of a stroke on a CT, but the CT eliminates the possibility that bleeding or brain tumor is present. Once those scenarios are eliminated the physician should proceed with an MRI.

MRI (magnetic resonance imaging) of the brain can be used to evaluate the brain immediately after a stroke and it will show the area where the stroke occurred or whatever else may be causing the patient's symptoms.

One might ask, why not do an MRI right away on everybody who has a stroke instead of a brain CT? For one thing, an MRI costs about $1,500 and the CT $1,000. Some hospitals don't have MRI technology, and not everybody is suitable for one.

Some people are claustrophobic; they just don't want to go into the machine. Some are too obese to fit into it. The maximum weight for an MRI machine is about 300 pounds. Open MRI is now available. Also, there are certain individuals who have metals implanted from previous surgery, making them unsuitable for the MRI machine.

The lists of metals in the body that can prevent an MRI from being done is quite long, but the most important ones are:
1. Aneurysm and hemostatic clips
2. Biopsy needles
3. Carotid artery vascular clamps
4. Dental implant devices and materials
5. Halo vests
6. Heart valve prosthesis

7. Intravascular coils, filters, and stents
8. Ocular implants
9. Orthopedic implants, materials, and devices
10. Otologic implants
11. Pellets and bullets
12. Penile implants
13. Vascular access ports

These devices could be dislodged or moved by the magnetic field of the MRI machine with disastrous consequences.

A thorough neurological examination is essential and indispensable in anyone who shows signs of a stroke. Black women are at high risk for strokes. In fact, black women are five times more likely to have a stroke, and die from it, than white women.[1] Black women are many times more likely to be hypertensive than white women and hypertensive black women are less likely to seek medical care for their hypertension. When treatment is given, it is less likely to be appropriate and, therefore, less effective. Here's why:

1. The incidence of obesity is quite high among black women. Approximately 50 percent of black women in the United States are obese. Obesity plays a major role in the elevation of blood pressure.

2. The high salt content in the diet many black women enjoy elevates blood pressure and its propensity to cause stroke.

3. Most black women are under stress because of their poorer educational status, economic status, social status, and overall living conditions as compared to other groups. A constant state of stress elevates hormones, such as epinephrine and norepinephrine. These raise blood pressure leading to subsequent stroke.

Until the above conditions improve, the incidence of stroke in black women the world over can be expected to continue unabated. Black women can decrease their high death rate by decreasing the amount of salt, fat, and carbohydrates in their foods; by exercising; and by practicing mental toughness and trading emotional support with one another to maintain a positive mental out-look.

Stressful Living

Black women may feel they have little control over their stressful lives, however they do have control over the foods they eat. It is a known fact that the poorer the individual, the less likely that he or she will be to afford nutritional food necessary to good health.

Sometimes it is not so much the quantity or quality of the food, but a combination of poor quality, high quantity, and poor preparation. The way one prepares food goes a long way toward good health. One should be careful to avoid foods that are too salty, greasy, or heavy in carbohydrates.

I'll go into more detail on diet in later chapters. My point is that clearly, diet and weight are important factors in the prevention of high blood pressure and stroke. As simple as it seems, a basic change in diet can be the first step toward prolonging the life of the African American woman.

High Cholesterol in African American Women

In 1996, 959,227 individuals died of cardiovascular disease in the United States, making heart disease the number one cause of death in this country.[1]

Coronary artery disease (plaques inside the vessels around the heart) has many risk factors including:

1. Hypertension
2. Hyperlipidemia
3. High triglycerides in the blood
4. High, low-density lipoprotein in the blood (LDL)
5. Low, high-density cholesterol in the blood (HDL)
6. High cholesterol in the blood
7. Family history of early heart attack, especially where a parent died of heart attack in his or her early forties to mid-fifties
8. Cigarette smoking
9. Diabetes mellitus
10. Elevated Lipoprotein A
11. Elevated Homocystein level
12. Elevated hs-CRP (C reactive proteins)
13. Obesity
14. Type A personality
15. Stress associated with work, bigotry, racism, illiteracy, poverty, and poor economic status
16. Alcoholism

According to a report in the *New England Journal of Medicine* Vol. 342 No. 12 (March 23, 2000), four new markers of inflammation were found to be predictors of future development of coronary heart disease. These are hs-CRP, serum amyloid A., interleukin-6, and sICAM-1. According to the authors of the report, the hs-CRP was the most sensitive predictor when found to be elevated.

Hyperlipidemia

Hyperlipidemia (too much fat in the blood) is a genetically transmitted disease. If a person's mother or father has too much fat in his or her blood, this trait is likely to be transmitted to the children. It can lead to the development of coronary heart disease, heart attack, and premature death. Hyperlipidemia is divided into:

1. High blood cholesterol
2. High blood triglyceride
3. High, low-density lipoprotein
4. Low, high-density lipoprotein
5. An abnormal high density lipid to cholesterol ratio, greater than 7.13.

(In a man if the LDL/HDL ratio is greater than 7.13 that is a high risk. In a woman if the LDL/HDL ratio is greater than 5.57 that is a high risk.)

Each one of the above components of hyperlipidemia represents an independent risk factor for the development of coronary disease.

Blood Cholesterol

Normal blood cholesterol is 130–200. Most people believe that blood cholesterol level is the only thing that matters when dealing with abnormal fat levels in the blood. But a person may have perfectly normal total blood cholesterol and yet significant hyperlipidemia, which predisposes them to coronary artery disease. Be aware that the quick cholesterol test may be misleading if normal. Blood cholesterol by itself does not indicate the presence of genetically transmitted abnormal lipids.

There are three basic cholesterols in the blood:

1. Total cholesterol
2. High density lipoprotein (HDL)
3. High LDL Cholesterol

HDL (high-density lipid) takes the harmful cholesterol from the blood, carries it into the bowel and the colon mixing it with stool, and carries it out of the body.

If the HDL is low, less than 45, then there is not enough of it in the blood to remove bad cholesterol from the body. The level of the bad cholesterol rises because the individual makes too much of a substance called HMG-CoA. HMG-CoA facilitates the production of bad cholesterol in the body.

These genetically transmitted lipid abnormalities are called **hyperlipoproteinemias**. When both the fasting cholesterol and the triglycerides are elevated, it is called hyperlipidemia.

The patterns of lipoproteinemia in the blood are:

1. Type 1, made up of high chylomicrons and high triglycerides
2. Type 2a, made up of LDL and high cholesterol
3. Type 2b, made up of elevated LDL and very low-density lipoprotein, (VLDL), elevated cholesterol, and triglycerides
4. Type 3, made up of a higher level of triglyceride and cholesterol
5. Type 4, made up of elevated VLDL and triglycerides
6. Type 5, made up of VLDL, chylomicrons, elevated triglycerides, and cholesterol

Secondary Hyperlipoproteinemia

Secondary Hyperlipoproteinemia is seen in association with several medical conditions.

In diabetes, three separate combinations of lipid abnormalities are seen. First, high triglycerides and VLDL are evident along with skin, eyes, and liver fat deposits. Second, VLDL and triglycerides get high in a diabetic person who develops ketoacidosis. Third, high triglycerides appear in the obese diabetic.

The use of birth control pills or ingestion of any estrogen-containing pills can raise the level of VLDL and triglycerides. It is important to know the lipid level in a person before he or she starts taking estrogen pills. If a woman has elevated lipid level, estrogen-containing medication may be harmful to her health because it's capable of pushing the blood lipid even higher, predisposing that individual to heart attack, stroke, phlebitis, pulmonary embolism, and more.

Alcohol abuse is also associated with elevated lipids in the blood. Triglyceride and in particular high low-density lipoprotein and chylomicrons will occur. Also Type 5 hyperlipidemia and sometimes Type 4 hyperlipidemia may be associated with alcohol abuse. Type 5 hyperlipidemia may cause acute pancreatitis, which is a very serious medical condition and if left untreated can be fatal.

Hyperlipidemia causes coronary artery disease because when lipid levels are high, the lipid is deposited within the lumen (cavity) of coronary arteries. The gradually narrowing vessels eventually block flow to the heart; thus the definition of **coronary occlusive heart disease**.

When the vessels around the heart become narrowed, the condition is called **angina pectoris** frequently develops. Angina pectoris is known as chest pain to you and me. The pain comes from lack of oxygen delivery to the heart muscle. It occurs when tissue is deprived of oxygen, causing a series of substances, called **kinins**, to be secreted in and around that tissue.

A good example of kinins is the familiar pain of a blister. If you burst the blister right away, the liquid that formed within it causes a burning sensation. That's because this liquid contains the kinins.

THE HEART ATTACK

What is happening when someone is having a heart attack? A clot forms as a result of either plaque or a fissure cracked open within a vessel. The end result is bleeding within the vessel, which develops into a clot. The clot closes the vessel, cutting off blood flow to the part of the heart muscle for which this vessel is responsible. It is no longer delivering oxygen and the end result is a heart attack.

The damaged muscle may die due to lack of flow of blood to it. Cardiac dysrrhythmias can develop resulting in all sorts of rhythmic disturbances such as atrial arrhythmias.

Arrhythmia such as ventricular tachycardia and ventricular fibrillation can cause immediate death. If a person arrives at the emergency room with chest pain and a physician administers **TPA** (Tissue Plasminogen Activator) to dissolve the clot, the death of the involved muscle can be prevented. This can actually stop the heart attack from occurring. From the time that the patient demonstrates symptoms until several hours later, the TPA can still be of help.

There is a high rate of cardiovascular associated deaths in black women due to the following factors:

1. High blood pressure
2. Obesity
3. High lipids in the blood
4. Smoking
5. Diabetes
6. Poor diet with too many fats, carbohydrates, and salt (Fifty percent of black women are obese in the United States. It is a major risk factor for coronary artery disease.)
7. Stress associated with racial discrimination, poverty, poor education, and poor economic status

All these factors exacerbate coronary artery disease in black women.

The premenopausal state prevents women from dying of coronary artery disease because estrogen is an anti-atherosclerotic hormone, meaning it breaks down accumulations of lipids. It has many side effects, but great value in the prevention of heart disease. However, when a woman becomes postmenopausal, whatever advantage she may have had from estrogen is over.

Estrogen protects a woman from osteoporosis as well as coronary artery disease. However, black women rarely suffer from osteoporosis and if they use estrogen, it will not benefit them because it causes them to retain salt, which will increase their blood pressure.[2] So, any advantage the estrogen would have provided for the heart is not only negated but can cause the situation to worsen.

It definitely increases the possibility of endometrial carcinoma and breast cancer. The use of estrogen is simply not wise in black women.

The following is a list of behaviors that decrease the incidence of coronary occlusive disease due to high lipids:

1. Maintain ideal weight
2. Exercise regularly
3. Moderate alcohol intake
4. Eat fruits and vegetables
5. Prepare foods with vegetable oils, particularly olive oil
6. Avoid butter when possible
7. Use skim milk
8. Avoid red meat as much as possible; decrease ingestion of pork, bacon, sausage
9. Avoid overloading on carbohydrates
10. Avoid fast foods
11. If cholesterol is a problem, avoid lobster, crab, shrimp, oysters, coconuts, and avocado. Eat foods with complex carbohydrates, such as yams, plantain, and sweet potato.

The most effective treatments of high cholesterol, high triglyceride, and hyperlipidemia are diet, exercise, and weight loss. However, when diet is no longer sufficient, medicine steps in.

MEDICATIONS

There are a series of medications referred to as HMG CoA reductase inhibitors. They are Lovestatin, Provestatin, Simvastatin, Lescol, and Lipitor. Medications such as Lopid and Tricor are excellent for bringing down the level of triglycerides. The HMG CoA reductase inhibitor actually inhibits the production of cholesterol in the liver. It removes cholesterol and LDL (low-density lipid) cholesterol from the blood, incorporating it into bile salts, which go to the gut to be mixed with stools and taken out of the body.

These medications work best when given in the evening because cholesterol circulates in time with the circadian system. That is to say, cholesterol level is highest in the evening when an individual eats their biggest meal. When cholesterol is plentiful, it is easier for it to be converted into bile acid, transported to the gut, and flushed from the system.

By the same token, drinking one or two glasses of wine at night increases the level of the HDL, the good cholesterol. It is not advised that people abuse alcohol, but studies clearly show that moderate ingestion of red wine in particular increases the level of the HDL cholesterol and decreases the stickiness of the platelets, which is important in preventing clot formation.

Dosage

Doses of the above medications are usually 10–20 mg per day for Lovestatin, 10–40 mg for Provestatin, and 5–20 mg for Simvastatin. The maximum dose of Lovestatin can go high as 80 mg daily, Simvastatin and Provestatin as high as 40.

These medications are quite expensive, but very effective in lowering cholesterol, LDL, triglycerides, and raising HDL, thereby decreasing incidence of coronary disease.

Lopid and Tricor are very good medications—they bring down the levels of LDL cholesterol and triglycerides. They have some side effects such as abdominal cramps and diarrhea. The usual dose of Lopid is 600 mg twice a day. For Tricor, 67 mg once a day.

These medications, in particular the HMG CoA reductase inhibitors, cause mild liver function test abnormalities so it is important to monitor the liver function tests every six weeks or every two months. These medications must be used in conjunction with a low fat, low carbohydrate diet, and exercise.

A warning: these medications can cause muscle and joint pain.

Some cases of muscle breakdown leading to **rhabdomyolysis** (a disorder caused by the toxic effects of the contents of muscle cells which could lead to kidney failure) have been reported, which if not recognized quickly and treated can lead to kidney failure.

DIET

Diet plays a major role in the prevention of obesity and in controlling hypertension. It also controls the levels of cholesterol and triglycerides in the blood. As I mentioned earlier, soul food has too much fat, carbohydrate, and salt. These foods taste exquisite. So eat them now and then; but when eaten on a daily basis, they raise blood pressure and cholesterol, leading to obesity, accelerating hypertension, and many other problems.

A combination of obesity, high blood pressure, and a high level of fat in the blood is responsible for the major incidence of coronary artery disease and deaths of blacks in the United States. To prevent these things from happening, the African American diet should be modified. Diet is very ethnic in origin, and that is fine, except that every culture should understand moderation.

To the African American woman, know this: an awareness of one's lifestyle and simple changes in it will help to reverse the extraordinarily high incidence of lipids and coronary heart disease seen in black women in the United States.

Obesity in African American Women

4

Obesity is a serious medical problem. When not associated with malfunction of the endocrine system, it is always the result of eating too much of the wrong foods. The wrong foods are those that are too rich in fats and carbohydrates.

In order for nutrients to be stored in the body, one needs a well functioning basal metabolism. The basal metabolism is a process through which the body burns calories that are ingested. If the basal metabolism is high, one burns calories too fast and stays thin. If the basal metabolism is too low, one burns calories too slow and remains overweight.

Slow basal metabolism, when not associated with medical problems such as hypothyroidism, is always genetically transmitted. There are several medical conditions associated with obesity; among them are:

1. Hypothyroidism
2. Cushing's disease (when the adrenal gland secretes too much adrenal hormone)
3. Gigantism—a person who is overgrown due to hyper-functioning of the pituitary gland

When a person is obese, medical conditions have been ruled out as a cause, and the person is not taking steroids or estrogen replacement medication, then the weight problem is because of low basal metabolism and ingestion of too many fats and carbo-hydrates.

Many factors conspire to create America's high degree of obe-sity. For instance, the diet industry spends somewhere between forty and fifty billion dollars a year selling products and programs for profit, but the medical profession devotes very little time to properly preventing obesity. Meanwhile the food industry spends around thirty-six billion dollars a year encouraging people to eat more. These are three big reasons behind the losing battle against obesity.

The reason the medical profession spends so little time man-aging obesity is because insurance companies will not pay for preventive programs. The federal and state governments are not doing very much either, because they feel it is adequate to spend their $50,000 a year on nutritional and other educational pro-grams. A pittance, really.

Almost seventy billion dollars was spent in 1990 in the United States to treat the complications associated with obesity. These complications include cancer, heart disease, adult onset diabetes, gallbladder disease, hypertension, stroke, and high cholesterol.

OBESITY IN BLACK WOMEN

Black women inherited low basal metabolism from their fore-bears in Africa. In ancient Africa and to a significant degree in the Africa of today, it was and is a sign of beauty to be big.

Genetic traits are adaptable, penetrating, and transmittable. African women adapted to the low basal metabolism gene and transmitted it to all women of African ancestry, disseminating the gene.

Another factor that plays a significant role in the development of obesity in black women is the food they eat as a result of sub-standard living conditions. Black women who live in Third World countries are by necessity forced to eat a meager diet. They are less obese than black women who live in developed countries like the United States.

In the third world, black women eat plenty of fresh fruits, grains, bananas, less red meat, and a lot of fish. These women exercise more because they have to walk long distances to the farm, long distances to the marketplace, long distances to fetch water...you get the idea.

All of these activities cause them to lose calories, which maintains weight. Nevertheless, African women carry the gene, and pass it on even though they manage to work off the fat that would deposit into their tissues, as predetermined by their hereditary trait.

Also, if a woman is overweight, she is likely to give birth to an overweight baby who carries the low basal metabolism gene. The baby will grow to become a fat adolescent and a fat adult unless it eats right and exercises.

Complex Carbohydrates

The foods that women in the third world eat are high in protein, vitamins, and fiber and low in fat and carbohydrates.

Complex carbohydrates satisfy hunger, but cannot be broken down and absorbed in the body. That is what makes them ideal food products. When prepared in vegetable oil, boiled, or broiled, they satisfy hunger, provide Vitamin A, Vitamin K, and the B Vitamins, including B_6, B_{12}, and so many more without threatening cholesterol levels.

On the other hand, simple carbohydrates, such as sugar and caloric foods are broken down in the liver and distributed through the tissues and muscles, resulting in obesity in the individual who consumes them all the time. Breast cancer, uterine cancer, colon cancer and cancer of the prostate can all be traced to too many of these kinds of fatty foods and to obesity.

The following diseases are associated with obesity:
1. Diabetes
2. Atherosclerotic heart disease
3. Hypertension
4. Stroke

    5. Arthritis

    6. Depression

What is the relationship between diabetes and obesity? When an individual is obese, fat cells are resistant to the effect of insulin, creating an insulin-resistant state in the body. The insulin cannot penetrate fat cells to metabolize sugar. Consequently, blood sugar rises. The rising blood sugar creates all sorts of disturbances to the system. Since the insulin has difficulty entering into the fat cells, it remains elevated in the blood stream. The high insulin level, in turn, forces the obese individual to crave sweets.

A vicious cycle begins. The more obese the person, the higher the level of insulin in the blood stream. The higher the level of insulin in the blood stream, the more the individual craves sweets, carbohydrates, and calories. The more the person eats them, the heavier they become, raising blood sugar even higher.

Obesity is associated with atherosclerotic heart disease, because consistently high levels of insulin cause plaques to develop within vessels throughout the body including around the heart. Sudden closure of one or several of these coronary arteries can result in a heart attack.

Diabetes is discussed in greater detail in Chapter Five.

OBESITY AND HYPERTENSION

Obesity goes hand in hand with hypertension, which is also quite common in black women. Three diseases that usually accompany obesity are diabetes, hyperlipidemia, and hypertension. This combination is called **syndrome X** or **metabolic hypertension**. Black women retain more salt in their bodies than white women do and, as a result, more fluid. The fluid retention causes elevation in the blood pressure. When a person who is obese loses weight, the blood pressure lowers and the need for medication decreases proportionately.

Obesity is commonly associated with stroke. Diabetes, hypertension, and hyperlipidemia are usually at the root of the problem in people who suffer from stroke. Because the three diseases accompany obesity, it follows that obesity can cause a high-risk person to have a stroke.

Obesity is associated with breast cancer in black women, in particular obese black women ages 38 to 49. The type of breast cancer seen in this group is extremely aggressive and resistant to treatments.

Obesity is associated with uterine cancer in a high percentage of black women (See Chapter 7).

Osteoarthritis of the shoulders, lower back, knees, and ankles is frequently seen in obese black women, because obesity causes a great deal of mechanical stress on these areas of the body. Such wear and tear causes severe pain as well as joint problems and osteoarthritis.

Many women who are obese feel a great deal of pressure in this society, which blatantly favors thin women. Sociological factors like this creates depression among obese black women. They have difficulty finding boyfriends and jobs, and face discriminations of all kinds.

Obese black women suffer more from discrimination than any other women in the American society, even black women who are thin and can at least conform in that way. It is a serious psychological problem with significant impact on the physical health of black women.

Black women must fight back, by eating a diet low in fat, low in salt, low in carbohydrates, and high in protein. It is important for black women to exercise at least three times a week. It is not necessary to spend money going to different exercise centers to exercise: these centers cost money. Walking one hour daily burns significant calories. Black women need to go back to basics. Learn to prepare healthy foods. A change in the eating habits of black women from soul and fast food will go a long way toward controlling obesity.

REVIEW:

Black women are obese partially because the obesity gene was inherited from their African ancestors. Understanding this fact and taking the necessary precautions is the best way to solve the obesity problems and their devastating consequences on black women.

Diabetes in African American Women

5

Diabetes is a very common disease in black women. Eight percent of the approximately sixteen million African American women in the United States have Type II diabetes. Of the general United States population 11.2 percent has some form of glucose intolerance.[1] The number of medically undiagnosed African American women with diabetes is believed to be two to three times the amount diagnosed.

According to the latest literature, diabetes has increased 600 percent in the United States since 1958. It is estimated that cases of diabetes will rise by 35 percent in the next ten years.

In the genetics of Type II diabetes one third of the offspring of diabetics have the propensity to become diabetic. Type I diabetes is a different disease altogether. It is believed to be caused by either an autoimmune phenomenon, disease, or some sort of a virus, but no one is quite sure. Type I diabetes usually begins during childhood.

African Americans as a group have twice the incidence of Type II diabetes than Caucasians.

WHAT IS DIABETES?

Diabetes is a condition in which the body is incapable of using sugar as a fuel due to lack of insulin. Two basic abnormalities cause it. One is abnormal insulin secretion and the other is a resistance to insulin. Resistance to insulin occurs in the tissues.

Diagnosis

Because diabetes is a condition in which the blood glucose is higher than normal, the glucose is drawn following an eight to twelve hour fast. Normal blood glucose is from 65 to about 116 mg/dL. If the fasting blood sugar remains abnormally high on more than three occasions, an individual can be said to have glucose intolerance and is suffering from diabetes in its earliest form.

Another way to test the blood is for the physician to order a two hour post-prandial (after eating) glucose test. Two hours after eating a meal containing sugar, a tube of blood is drawn from the individual and if the blood glucose is 140 mg/dL or greater, then that individual is said to have glucose intolerance or early diabetes.

Usually insulin-dependent diabetes, or Type I diabetes, occurs before age forty. Non-insulin-dependent diabetes occurs later, with some exceptions. For the most part insulin-dependent diabetes appears before age twenty, but can occur later.

By and large, age forty is the cut-off point for someone to have Type I or insulin-dependent diabetes. If the individual is older, the diagnosis is most likely going to be adult onset diabetes, or Type II.

TYPE II DIABETES

There are different types of Type II diabetes. The most common happens because of the inability of the pancreas to secrete insulin. In people who have chronic pancreatic inflammation, its failure results in Type II diabetes. Diseases associated with Type II diabetes are obesity and Cushing disease. Steroids can cause chemically induced secondary diabetes, but it is transient.

What is happening in the body of the individual to cause her to become diabetic?

The pancreas is an organ located on the left side of the abdomen. It has several functions to perform for proper health, among them the secretion of insulin.

What is insulin?
Insulin is a hormone produced by the body.

How is the pancreas able to produce insulin?
A group of cells called beta cells are located within the area of the pancreas referred to as the Island of Langerhans. They produce insulin. Once produced, insulin, along with several other juices made by the pancreas, is secreted into the stomach and blood-stream.

What is the role of the insulin?
The job of the insulin is to metabolize (break down) sugars and other carbohydrates, so that the body can use them. It moves glucose into cells where it is used for the multitude of functions necessary to the body.
There are two key roles played by sugar in the human body once it's under the influence of insulin:
1. Sugar is used as fuel for the body. It gets the bulk of its energy when it's broken down under the influence of insulin.
2. Sugar is needed to carry oxygen to different tissues and organs, most importantly the brain. Without sugar, we cannot carry the appropriate amount of oxygen needed to remain alert.

When the body is not able to use sugar because of lack of insulin, it is forced to use fat for fuel. When used in this manner, fat produces byproducts called ketone bodies that are very toxic when dumped into the blood stream.

Hemochromatosis
There exists another common type of Type II diabetes. It is due to **hemochromatosis**, a condition that brings on iron over-

load. Recently, a genetic test has identified a gene called C282Y, known to cause hemochromatosis in Caucasians. Many individuals who have Type II diabetes believe the diabetic gene was passed to them by their parents when in fact, it is the hemochromatosis gene.

The iron overload, set off by the gene, accumulates in the pancreas. Ultimately damage within the pancreas destroys the beta cells (cells that produce insulin) and the result is diabetes.

The percentage of African American men or women who have hemochromatosis is not known. It was believed that hemochromatosis was seen mainly in European Caucasians but that is not the case. There are African men and women and other black men and women in the Americas who have primary hemochromatosis although these individuals are negative for the C282Y gene.

The gene that causes hemochromatosis in blacks has not been identified. More genetic research should be done to pin down the gene that causes hemochromatosis in people of African ancestry.

Testing

The serum ferritin test costs about $60 and is routinely available. An elevated serum is suggestive of hemochromatosis. Women who are menstruating lose iron every month, which may hide the fact that they have hemochromatosis. However, once they become postmenopausal the ferritin level starts creeping up and suddenly iron overload is a problem. Women who had an early hysterectomy and are no longer menstruating may be surprised to find that they have hemochromatosis.

REVIEW:

Iron is a very toxic material. When it is broken down it releases free radicals in the body resulting in severe tissue damage. It is the free radicals that cause damage to these tissues.

The iron causes the release of these free radicals, which gradually destroy the beta cells responsible for the production of insulin. Once the beta cells are damaged, elevated blood sugar begins to develop and the end result is a form of Type II diabetes.

Obesity-Related Diabetes

Obesity-related diabetes develops particularly in black and Hispanic women, since they tend to be more obese than Caucasian women[1]. If the condition of obesity persists for a long time, the pancreas will ultimately fail because it oversecretes insulin to keep the blood sugar under control. Diabetes sets in as a result of pancreatic exhaustion.

Diabetes, Obesity, and Treatment

Insulin is an anabolic hormone, meaning the more insulin is injected exogenously (from the outside) into the obese diabetic, the more they eat. The more obese they get, the more insulin resistant. The only way to break this vicious cycle is to treat the obese diabetic with a strict dietary program that can decrease the weight and increase the insulin sensitivity.

If at all possible, it is best to treat the obese diabetic person by combining an oral hypoglycemic agent with diet. There is a long list of oral agents available on the market. All of them are good. Some are Diabeta, Glucotrol, and Glucophage. These oral agents, except Glucophage, work by stimulating insulin secretion from the pancreas.

Glucophage works by making it easier for a person to use insulin in the blood stream. It does not work at the level of the pancreas; rather, it increases usage of insulin right in the blood stream. Because of that, Glucophage can be used in conjunction with insulin. It can also be used in conjunction with oral agents.

Gestational Diabetes

Another commonly seen diabetes is gestational diabetes. Pregnancy causes a state of insulin resistance in some women. In this situation, the amount of insulin needed to break down sugar is not sufficient to meet the demands of pregnancy.

If a woman is overweight when she becomes pregnant, it increases her chances of developing gestational diabetes because she is already in a state of insulin resistance. The reason that it is important that gestational diabetes be recognized early in pregnancy is that if the blood sugar remains elevated, it causes a state of increased insulin secretion. The elevated blood sugar then crosses the placenta, which causes increased insulin secretion in the unborn fetus. Fetal macrosomia (increased size of the fetus) develops, and the baby has to be delivered by caesarian section.

To diagnose gestational diabetes, a glucose tolerance test is usually done by the twentieth week of pregnancy. If the one-hour glucose test exceeds 140 nanograms/dL, then a 100-gram oral glucose tolerance test is performed. A diagnosis of gestational diabetes usually can be made after two abnormal results.

Gestational diabetes is first treated with diet, but if diet is insufficient to control the blood sugar then insulin must be dispensed. It is said that 30 percent of women who have gestational diabetes will ultimately develop true diabetes within five years after delivering the baby.

Early signs of diabetes in women may be recurrent fungal vaginal infection, recurrent fungal toenails, fingernail infection, recurrent paronychia (infection in the bed of the nails), recurrent groin fungal infection, and recurrent infection under the breasts. Infertility may be due to dormant diabetes. Also, frequent spontaneous abortions may be due to evolving, dormant, or overt diabetes.

Diabetes is a very complicated and complex disease that affects all organs in the human body in some way. However, the organs that suffer most from the devastation of diabetes are the end organs (the heart, brain, kidneys and eyes).

Other organ systems affected by diabetes are the nervous system, causing peripheral neuropathy with pain; numbness; and coldness in the toes, feet, and fingers. If severe enough, diabetic neuropathy can keep the patient from walking.

Some of the acute symptoms of diabetes are:
1. Weight loss
2. Thirstiness
3. Blurred vision

4. Urinary frequency
5. Tiredness and malaise

If these symptoms are not recognized, then the patient may go on to develop diabetic ketoacidosis, which can lead to death.

There is a subgroup of diabetes called **hyperosmolar-nonketotic diabetes**. It is a condition in which the individual loses so much water that the blood sugar can exceed 1,000 and sometimes 1,500 to 2,000. Because they have lost so much water, the brain becomes dehydrated and they skip diabetic ketoacidosis, falling directly into a coma. This is a very serious condition and if it is not recognized right away kidney failure from dehydration will result.

Some of the late symptoms of diabetes are:
1. Blindness
2. Chronic kidney failure
3. Coronary artery disease
4. Recurrent leg and feet ulcers with frequent loss of lower limbs
5. Peripheral neuropathy
6. Sexual impotence
7. Loss of libido
8. Gastroparesis

Problems associated with diabetic failure are: Dyspepsia (bad taste in the mouth and indigestion) due to a condition called **gastroparesis**. This is the inability of the smooth muscle of stomach to contract properly. It causes retention of food material in the stomach resulting in nausea, sometimes vomiting, and heartburn.

Another problem is urinary tract infection because diabetes damages the smooth muscle within the bladder preventing the complete excretion of urine. The residual urine allows for bacterial growth in the bladder, followed by urinary tract infection.

Constipation occurs because the nerves that control smooth muscles in the walls of the large bowel are damaged. Proper contraction cannot take place to propel stools downwards.

The Kidneys and Diabetes

Renal failure occurs in diabetics because high sugar in the blood damages the small vessels within the delicate and important structures inside the kidneys. Plaques (from the damage) cause them to become narrowed, preventing proper oxygen delivery to kidney tissues.

Roughly 60 percent of the blacks on dialysis in the United States receive this dialysis because of the effects of diabetes on the kidneys. Renal insufficiency ultimately leads renal failure.

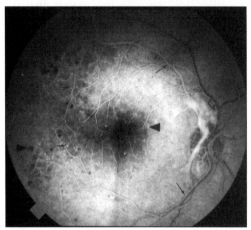

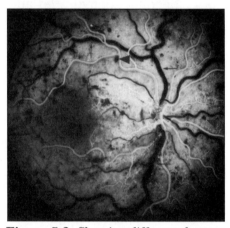

Figure 5.1: Showing different degrees of abnormalities in the eye of a patient with diabetes mellitus (diabetic retinopathy). Fluorescein angiogram shortly after injection of dye in patient eye.

Dye in arteries (white) and just starting to enter veins (large arrow). White area off NH is neovascular tuff (open arrow). Black spots are hemorrhages (arrow heads). Tiny white dots are Microaneurisms (small arrow).

Figure 5.2: Showing different degrees of abnormalities in the eye of a patient with diabetes mellitus (diabetic retinopathy). Large arrows showing dilated veins. Arrow heads showing hemorrhages inside the eye.

Why is diabetes so prevalent in African American women?

The answer lies partly in the fact that fifty percent of African American women are obese, and obesity has a high association with diabetes[2]. Obesity and certain forms of adult onset diabetes are closely linked and genetically transmitted. It's not surprising that they're prevalent in black women.

It is much more difficult to provide care for the patient who is both obese and diabetic.

Diabetes and Stress

Stress causes a person to secrete a series of hormones called counterregulatory hormones, which include **adrenaline** and **noradrenaline**. When secreted in large amounts insulin and noradrenaline can negate the effect of normally secreting insulin, making it difficult to lower a person's blood sugar. Most counterregulatory hormones, including cortisol, counter insulin's ability to do its work properly in the body.

The African American woman who is obese, diabetic, *and* living under stressful conditions has a constant interplay of oversecretion of adrenalin with insulin that is unable to penetrate the fat cells in order to lower blood sugar. All of this makes the management of their diabetes a challenge that is unique to their culture. Their treatment should reflect this special need.

What can black women do to decrease the incidence of diabetes and what can those women who are genetically predetermined to develop diabetes do to delay the onset of the disease?

The first thing for black women to do is to learn about their family health history. Knowing the family history may save lives. If either parent has diabetes, or if both parents are diabetic, then these women must be ever so careful and must see their physicians regularly for evaluation of their blood sugars. These are necessary precautions to delay the onset of diabetes and its complications.

Some of the precautions to control blood sugar are:

1. A diet rich in fruits, vegetables, protein, high in complex carbohydrates, and low in fat, simple sugar, and salt

2. Exercises to control weight, increase insulin sensitivity, and decrease blood sugar

Increasing insulin sensitivity decreases the level of insulin in the blood, which in turn decreases appetite and craving for carbohydrate containing foods. There are some Type II diabetics who need insulin in order to survive, because the pancreas is no longer able to produce it. On the other hand, there is another group who is non-insulin requiring. This means they still have enough beta cells left in their pancreas to be stimulated by oral agents to secrete insulin.

The way one finds out which group they're in is by trial and error. The patient's physician and the patient determine the types of insulin that are appropriate.

EMERGENCY TREATMENT

When a diabetic first shows signs such as elevated blood sugar, dehydration, thirst, etc., they are placed in the hospital for fluid replacement, electrolyte replacement, and I.V. insulin drip or subcutaneous insulin. If suffering from diabetic ketoacidosis, the patient should be treated with IV fluid, electrolytes, and regular insulin, either by I.V. or injection. If the person is in shock, it is inappropriate to give that person insulin subcutaneously. Insulin should be given intravenously so that it can get right into the bloodstream.

The treatment of diabetes and its associated problems is very complex and takes an experienced physician and/or expert in diabetes to properly manage. A general internist is a good choice.

Type I diabetes mellitus and juvenile onset diabetes are both treated with diet and insulin. Oral agents are not appropriate because there are no insulin-producing cells left in the pancreas for an oral agent to help secrete insulin in the bloodstream.

Diabetic patients should also have their eyes examined to be certain that they do not have diabetic retintopathy. Diabetics do not heal very easily due to poor circulation secondary to the effects of diabetes on the vascular system.

It is a good idea also for the diabetic patient to get in contact with the American Diabetic Association to become familiar with all the different programs that are available to help them. It is also very important for the diabetic patient to wear a medical identification bracelet in the event that they have a hypoglycemic episode in public or on the job.

A hypoglycemic episode, related to the condition of diabetes, consists primarily of dizziness, sweatiness, or a feeling of impending doom. Hypoglycemia (low blood sugar) that occurs on a repeated basis is very dangerous because sugar is needed to carry oxygen into the brain. When the patient is having repeated episodes of hypoglycemia, the brain is being deprived of insulin. In other words, when the diabetic person feels sick, it is best for him or her to ingest sugar because it is easy to bring the blood sugar down.

Hypoglycemia

It is much more difficult to treat the condition of low blood sugar or hypoglycemia. It must be treated in a hospital because it could take days to raise the level of the blood sugar. The half-life of hypoglycemic agents can be quite long.

Diabetes mellitus, while not a curable disease, is definitely a treatable one. There are plans underway for pancreatic transplants and if these become successful, then the disease can be considered curable. Insulin pumps are already in use. These pumps add a great deal to the treatment of the diabetic patient requiring insulin.

There is research underway to determine the cause of Type I diabetes and some day the answer to these problems will be found. Meanwhile, it is important for the diabetic patient to learn as much about both types of diabetes as possible.

Heart Disease in African American Women

6

Heart disease is the leading cause of death among black women and men in the United States, and the same is true for white women, white males, Hispanic males, and Asian and Native American men and women[1]. Every thirty seconds someone dies of cardiovascular disease in this country.

The death rate due to heart disease is much higher in black women than white. According to studies, in 1990, the incidence of black women who died as a result of cardiovascular disease in the United States was 67 percent higher than that of white women during the same time period.

What are the reasons for the marked difference?

- Black women are more obese than white women
- Black women suffer more hypertension than white women
- Black women are less likely to receive medical attention at an earlier age than white women
- The diet that black women eat contains more fat
- Black women are more likely to ignore the symptoms of shortness of breath, chest pain, and other cardiac symptoms than white women
- Black women are less likely to get proper medical attention at the emergency room
- Many black women live under conditions that are more stressful than many white women, thereby exposing them more to the possibility of sudden cardiac death

To add to the greater cholesterol, obesity, stress, and psychological problems with which black women must cope, there is a higher incidence of cigarette smoking among African American women than white women.

Repressed emotion could predispose African American women to high blood pressure and cardiovascular trouble. It has been documented that black women who live in the eastern part of the United States have less high blood pressure and fewer incidences of cardiovascular disease than black women from the south, due, in part, to the fact that black women in the east are in a better position to voice their opinions[2].

Females in general, are less likely to be taken seriously as compared to white males in the emergency room. They are less likely to be admitted to a Coronary Care Unit and less likely to undergo cardiac catheterization and coronary bypass.

How does hypertension cause cardiovascular heart disease?
Hypertension takes various routes in causing heart disease. First, having a high pressure within a vessel while the blood passes through causes the lumen (inside) of the vessel to get damaged. The damaged area traps debris as the blood passes through and platelets and lipid particles settle into it, resulting in a **nidus** (cavity which holds bacteria). Once a nidus is formed, plaque develops in it.

The plaque narrows the vessel, particularly in the coronary arteries. The narrow coronary artery prevents blood and oxygen delivery to the heart muscle, causing symptoms of coronary heart disease. If blood pressure stays high for a long time the heart muscle becomes **hypertrophied** (enlarged).

How does diabetes cause cardiovascular disease?
The high level of blood sugar in the circulating blood damages blood vessels, including the vessels around the heart (coronary arteries). Sorbitol is a sugar whose level becomes quite elevated in uncontrolled diabetes and it has a very toxic effect on different vessels in the body.

How does obesity cause cardiovascular heart disease?

Obesity is associated with cardiovascular heart disease by being associated with diabetes, hyperlipidemia, and hypertension (syndrome X, see page 00). A sedentary lifestyle associated with obesity increases the chance of cardiovascular heart disease. Obesity is associated with cardiovascular disease, not because the person is so obese that the heart has to pump so much harder, but because it is associated with a high level of circulating insulin.

Insulin causes plaque to develop within the vessels of the heart, resulting in coronary artery disease. The higher the level of circulating insulin, the higher the likelihood that the affected individual is developing coronary occlusive disease.

The more obese the person, the more insulin-resistant he or she is likely to be. According to studies, insulin causes plaques to develop around an individual's heart resulting in coronary occlusive disease.

How does the poor diet of African American women contribute to the higher incidence of atherosclerotic heart disease among them?

Fatty diets lead to higher lipid levels and heart disease. Higher carbohydrate-containing diets result in obesity, and its propensity to the development of heart disease. A diet high in salt contributes to the development of hypertension and high blood pressure.

Low fat diet and exercise decrease the bad cholesterol level. Here is the lipid profile.

- Cholesterol
- Triglycerides
- High-density lipoprotein (HDL)
- Low-density lipoprotein (LDL)
- HDL/cholesterol ratio

Each one of these five components of the lipid profile is a risk for cardiovascular heart disease when it's abnormal.

1. Cholesterol is considered abnormal when it is too high—greater than 200
2. the triglyceride, when it is too high

3. the HDL, when it is too low
4. the low density (LDL) when it is too high
5. the ratio of HDL to cholesterol when it is too high

(Coronary Artery Angiogram of Women with High Cholesterol)

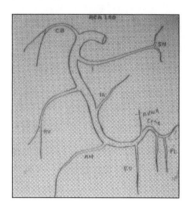

Figure 6.1: Once plaques develop then atherosclerosis follows and the end result is narrowing of the coronary arteries and arteriosclerotic heart disease and its multitude of symptoms and consequences.

How Does An Elevated Level Of Adrenaline Brought About By Stress Cause Cardiovascular Disease?

Stress induces the activation of the sympathetic nervous system. Activation of the sympathetic system leads to a release of adrenaline and other counterregulatory hormones. As the level of adrenaline goes up in the blood stream, it elevates blood pressure. Black women are already predisposed toward hypertension, so it is prudent for them to try to avoid stressful situations that put adrenaline to negative use.

If a black woman suffers from hypertension, each time she faces a situation that brings about anger her high blood pressure is made worse by the addition of adrenaline. The more frequently her anger is provoked in situations, the higher her blood pressure stays. If she faces racial discrimination in the workplace, for example, her blood pressure stays up for that period of time.

If she is taking medication, that may neutralize the problem, but if she is not taking medication—often the case—then her cardiovascular system experiences the full effects of high blood pressure. It is amazing black women survive as well as they do! Having such stamina proves that with a little preventive care they can transcend these health problems.

The elevation of adrenaline can help motivate black women to produce extraordinarily in the intellectual field, in the arts, in sports, and professionally. That is an effective way to use it, as a motivator to accomplish goals.

Adrenaline and Heart Disease

When one's level of adrenaline is increased as a result of stress, it causes the heart rate to go faster than normal. The fast heart rate causes an already sick heart to beat not only faster, but also in an irregular fashion. The fast and/or irregular heart rate is referred to as **cardiac arrhythmia**. There are many different types of cardiac arrhythmias, such as sinus tachycardia, paroxysmal atrial tachycardia (PAT), paroxysmal ventricular tachycardia (PVC), atrial paroxysmal tachycardia (APC), supraventricular tachycardia (SVT), bigeminies, trigeminies, quadrigeminies, couplets, atrial fibrillation, ventricular fibrillation, and on and on.

The vast majority of individuals die of coronary heart disease as a result of serious arrhythmia. Most heart attacks occur in the early morning hours. The level of adrenaline is highest around three or four o'clock in the morning, preparing the body for the day. This is known as the circadian system.

A sick heart with precarious oxygen delivery, as a result of underlying coronary artery disease, cannot tolerate the demands brought about by a high level of adrenaline. Stress can both cause cardiovascular heart disease and make preexisting disease worse.

Some symptoms of cardiovascular disease:
1. chest pain—most common
2. shortness of breath
3. pain in the left shoulder, radiating down left arm, with numbness and shortness of breath
4. a combination of the three previous symptoms
5. worsening of these symptoms upon exertion

6. irregularity and rapid heartbeat, sometimes slow heartbeat (**bradycardia**)

7. chest pain with dizziness, sweating, and shortness of breath, which can often mean that the patient is in the process of a heart attack

8. shortness of breath along with accumulation of fluid in the lungs

HOW TO DIAGNOSE CARDIOVASCULAR HEART DISEASE

To diagnose cardiovascular heart disease, the physician must:

1. take a good history
2. carry out a thorough physical examination
3. do an electrocardiogram (EKG)
4. follow up with a chest x-ray

These are required in the emergency room as well.

Based on these tests, the physician may prescribe a beta-blocker (a class of drugs that slow heart action), nitroglycerin, and aspirin (if there is no contraindication to aspirin in other words if aspirin is advisable). Arrangements can be made for the person to undergo a stress test provided they are not experiencing active chest pains. If the cardiac stress test along with an echocardiogram suggests the possibility of a coronary occlusive disease—artherosclerotic heart disease—then the patient may be referred to the cardiologist for a cardiac catheterization.

For the patient with chest pain in the ER a new test called Troponin-1 can be done. It is quite sensitive. Troponin-1 is a substance secreted by a cardiac muscle that has just become damaged. It is the first cardiac enzyme to rise when an acute heart attack has occurred. It rises one hour to six hours after heart muscle damage (Normal Troponin-1 is 0-0.4).

A more conventional group of blood tests that determine myocardial infarction are referred to as CPK. The total CPK is usually from 20–225 i.u. per milliliter. There are three different types of CPK that are measured; the MM which comes from skeletal muscle, the BB that comes mostly from the brain, and the MB CPK, which comes from heart muscle.

There are a few other conditions that can cause the MB fraction of the CPK to go up. They are Duchenne's muscular dystrophy, dermatomyositis, myoglobulinuia, polymyositis, rhabdomyolysis, Reye's syndrome, or Rocky Mountain spotted fever.

In a heart attack where there is heart muscle damage the MB CPK is elevated, so laboratories look for MBs higher than five percent. Most hospital laboratories are set up to do electrophoresis on the CPK MB fraction. Ordinarily the CPK is tested three times during hospitalization. It usually goes up between twelve to twenty-four hours and starts coming back down over twenty-four to forty-eighty hours.

There are two other enzymes (beside the CPK) in the blood whose levels go up after a heart attack. They are lactic dehydronase (LDH) and serum glutamic-oxaloacetic transaminase (SGOT). Of these three blood enzymes, the first to rise is the CPK, followed by the SGOT, and then the LDH. They go back down in the same order.

There are classic abnormalities seen on the EKG tracing when a myocardial infarction is about to occur, or has just occurred. The EKG might show what is called inversion of the T-wave. The physicians are able to map out the circulation of the heart as it relates to coronary artery, based on the 12 lead EKG.

It is very important to know how to read an EKG properly because infusing TPA prevents the heart attack from taking place. In fact, TPA can still dissolve the clot up to six hours after a heart attack has occurred. It opens up the vessel and prevents further damage. Often, knowing when the patient started to experience chest pain, shortness of breath, sweating, or just severe pressure in the chest along with the EKG finding prevents a heart attack from occurring.

If the EKG findings and the history are not consistent with a myocardial infarction, then the person is said to be having angina, unstable angina, or preinfarction angina. How a physician is able to determine if an individual has had or is having a myocardial infarction, angina, unstable angina, or preinfarction angina is based on the experience and clinical judgment of the physician.

71

A large percentage of individuals get admitted to intensive or coronary care units who are not having myocardial infarctions, or for that matter, no heart-related chest pain. On the other hand, some people get sent home because the physicians don't catch the signs. They end up having heart attacks at home. Women and minorities, as stated before, are frequently victims of these types of misjudgments.

Many articles contend that women—in particular black women—receive less attention in the Emergency Room with regard to chest pain. Black women also get referred less often for invasive cardiac tests such as cardiac catheterization to determine whether or not they have coronary disease. Yet cardiovascular disease is the number one cause of death in women, and the number one cause of death in the country.[3]

There are several possible scenarios when a person comes to the Emergency Room with chest pain:

• He or she is evaluated and sent home with instructions to see his or her doctor for follow-up, or is referred to a medical clinic for follow-up.

• The person is evaluated and admitted for further observation in a telemetry unit.

• An echocardiogram may be done to rule out other causes of chest pain such as mitral valve prolapse, myocarditis, pericarditis, etc.

• The physician feels that the person has preinfarction angina and is admitted for treatment in the Coronary Care Unit. Heparin and aspirin are administered intravenously or by injection. In addition, three sets of cardiac enzymes and Troponin-1 tests ordered. An EKG is taken for three days to be sure that a myocardial infarction has not occurred.

• The person found to have had a heart attack by EKG or by the first elevated CPK value, or the Troponin-1 value is admitted to the Coronary Care Unit for a myocardial infarction. TPA can be administered—if there is no contraindication—to begin dissolving the clot.

When a myocardial infarction has been ruled out, after three sets of enzymes and an EKG that is unremarkable, a decision has to be made about how to proceed. One approach is to do a nuclear adenosine, or MIBI test, a Persantine MIBI test or a stress echocardiogram—whichever the testing physician prefers.

If the results are negative, then the patient is assumed not to have coronary disease. They are sent home and taken off myocardial medication like beta-blockers and nitrates. These tests, though excellent, are not 100 percent foolproof.

If the patient continues to have chest pain and shows no clear evidence of acute myocardial infarction, then that patient is a candidate for immediate cardiac catheterization. That is when a tube is fed into the heart and injected with dye to highlight the vessels around the heart. An image of damaged vessels will indicate that the patient has coronary disease.

It is not safe to do a stress test on someone suffering active chest pain. Someone may have less than 50 percent plaque in a coronary vessel and this can be missed by a stress test. Yet, they will still be in significant danger for the following reasons.

A fissure can develop in a plaque as a result of certain enzymes produced by anaerobic bacteria from the mouth. The plaque then causes acute bleeding which in turn can result in clot formation, closing off coronary vessels. Bingo, a myocardial infarction occurs.

In a sense, 30 to 40 percent plaque in one's coronary vessel is more dangerous than eighty percent plaque because it takes a long time to develop that high an amount.

By the time it's 80 percent, collateral (auxiliary) vessels would have had time to develop which can protect the heart by providing new vessels through which blood continues to flow. When one has thirty percent plaque, there has not been enough time for collateral vessels to develop. As soon as a fissure develops in a vessel, the bleeding has no alternative routes and clots in the vessel much faster.

As an anti-inflammatory, aspirin may protect against coronary artery disease. Anaerobic bacteria bring on inflammation in the damaged blood vessels that feeds on ruptures in it. If the vessel is less inflamed it is less liable to blockage.

Stress Tests

Treadmill stress tests have some value in evaluating someone for coronary insufficiency, but they have a high potential for false results, especially in women, that they're inappropriate for evaluating chest pain. Nuclear cardiac imaging has replaced treadmill stress tests. The regular treadmill stress test is appropriate for someone in the thirty-five-to forty-year-old range being evaluated to fly planes, race, start a jogging program, or something along those lines.

Nuclear stress tests that evaluate the heart include:
1. The MIBI myoview stress test
2. IV Persantine or IV Adenosine
3. IV Dobutamine or IV Arbutamine
4. Resting Thallium distribution stress test
5. Stress Echocardiogram

In certain circumstances, a gated blood pool, known also as a MUGA, is also done.

The persantine MIBI stress test or adenosine stress tests are suitable for individuals who are able to exercise and need a stress test. One should abstain from certain medications for roughly two days prior to having these stress tests. Among these medications are beta-blockers (Tenormin, Atenolol, Metoprolol, Propanolol) and alpha-blockers (Coreg, Labatolol). Some calcium channel blockers should be stopped (Cardizem, Nifedipine, and Verapamil). Aminopylline, and Theophylline must be stopped, as well as coffee, tea, decaffeinated coffee, and other beverages with caffeine.

It's important that the heart pumps forcefully without interference. The higher the heart rate during exercise, the more stress on the heart. The more stress there is on the heart the better the evaluation of it. Anything that suppresses the contractile effort of the heart impacts the evaluation negatively.

The MIBI nuclear stress test or the Adenosine stress test

shows both angina and/or previous myocardial muscle damage. The sestamibi, or thallium test, has the same chemical properties as potassium; dead tissue cannot pick up potassium. The nuclear material is injected into the blood and the substance acts as a tracer in the patient's bloodstream. The entire process is computerized; color pictures of the heart gauge important characteristics such as the ejection fraction of the heart.

The nuclear cardiac stress test enables cardiologists to differentiate between normal heart muscle, scarred heart muscle, and heart muscle that is not receiving sufficient blood and oxygen. Physicians can tell exactly which coronary artery or arteries are diseased with plaques based on the result of the MIBI stress test.

During exercise, the area of the heart supplied by a plaque-containing coronary artery fails to deliver sufficient blood and oxygen to that area. It shows up in the test as an emptiness or lightness. The reason the area remains unchanged is because the muscle is scarred and, therefore dead. If the abnormal area remains unchanged, both at rest and during exercise, it means that this person has had a previous myocardial infarction that they may not have known about.

Another nuclear stress test is the Persantine MIBI stress test. This test is suitable for individuals with infirmities that prevent them from being able to use a treadmill. They might suffer from arthritis, be markedly obese, have had a stroke, or are advanced in age and unable to exercise.

The difference between the regular MIBI stress test as compared to the Pesantine MIBI stress test is that persantine is given to dilate the coronary arteries. The dilatation causes the heart to beat very fast, resulting in stress. The end-result is the same as exercising on the treadmill to raise the heart rate. An advantage of the persantine stress test is that beta-blockers and calcium channel blocker medications can be continued throughout its dispensation.

When the Test Results are Negative

If the person continues to have chest pain, then it's time for an abdominal ultrasound to evaluate the gall bladder. Gall bladder disease, such as gallstones, can cause chest pain similar to coronary heart disease. Medication like nitroglycerin, which relieves anginal chest pain, also relieves chest pain stemming from gall bladder disease, thus confusing the whole situation.

Gall bladder disease is quite common among black women. Thirty-to forty-year-olds who are obese and fertile are often affected. Black women are more likely than white women to have gallstones because of their tendency toward obesity. Obesity is highly associated with gallstones.

Some black women are more likely to have abnormal hemoglobin in their blood. Abnormal hemoglobin forms bilirubin stones. It is the dumping of bilirubin in the bloodstream that ultimately leads to bilirubin gallstones. This is why gall bladder disease is frequently seen in men and women who have hemolytic anemia.

If the abdominal sonogram is negative—ruling out gallstones—then an upper G.I. series must be done to look for diseases such as hiatal hernia (with or without reflux), esophagitis or stomach ulcers. Any one of these can cause chest pain similar to that caused by heart disease.

Mitral valve prolapse (seen on echocardiogram) and costochondritis (detected by physical examination) should be considered as well. Costochrondritis is a condition that causes pain in the ribs and upper chest. When the physician touches these areas with the examining finger, it is quite tender. It is the inflammation of bones in the chest wall that causes pain to occur. Conditions such as arthritis and bursitis of the left shoulder with radiating pain down the arm can simulate cardiac pain.

A Pulmonary embolism can be diagnosed by a lung scan. A condition called **Pericarditis** (fluid around the heart, within the sac in which the heart sits) can be due to viral illness or conditions such as system lupus erythematosus (SLE) or rheumatoid arthritis. These conditions can be diagnosed by blood tests (vital titers, erythrocyte sedimentation rate (ESR), antinuclear antibody (ANA).) Echocardiogram might show fluid around the heart and EKG might show certain ST-T wave abnormalities.

Pleuritis is an inflammation in the sac that houses the lungs.

The sufferer feels pain when breathing in. Viral, bacterial, or fungal infection, as well as collagen vascular disease can cause Pleuritis.

Chest pain can come from cancer of the lung, therefore a good chest X-ray must be done to rule out that possibility.

There are many conditions that cause chest pain, but the point is that the physician must keep an open mind and properly evaluate for these possibilities before proceeding to more invasive tests. It is neither too expensive or time consuming to do these things.

Sometimes the pain is extreme and frightening. In this case, the patient must immediately have a coronary angiogram to be certain that coronary artery disease is not the cause. It would be rather dangerous to wait to do a prolonged G.I. work up while the patient is having pain that could be risking the possibility of a heart attack.

Cardiac Catheterization

Before offering a patient cardiac catheterization, a thorough medical evaluation must first be completed. It is ill advised to do a stress test on a patient while he or she is having active chest pain, as the stress test might precipitate a heart attack.

Ordinarily cardiac catheterization for the possibility for coronary occlusive disease is undertaken when the patient has a positive stress test and has failed medical management. If the patient has major risk factors such as smoking, hypertension, hyperlipidemia, and a family history of coronary artery disease, in conjunction with the above, then this patient should be offered cardiac catheterization.

If the individual agrees, then they will be informed about catheterization and its possible side effects. It is a procedure that is done by highly qualified cardiologists as a subspecialty of cardiology. The procedure takes place in a special operating room, well equipped to provide care for the heart in case anything happens.

The Procedure

The procedure is done by making a needle size puncture in the groin, where the femoral artery is located. First the area is shaved and cleansed, and then anesthetic is injected. A puncture is made with a needle through which a catheter is threaded. The catheter is threaded into the heart, where it can be moved to different parts of its chambers. A dye which highlights the coronary arteries around the heart is then injected through the catheter.

A multitude of very important information can be obtained during the cardiac catheterization. The displaying of the coronary arteries may show evidence of plaques and narrowing in the coronary arteries. If the cardiac catheterization is negative for occlusive coronary disease, it means no gross coronary artery disease is present.

Coronary spasm can be seen or induced accidentally during cardiac catheterization. It can cut off blood and oxygen flow to the heart muscle sometimes, resulting in acute myocardial infarction.

Recently a condition has been described in individuals who suffer from long-term hypertension. Women, in particular, who suffer from long-term hypertension can develop this type of hypertensive cardiovascular disease. It involves the enlargement of the left ventricle and increased end diastolic pressure, suggesting that these individuals have what is called small vessel myocardial disease. Black women, because of their greater propensity for hypertension are quite prone to having this condition.

After completion of the cardiac catheterization, the results are evaluated and a determination is made as to whether the abnormalities found can explain the person's symptoms. In the case of chest pain, the key finding is coronary artery narrowing due to plaques of different degrees.

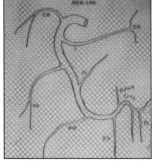

Figure 6.2: A normal right coronary artery.

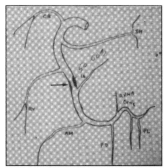

Figure 6.3: Big arrow shows 50 to 60% occlusion in the mid-portion of a right coronary artery.

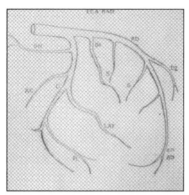

Figure 6.4: A normal left coronary artery.

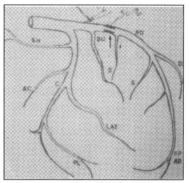

Figure 6.5: A 50% occlusion of a left anterior descending coronary artery, in a patient with both high cholesterol and hypertension.

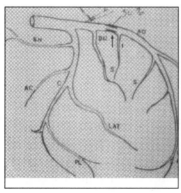

Figure 6.6: Big arrow showing 40-50% of the proximal portion of the right coronary artery. Small arrow showing 70-75% occlusion of the distal right coronary artery. This right coronary artery has diffused atherosclerotic changes in other areas.

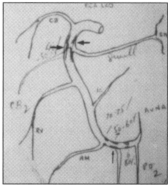

Figure 6.7: Small arrow shows 40% occlusion of the proximal left anterior descending artery. There is a 30% occlusion of the LAD in its proximal portion just before the first major septal artery and also there is a 40% occlusion in the mid-portion of the LAD. The big arrow shows 50-60% occlusion of the epical diagonal branch of the left coronary artery. There are several areas of diffused atherosclerotic changes involving this left coronary artery.

Based on the findings of the cardiac catheterization as mentioned above, recommendations are made to what course of action to follow. If for example, the coronary arteries are found to have plaques in them, then the possibilities are:
1. angioplasty
2. cardiac bypass
3. medications, when the disease cannot be approached surgically and/or the patient refuses to have the angioplasty or cardiac catheterization
4. contraindications to either number 1 or 2

Angioplasty is simpler than coronary bypass, but it also has a higher rate of recurrence. The act of entering through the vessels to push aside plaques can scrape the inside of the vessel, creating rifts where new plaques can form.

Sometimes a stent (a metal rod used to keep a coronary vessel open) is used inside the vessel to try to keep it open. It decreases the possibility of new plaques forming. These individuals are frequently placed on antiplatelet medications such as Ticlid, sometimes in conjunction with aspirin, for several weeks to prevent platelet aggregation. Angioplasty is done in the cardiac catheterization lab by the same cardiologist who performs the cardiac catheterization.

On the other hand, coronary bypass requires open heart surgery. It is major surgery and the hospital stay is longer and it costs more. The success of coronary artery bypass surgery is quite good, though some say that coronary bypass relieves symptoms but does not prolong life.

After angioplasty or coronary bypass, cardiac medications are continued. The list of medications used in cardiovascular disease is very long. The following is a list of different cardiac medications presently in use:
1. Aspirin
2. Ticlid
3. Nitroglycerin
4. Beta-blockers

5. Calcium channel blockers
6. Alpha channel blockers
7. Digitalis
8. diuretics
9. Nitropaste
10. Betapace
11. antiarrythmics such as Lidocaine, Quinidine, Procainamide
12. pacemakers (these play a major role in the management of patients with heart disease)

How do these medications work to treat heart disease?

Aspirin and Ticlid treat heart disease by preventing clot formation within the lumen of the vessels surrounding the heart. They do so by preventing platelet clumping, which enables such clots to form.

Aspirin both prevents and treats coronary disease. When a patient arrives at the hospital in the process of a heart attack, two aspirins added to heparin can ease damage to the heart. If TPA is injected into the patient within the first hour of an approaching heart attack, a great deal of heart muscle can be spared.

Beta-blockers are a group of essential medications as well. Among the most commonly used beta-blockers are:
1. Inderal
2. Lopressor
3. Tenormin

Beta-blockers mainly affect the sympathetic system, decreasing heart stimulation. They also decrease the forcefulness of its pumping, sparing the need for greater oxygen delivery. Beta-blockers are also antiarrhythmic (they prevent arrythmia).

The long acting beta-blockers in the Lopressor family actually cut down on the amount of adrenalin the body can secrete, and that decreases the incidence of death from myocardial infarction. That is why long acting beta-blockers are used to protect the heart when a person is sleeping. They respond to the body's 3:00 or 4:00 A.M. burst of adrenaline.

The harder the heart pumps the more blood and oxygen is

needed. If plaques narrow the vessels around the heart, that demand for blood and oxygen cannot be met. Beta-blockers, by cutting down the adrenaline secreted, spare the heart excess stimulation. In this way Beta-blockers prevent sudden death during sleep.

Beta-blockers also slow the heart rate or at least regulate it, preventing cardiac arrhythmias. A complex abnormal rhythm prevents proper pumping, and arrhythmias are frequently what stops the heart after an attack. In fact, using long acting beta-blockers, especially a 24-hour dose, will cover abnormalities and early morning attacks all at once.

Another group of medications used in coronary disease is nitrates. Nitroglycerin is in this group. Nitrates come in different forms, from sublingual nitroglycerin to nitroglycerin capsules, nitroglycerin patches, nitroglycerin paste, and nitroglycerin liquid that can be used intravenously. It relieves symptoms of angina pectoris by dilating the smooth muscles inside the coronary arteries, allowing for better blood and oxygen flow around the heart.

Calcium channel blockers are excellent medications that have multiple uses in the treatment of cardiovascular disease. Nifedipine, Cardizem, Verapamil, Norvasc, and so on, block the effects of calcium to the smooth muscle inside the coronary arteries around the heart. Calcium is involved in muscle contraction, and muscle contraction causes vasoconstriction. (Vasoconstriction means that the inside of the blood vessel becomes narrowed.)

The narrowing of the blood vessel prevents proper circulation of blood, thereby preventing proper delivery of oxygen to the heart muscles. When oxygen fails to reach the heart muscle a person feels intense chest pain.

Calcium channel blockers also decrease blood pressure because the relaxation of smooth muscle lowers blood pressure.

In black men and women, these medications must be combined with diuretics—if a patient is not in renal failure—to control blood pressure. Verapamil IV or Cardizem IV is used extensively in the emergency room for cardiac dysrhythmias.

Diuretics' importance in the treatment of cardiovascular heart disease may be puzzling at first. Heart failure causes fluid to be accumulated in the lungs, the abdomen, the legs, and the ankles. Loop diuretics, such as Lasix and Bumex, remove the fluid from the body, improving heart function and relieving symptoms of fluid overload.

Fluid retention brings us back to the issue of salt. Salt plays a major role in accumulating fluid in the body; therefore the intake of salt must be curtailed significantly in a heart patient. Anyone who has chronic congestive heart failure by definition has elevated sodium levels.

HEART FAILURE

Heart failure is rife with complications. When treated improperly, long-term hypertension causes the heart to become enlarged: its muscles have been stretched to the limit and it is incapable of pumping properly. Once the heart loses this ability fluid backs up in the body restricting breath. For example, a heart failure sufferer is unable to lie down flat.

Failure can also occur as a result of chronic damage from previous heart attacks, where damaged and scarred muscles lose their ability to pump properly. A combination of an enlarged heart, a condition referred to as **cardiomegaly** and **hypertrophy** (abnormal enlargement) of the muscles of the heart qualifies as heart failure. In 1998, 260,000 individuals died as a result of heart failure and each year 550,000 people are diagnosed with it.

MORE ABOUT MEDICATIONS—HOW THEY WORK

Digitalis is a medication that has been around for many years. If the heart is enlarged and the person has congestive heart failure, digitalis is quite effective in helping it pump.

Lidocaine is a very important medication; it is used for those who develop ventricular arrhythmias after repeated heart attacks. It is important to realize that after heart attack, it is often the arrhythmia that causes the person to die. If a physician can get to someone having a heart attack and inject lidocaine, his or her life can be saved.

Antiarrhthymic medications such as procainamide and quinidine are used for both atrial and ventricular arrhythmias. Quinidine can also be used to get the rhythm of the heart back to normal during atrial fibrillation.

ACE inhibitors. Captopril is a prototype of this family of medications. Literature has shown that when used for congestive heart failure, inhibitors not only improve the condition, but also can prevent a heart attack. It has been shown that aldactone results in markedly improved survival of patients with congestive heart failure.

These types of medications, and many others, are very effective. Different cardiovascular diseases require different medications used in combination in order to make the heart function properly.

The Pacemaker

Some patients will not need a permanent pacemaker. As their hearts recover, the problem that caused the slow pulse may resolve itself.

Pacemakers are inserted for different reasons. Clinically the patient has "sick sinus disease." That is when the area of the heart where the electrical system is located degenerates, resulting in heart blockages. A pacemaker must be inserted to take over the electrical functioning of the heart.

One of the most common symptoms of sick sinus disease is dizziness, tiredness, general malaise, and fainting spells. A person may feel that he or she is blacking out and may actually lose consciousness. This happens because the person's pulse has become too slow, sometimes less than 30 beats per minute. At this rate the heart cannot pump enough blood to the brain.

This happens in someone who has had chronic heart disease, or as a result of the aging process, or as a result of a heart attack. Sometimes a pacemaker or defibrillator is used to treat arrhythmias that have failed to respond to medications.

It is important to realize that the pacemaker can be tested even after insertion. When the patient is at home or traveling, it can be tested on the telephone. Such machinery is being modified all the time. Pacemakers can do wonders to keep people alive.

Valve Replacement

When an individual damages a heart valve during heart attack, it will bring on heart failure. It is important for it to be detected quickly so the valve can be replaced. The different valves of the heart can be damaged as a result of infection or of the aging process. Some get damaged because of congenital problems. Cardiovascular surgeons replace the valve to make the heart function better.

REVIEW

In recent years more women than men have died of cardiovascular disease. A larger percentage of black women have died of cardiovascular disease than white women. Therefore, it is very important that black women especially take precautions to prevent the ravages of cardiovascular disease. Pay special attention to the following advice, in addition to following a proper diet to prevent weight gain.

1. Exercise
2. Visit the doctor frequently to have blood pressure checked for hypertension
3. Take chest pain seriously and have it evaluated with a stress test
4. Don't smoke

Women's symptoms are not always the classic ones. They are not always the same as in men. They may be just shortness of breath. It may be a little pain in between the breasts or near where the upper part of the stomach is located. If the black woman has family members who suffer from heart disease, it is very important that she mention this to the doctor to ensure that she is properly evaluated for the existence of heart disease.

The incidence of heart disease in black women and the incidence of death from heart disease in black women can be brought down significantly, provided black women understand the gravity of the situation and do what's necessary to maintain health.

Cancer in African American Women

7

In the year 2000, it is expected that 1,220,100 individuals will be diagnosed with cancer in the United States. In 2000, according to the American Cancer Society, 552,200 persons are expected to die of cancer in the United States. This means that more than 1,500 individuals will die daily. One in every four deaths in the United States is due to cancer. In a lifetime, a man has a 1 in 2 chance and a woman has a 1 in 3 chance of developing it.

Blacks in the United States are more likely to develop cancer than any other racial group. From 1990 to 1995, the incidence of cancer among whites and Hispanics decreased, while the incidence of colon, rectal, and lung cancer increased among black women.

Overall, according to figures published by the American Cancer Society, African Americans are about 34 percent more likely to die of cancer than whites in the United States. This is an astonishingly large disparity. There is a comparably large difference in the cancer death rate between black women and white women.

Cancer is the second leading cause of death in the United States next to cardiovascular heart disease. It's also very costly to treat.

WHAT IS CANCER?

Cancer develops when a cell loses its ability to grow and multiply in a normal pattern. A good example of this is **contact inhibition**. When a normal cell is placed in contact with a hard surface in a petri dish, the normal cell stops growing. However an abnormal cell continues to grow. It has lost its contact inhibition ability.

The uncontrolled growth develops into a cancer growth. The cancer cells fail in the process of cell-to-cell interactions. There is normally a balance between **growth promoting genes** and **growth suppressive genes**, but once mutation occurs for one reason or another, the growth promoting genes halt the effects of the suppressive genes. The ultimate goal of cancerous cells is to destroy the body in which they are growing.

All of the following can damage the DNA/RNA materials in a cell (which results in malignancy):

1. Transmission of a hereditary cancer oncogene
2. Exposure to oncogenic viruses such as Epstein bar, which can cause nasopharyngeal carcinoma
3. Exposure to human papilloma virus, which causes cervical cancer.
4. Exposure to either hepatitis B or C virus, can cause liver cancer
5. Exposure to HTLV-I and HTLV-II which can cause T cell leukemia/lymphoma
6. Sun exposure causing basal cell carcinoma of the skin
7. Exposure to carcinogens such as tobacco
8. Exposure to ionizing radiation; it causes leukemia, lymphoma, and other cancers
9. Exposure to toxic chemicals such as benzene, which causes malignancies
10. Consumption of excessive alcohol resulting in cancer of the mouth, throat, and esophagus
11. Exposure to estrogen causing increased incidence of breast cancer and uterine cancer in women
12. Consumption of too much red meat resulting in increased

incidence of breast, uterine, prostate, and colon cancer

13. Long-term exposure to toxic pollutants and chemical solvents in the workplace

14. Nonacquired immunodeficiency and its propensity to cause malignancies

Cancer Genetics

Examples of cancers that develop genetically are:

• Multiple endocrine neoplasia (MEN) type 2a and type 2b—thyroid, pheochromocytoma, and hyperparathyroidism.

• MEN 2b—medullary carcinoma of the thyroid, pheochromocytoma, mucosal Neuromas, and bony abnormalities.

Cancers that occur as a result of damaged DNA and failure of DNA repair include:

• Hereditary nonpolyposis colon cancer (HNPCC). This abnormality is responsible for about 10–15 percent of colon cancers and is associated with ovarian, endometrial, and cancers of the urinary tract.

Other genetically associated cancers include neurofibromatosis 1 and 2, hereditary Wilm's tumor, LiFraumeni syndrome, and familial adenomatous polyposis of the colon. Treatment usually requires the affected individual to undergo total removal of the colon by 20 to 30 years of age.

Breast Cancer

In breast cancer, the BRCA 1 and the BRCA 2 genes have been discovered. Women who inherited these genes have an 85 percent susceptibility of developing breast cancer in their lifetime. The BRCA 1 and BRCA 2 genes are also associated with ovarian cancer.

Many more genes that have been discovered may be linked with cancer. Gene therapy is being actively investigated in the hope that treatment will become cure in the near future.

The cancers most common to women:

Type of Cancer	Cases Per Year
Breast cancer	175,000
Lung cancer	77,000
Colon and rectal cancer	67,000
Cancer of the cervix	12,800
Cancer of the uterus	37,400
Cancer of the ovary	25,000
Cancer of the urinary bladder	14,900
Cancer of the pancreas	14,600
Non-Hodgkin's lymphoma	24,200
Melanoma of the skin	18,400
Thyroid cancer	13,500

Different cancers have different predisposition and risk factors. One in nine women in the United States will develop breast cancer. The risks and predisposing factors for breast cancer in women are: genetic predisposition, such as a mother, maternal aunt, sister, or a grandmother with breast cancer carrying the BRCA 1 gene.

Additional risk factors for breast cancer are: menarche (first menstruation episode) at an early age (8–9 years); late menopause; childlessness; obesity; poor diet; birth control or estrogen-containing medications; cancer of the ovary, colon, uterus, or any other cancer; and exposure to carcinogens.

The mechanisms through which these risk factors cause breast cancer are:

1. Heredity: This plays a role in the causation of breast cancer by mothers transmitting the breast cancer genes to their daughters. Ten to fifteen percent of women have this form of breast cancer.

2. The earlier a girl begins to menstruate, the earlier her breast tissue is exposed to the effects of estrogen.

3. No pregnancy: When a woman is pregnant, breast tissues are less exposed to the effects of estrogen. It gives these tissues a rest from estrogenic effect.

4. Obesity: excessive estrogen is produced when a woman is obese. The increased production of estrogen comes from the cholesterol portion of fat. Estrogen is a hormone and cholesterol is the first step in the production of any hormone. Further, when an obese woman becomes menopausal, her breast tissues do not get any rest from the effects of estrogen because the excess fat is converted to estrogen under the influence of the adrenal glands. Estrogen, in turn overstimulates the breast tissues. Since 50 percent of African American women are obese, the incidence of breast cancer in this group of black women is high.

5. Excessive consumption of red meat and other fatty food increases the incidence of breast cancer because the excess fat increases the level of estrogen in the body, which in turn overstimulates breast tissue, increasing the incidence of breast cancer.

6. Birth control pills and other estrogenic medications overstimulate breast tissue, increasing the risk of breast cancer.

7. Exposure to carcinogens in the air, in the water, and in foods can cause DNA damage, which in turn can lead to increased incidence of breast cancer.

It is important that women whose mothers, grandmothers, sisters, and/or aunts have breast cancer be very vigilant about the health of their breasts. All women, in particular those who are at high risk for breast cancer, must learn how to do breast self-examinations. These women must have their breasts examined two or three times a year by a physician.

Breasts examinations should be started in at-risk women during their twenties. Women who have fibrocystic disease (benign cysts of the breast) should have their breasts examined 2–3 times per year because these cysts can confuse the detection of breast cancer.

These cysts are not cancer and do not develop into cancer, nor is there an increased incidence of breast cancer in women who have cystic breasts. The problem is the confusion that these cysts cause upon examination and in mammograms.

Fibrocystic diseases of the breasts tend to be found in females on birth control pills and estrogenic containing medications. Caffeine makes these cystic nodules worse. When a women is premenstrual or is menstruating, these cysts get larger because of estrogen's effect on the breast tissue.

One in nine women in the United States will have breast cancer. Therefore, it is important for women to be vigilant in self-examination and have frequent mammograms, starting at age forty. By age fifty, every woman should have a mammogram every year.

Figure 7.1: X-ray picture of positive mammogram for cancer

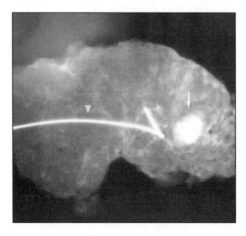

Figure 7.2: Needle biopsy of a breast cancer mass

Symptoms of breast cancer are: lumps, tenderness, skin retraction, discharge from the nipple, and/or pain in the nipple. Frequently, cancer is found on a mammogram without symptoms. Conversely, symptoms can occur when no breast is cancer present.

A Lump in the Breast

Once a lump is discovered a mammogram should be done, followed by a biopsy, or if it is a fluid-filled cyst, an aspiration of the cyst. The fluid is sent for a cytological evaluation.

There are different methods of doing a breast biopsy. One is a needle-guided biopsy. (See Figure 7-1, Cancer on mammogram and Figure 7-2, needle guided biopsy of breast cancer. The second is a straight needle biopsy of a breast mass under anesthesia.)

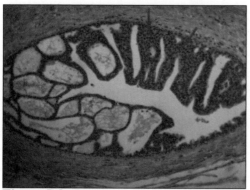

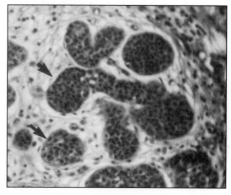

Figure 7.3: showing intraductal carcinoma of the breast

Figure 7.4: showing lobular carcinoma of the breast (arrows)

Once it is determined that a woman has breast cancer, an evaluation must be undertaken to be sure that she does not have metastatic disease. A metastatic evaluation for breast cancer includes:

1. Complete blood count, liver function tests (LDH, SGOT, SGPT, bilirubin, and alkaline phosphatase). If the alkaline phosphatase is elevated, it may mean that cancer has gotten into the liver or the bone—or it may mean that the patient has some other problem that causes her alkaline phosphatase to

be elevated, such as chronic hepatitis, gall bladder disease, or Paget's disease.

2. Bone scan.

3. Abdominal CAT scan or abdominal sonogram to look at the liver.

4. Chest x-ray or chest CAT scan.

If all these tests are normal, indicating that the breast cancer is localized. It's time for either a lumpectomy or mastectomy. The decision as to which is done is based on the size of the tumor, the decision of the patient, or the extent to which the cancer has spread.

STAGES OF BREAST CANCER

Stage I breast cancer is a breast cancer that is 2 cm or less.

Stage IIA breast cancer is a tumor that is greater than 2 cm and less than 5 cm.

Stage IIB breast cancer is a tumor that is greater than 2 cm and less than 5 cm and metastasis is found in node or nodes on the side of the malignant breast, or the tumor is found to be greater than 5 cm in size with no metastasis to regional or distant nodes.

Stage IIIA breast cancer has multiple scenarios.

1. Metastasis to node or nodes or other structures on the same side as the tumor.

2. Tumor no greater than 2 cm with positive lymph node or nodes on the same side as the tumor.

3. Tumor greater than 2 cm with metastasis to node or nodes on the same side as the cancer.

4. Tumor greater than 5 cm with metastasis to node or nodes on the same side as the tumor.

Stage IIIB A tumor with direct extension to the chest wall with metastasis to the lymph node or on the same side as the tumor or metastasis to mammary lymph nodes.

Stage IV is distant metastasis to other parts of the body such as the lungs, liver, bones, or brain.

Some of the most important markers that are used to evaluate and treat breast cancer are:
1. Estrogen receptor
2. Progesterone receptor
3. HER-2

TREATMENTS FOR BREAST CANCER

Different stages of breast cancer are treated differently. For patients who choose lumpectomy with axillary node dissection, post surgical treatment with two cycles of chemotherapy are followed by radiation therapy, then four more cycles of chemotherapy.

Adjuvant tamoxifen is used in estrogen receptor positive postmenopausal women. Tamoxifen can be used while they are receiving chemotherapy. Tamoxifen is usually used for 5 years and the results so far have been very good in preventing recurrence of breast cancer. The benefit of Tamoxifen in premenopausal women or those with an estrogen receptor negative tumor is not conclusive.

There is an increased risk of endometrial cancer in women taking tamoxifen. Tamoxifen is an estrogen-like medication and its stimulation of the lining of the uterus increases the development of endometrial cancer. There is also an increase in clot formation in the legs in women on Tamoxifen. Other side effects of Tamoxifen include vaginal bleeding, easy bruising, and **hypercalcemia** (high serum calcium).

Chemotherapies used in breast cancer and their major side effects
Cytoxan

Bone marrow suppression with low white blood cells, low platelets, low red blood cells, hematuria (blood in urine), alopecia (hair loss), nausea, and vomiting.

Methotrextate

Bone marrow suppression with low white blood cells, low red

blood cells, and low platelets. Nausea, vomiting, and sores in the mouth.

5-Fluorouracil

Bone marrow suppression with low white blood cells, low red blood cells, and low platelets. Nausea, vomiting, sores in the mouth, alopecia (hair loss), and darkness of the skin at the back of hands and nails. Chest pain.

Adriamycin

Bone marrow suppression with low white blood cells, low red blood cells, and low platelets. Sores in the mouth, nausea, vomiting, darkening of the skin, burning at the site of injection, danger of cardiac toxicity.

It is recommended a test called REST MUGA is done before starting Adriamycin to evaluate the ejection fraction of the heart (work the heart is capable of doing in one second). REST MUGA is done periodically during the treatment with Adriamycin and if the ejection fraction is shown to be dropping (indicating cardiac malfunction) treatment is ceased.

Herceptin

The main side effects of Herceptin occur to the heart, and that being the case, REST MUGA is done before Herceptin is started and repeated periodically, during its usage.

Taxol

The main side effect of Taxol is **neutropenia**, low white blood cell count; another frequent side effect of Taxol is **peripheral neuropathy**. Loss of hair also occurs in most patients receiving Taxol.

REVIEW

Women must do breast self-examination and get yearly mammograms beginning at 50. At age 40 women get their first mammogram unless they are at high risk for breast cancer. If at risk they should get a mammogram at an age that is appropriate for their situation.

LUNG CANCER IN WOMEN

According to the American Cancer Society in 1995, there were 47 million adult smokers in the United States—24.5 million men and 22.5 million women. African American men and women smoke more than whites.

The cancer causing material in tobacco is responsible for the high incidence of cancer seen in women and the high death rate from lung cancer. Other risk factors include exposure to industrial substances like toxic chemicals, arsenic, asbestos, air pollution, and the lung scarring which occurs as a result of tuberculosis.

Smokers exposed to asbestos have a greater likelihood of developing the lung cancer **mesothelioma**. A common characteristic of mesothelioma is calcification either in the lung or the diaphragm.

The most common signs and symptoms of lung cancer are chronic cough, coughing sputum with blood in it, chest pain, recurrent pneumonia, or recurrent bronchitis. Sometimes, lung cancer is discovered on a chest X-ray without any symptoms. Early detection is crucial in increasing the chance of curing lung cancer.

A chest X-ray is the first test. It is done either as part of a routine examination or because the patient suffers the symptoms described above. What is seen on the chest x-ray or CT scan in primary lung cancer is a mass or fluid in the lung, an infiltrate, or in some cases calcification (mesothelioma).

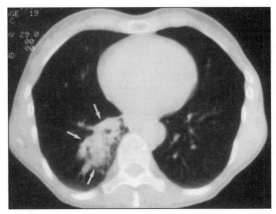

Fig. 7.5

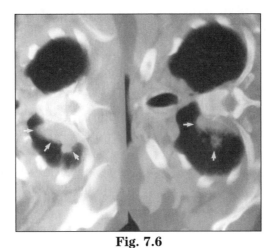

Fig. 7.6

Figures 7.5 & 7.6: are CAT Scans of the chest showing cancerous lung lesions

DIAGNOSING LUNG CANCER

There are two types of lung cancer, large cell lung cancer and small cell lung cancer. Large cell lung cancer includes adenocarcinoma of the lung, squamous cell carcinoma of the lung, and scar carcinoma of the lung. Mesothelioma is a form of lung cancer associated with asbestos exposure. Another name for small cell carcinoma is oat cell carcinoma.

In primary cancer of the lung, the chest X-ray shows a mass. Once cancer of the lung is suspected on a chest x-ray, the next test to be done is a CAT Scan of the chest.

See: CAT Scan of the chest lesion in inferior segment of the lower lobe of the lung. Squamous cell carcinoma (cancer) in a smoker, Figures 7.3; CAT Scan of the chest showing lobulated mass (cancer) in the right upper lung in a patient who smokes, Figure 7.4; and CAT Scan of the brain, Hypodense mass left cerebellar hemisphere-Metastatic cancer to the brain from a lung primary cancer in a smoker, Figure 7.7.

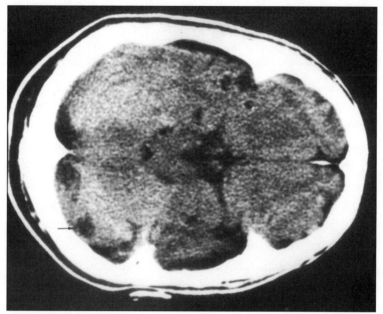

Figure 7.7: CAT Scan of the brain showing hypodense mass in left Cerebrallar Hemisphere (arrow). Metastatic Cancer of the brain from a lung primary in a smoker

Following the CAT scan of the lung, the patient is referred to a pulmonary specialist for a bronchoscopic examination. Another approach is to refer the patient to a chest surgeon, depending on the location of the mass. Some are located so peripherally that they cannot be reached via bronchscopy (see below).

Bronchoscopy

This is a procedure in which a tube is introduced into the lung. During the bronchoscopy, either a biopsy or washing is taken from the mass in the lung and sent to the pathology lab for examination.

If it is cancerous, then a chest surgeon may proceed to remove the segment of the lung that contains the cancer. During the procedure, several lymph nodes are taken out from the surrounding area to check for cancer in them.

Another method used to diagnose lung cancer is a CAT- or sonogram guided needle biopsy to obtain tissue for diagnosis. This invasive procedure is carried out by a radiologist with great precision. It saves the patient a bronchoscopy or open chest surgery.

It is very important to know in advance what cell type lung cancer the patient has in order to know how to proceed with further treatment. Knowing whether a person has small cell (oat cell) lung cancer or large cell lung is important because small cell cancer has almost always spread by the time a mass is seen on the chest x-ray.

The approach to the evaluation and treatment of small cell cancer is different from any other lung cancer. In fact, it is almost a given that by the time a coin-size lesion is found in the lung of a patient that turns out to be oat cell, the cancer mass probably has already spread to the brain and other organs.

On the other hand, once a tissue diagnosis is made that the cancer in the lung is of the large cell type, the decision is usually to remove the cancer because the chances of cure is better. Though it must be remembered that in 20–25 percent of people with the large cell type of lung cancer, the cancer has already spread into the brain by the time of diagnosis.

Evaluation of lung cancer includes:
1. History and physical examination
2. Chest x-ray
3. Chest CAT scan
4. Sputum for cytology
5. Lung biopsy
6. Abdominal CAT scan to look at the liver
7. Bone scan to be sure that the cancer has not spread to the bone

8. Brain CAT scan with contrast because a brain CT without contrast will likely miss disease of the brain. In certain difficult cases a PET scan can be done

Treatment of lung cancer includes:
1. Surgical resection of the cancerous mass
2. Adjuvant radiation therapy, after surgical resection
3. Adjuvant chemotherapy

Some frequently used chemotherapeutic agents for large cell lung cancer are:
- Cytoxan
- Doxorubicin
- Cisplatinium
- Etoposide

These are used in different combinations.

Some of the commonly used chemotherapeutic agents in small cell lung care are:
- Cyclophosphamide
- Doxorubicin
- Vincristine
- Etoposide
- Cisplatin
- Methotrexate

COLORECTAL CANCER

In 1999, there were more than 100,000 cases of colorectal cancer in the United States; 67,000 women and 62,400 men. It is expected that more than 50,000 individuals will die of colon-rectal cancer a year. Statistics show colon and rectal cancer to be more common in African American women than in white women. Consequently, their death rate surpasses that of white females as well.

Risk factors for colon cancer include a family history of it, inflammatory bowel disease (ulcerative colitis and Crohn's disease), familial polyposis, consumption of too much red meat and recurrent polyps in the colon.

Anyone with a family history of colon cancer should be carefully monitored for it, starting at age 35 with yearly examinations. A stool **hemoccult** (a test for hidden blood in stool) and **flexible sigmoidoscopy** (a test which allows doctors to look at the lining of the lower part of the bowel) should be done. Beginning at age 40, a yearly **colonoscopy** should be performed. Patients whose family have the gene for familial polyposis should be evaluated starting in the teenage years. Patients with ulcerative colitis or Crohn's disease must be closely monitored with yearly colonoscopy because inflammatory bowel disease predisposes them to the development of colon cancer. It is very important to monitor closely the stools of people who have the hereditary predisposition to colon cancer. People in the colon cancer age group are from 35 to 100 years old.

Too many fatty foods put one at risk for colon cancer, because when fat is ingested, large amounts of bile are required to digest them. Bile is quite irritating to the tissues in the large bowel, and it puts them at risk for an invasion of cancer.

Diagnosing Colon Cancer

To diagnose colon cancer, a complete history and physical examination needs to be carried out. As part of this examination, a digital rectal examination should be done and the stool tested for blood. Sometimes, a person might say that he or she has had hemorrhoids for a long time and suddenly the hemorrhoids have come out and are now bleeding. Sometimes a woman in her 40's comes to the conclusion that he or she has just developed a hernia.

In all these instances, a complete lower bowel evaluation should be done for colon cancer. When testing the stool for blood one should stay away from aspirin or nonsteroidal anti-inflammatory drugs (NSAIDS) for 7-10 days and 3-4 days respectively. It is also important to avoid red meat for 3 days prior to the test.

The tests most effective in evaluation of colon cancer are:
1. Barium enema

2. Colonoscopy

3. Flexible sigmoidoscopy

4. Rigid sigmoidsocopy

The barium enema is a sort of X-ray test during which the bowel is cleansed with cathartics and enemas. barium is put in the bowel from the rectum, and the x-rays show abnormalities. There are, however, a couple of limitations with the barium enema:

1. Retained stools in the bowel

2. Inability of the barium enema to diagnose cancer in the lower part of the bowel (cancer is best discovered in that area by sigmoidsocopy or colonoscopy)

Colonoscopy is the best way to evaluate the colon because the gastroenterologist can see the entire lower bowel and can biopsy any lesion or polyp that is there.

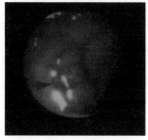 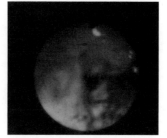

Figure 7.8: Colon cancer: sessile lesion of the colon (arrow)

Figure 7.9: Large obstructing colon cancer with bleeding (arrows)

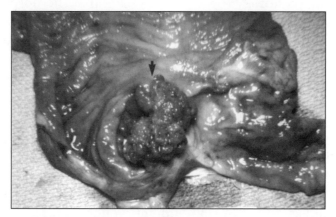

Figure 7.10: Carcinoma in papillary adenoma of cecum (arrow)

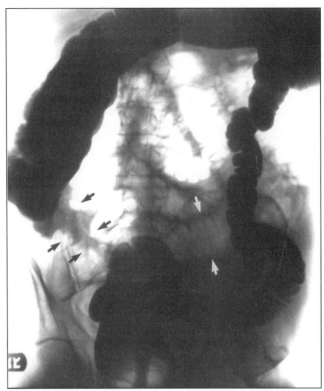

Figure 7.11: Barium enema: Apple core lesion of the cecum (black arrows) with small bowel obstruction (white arrows).

After the Test

If the pathology report comes back that the polyp removed is negative for cancer, then in about two years the individual should have another colonoscopic examination. Some people are prone to developing polyps in their colon. It takes about 3-5 years for a precancerous polyp to develop into cancer. The FDA has just approved Celebrex, a Cox 2 inhibitor used for arthritis, to prevent polyp formation in people who are prone to develop them.

The metastatic evaluation for colon cancer includes:
1. Complete blood count.
2. Liver function tests such as SGOT, SGPT, Alkaline phosphatase, and CEA (carcinoembryogenic antigen).
3. Abdominal CT to look at the liver and the retroperitoneal

area etc. or abdominal sonogram.

4. Chest X-ray or CAT scan of the chest and bone scan.

If all these tests are normal, then the assumption is made that the cancer has not spread to these organs and the patient is then scheduled for surgical resection of the cancerous mass.

Another form of cancer that develops in the large bowel is carcinoid tumor. The treatment approach is the same: first, surgical resection followed either by radiation therapy or chemotherapy depending on the histology and the extent of disease found at surgery.

Radiation Therapy

Radiation therapy plays a significant role in the postsurgical care of cancer of the colorectal areas of the bowel. Radiation therapy is more effective in cancer of the rectum than cancer of the colon. Whether or not a patient needs a colostomy depends on the location of the cancer in the colorectal areas. Sometimes the colostomy is temporary and sometimes permanent.

Colorectal cancer is curable when found early. Therefore, yearly rectal examination and testing of the stools for blood as well as a complete blood count can help prevent colon cancer from becoming deadly. If the treating physician does these tests and follows up on the results, pre-cancerous lesions of the colon and rectum can be discovered early and treated appropriately.

CANCER OF THE CERVIX

In 1999, over 12,000 women were diagnosed with cancer of the cervix. More than 4,000 were expected to die of the disease.

Risk factors for cervical cancer include: early sexual intercourse, multiple partners, a partner with multiple partners, sexual intercourse with men who are uncircumcised, and exposure to sexually transmitted diseases. Gonorrhea, Chlamydia, human papilloma virus, and Herpes are all sexually transmitted. Douching with corrosive solutions like vinegar and other homemade concoctions puts one at risk too.

Some of the signs of cancer of the cervix are abnormal vaginal bleeding and discharge. When cancer of the cervix is advanced, these symptoms are accompanied by pain.

When a girl begins sexual intercourse at an early age, the cervical tissues are immature. Trauma associated with the act of sexual intercourse damages them, increasing vulnerability to cervical cancer. When the cervical tissues are exposed to the irritating effects of sexually transmitted diseases (STD), dysplasia can occur, which in turn can lead to cervical cancer.

Tissue exposure to Human Papilloma Virus (HPV) is notoriously associated with the development of cervical cancer. Patients infected with the AIDS virus are also at risk for cancer of the cervix.

The uncircumcised penis carries a thick secretion under its foreskin. It is believed to cause cervical cells to become abnormal when they are exposed to it regularly. The labia minora and the clitoris of the female genitalia also produce the secretion seen in the uncircumcised penis.

Low socioeconomic status is associated with a higher incidence of cervical cancer. Poor women, generally minorities, do not go for regular Pap smears as often compared with thos women whose socioeconomic status is higher. All sexually active women should have a pelvic examination and a Pap smear annually.

Evaluations and Treatment of Cervical Cancer

Cancer of the cervix, if detected early, is curable. However, if the cancer is detected in an advanced stage, it becomes very difficult to treat and cure.

A cervical Pap (Papanicolaou) smear should be done to look for abnormal cells that may be precancerous or cancerous. It involves scraping of the woman's cervix when not menstruating and free of yeast infection. The procedure is carried out with an instrument called a speculum. While lying on the examining table, feet properly in stirrups, the physician is able to see the cervix. Multiple scrapes are taken throughout the vagina and sent to the cytology laboratory to be prepared for microscopic examination by a trained cytologist/pathologist. The Pap smear is very accurate when performed appropriately. It is graded from Class I through Class V. Class I is normal. Class II may be abnormal, sometimes due to an inflammation or infection. If either an inflammation or infection is found which causes a Class II Pap smear grading, it is recommended that it be treated and then the Pap smear repeated.

If the Class II grade reverted to Class I after treatment it is considered normal. If, on the other hand, the Class II grade persists, then further gynecological evaluation of the cervix is required. Class III to V requires cervical biopsy.

Recommendations for Pap Smear

It is recommended that all sexually active women have a Pap smear every year. If a woman is not sexually active and has had two consecutive yearly Pap smears that are normal, then she can have a Pap smear every other year thereafter. A Pap smear is necessary in women up to 60-70 years old. It is always important to get a vaginal pool along with the cervical smear. The vaginal pool detects cancer of the vagina. This is why two smears are taken, one of the cervix and the other of the vagina.

As is the case with many other cancers, cervical cancer is usually found in a more advanced stage in black women than in white, because many black women do not seek treatment until their cancer is far more advanced. In all stages of cervical cancer, white women have a 67 percent five year survival rate. On the other hand, black females have a 59 percent five year survival rate.

Black women generally have Pap smears less frequently so their cervical cancers are detected at a more advanced stage, followed by the lower survival rate.

Treatments of cervical cancer

Preinvasive cancer of the cervix is treated with laser or

cryosurgery, or with loop excision of the entire zone. After either of these treatments, the patient must remain under gynecological surveillance for life, with frequent vaginal examinations and cervical Pap smears.

Many factors enter into the types of treatment that are offered to a woman with cervical cancer: the size of the tumor, histology and stage of the tumor at diagnosis, lymph node involvement on abdominal CAT scan, ability to withstand surgery, the risk of radiation, and what the patient prefers. All issues must be brought into the discussion before deciding how to proceed with treatment.

Stages IA1, IB1, and IIA of cervical cancer are usually treated with either radical hysterectomy or radiation therapy. Stages IB2 through IVA are usually treated with radiation therapy. More advanced stages IIB, IIIB, IVB, and IVA, etc. are treated with radiation therapy in association with chemotherapy and pain management.

Chemotherapy for cervical cancer is not very effective. The chemotherapeutic agents used in advanced cervical cancer include: Cisplatin, Bleomycin, Methotrexate, 5FU, and Isophamide. Cancer of the cervix is a curable disease when discovered early with Pap smear and appropriate gynecological treatment.

CANCER OF THE UTERUS

The early symptoms of uterine cancer are abnormal uterine bleeding or spotting. Pain in the lower abdomen may be a late sign of cancer of the uterus. The best way to diagnose cancer of the uterus is to do an endometrial biopsy. Vaginal bleeding in postmenopausal women requires this procedure. If a woman is experiencing vaginal bleeding in between menstrual periods, a pelvic examination with Pap smear should be done, followed by a D&C, (dilation and curettage) or endometrial biopsy. If the biopsy is abnormal because of the presence of cancerous cells, then the abnormality has to be staged in order to determine the appropriate treatment.

In 1999, there were over 35,000 new cases of cancer of the uterus, and 6,400 women were expected to die from it. The incidence of uterine cancer in African American women is twice that of white women.

The earliest signs of uterine cancer are abnormal vaginal bleeding and frequent spotting in between menstrual cycles. The major risk factors are: estrogen therapy, treatment with Tamoxifen, childlessness, early menarche, and late menopause.

Estrogen increases the incidence of cancer of the uterus because it affects the lining (the endometrial lining). Because **Tamoxifen** has estrogenic effects, it damages the lining of the uterus, increasing the propensity of the uterine tissues to become cancerous.

Women who haven't given birth show an increased incidence of endometrial cancer because their uterus is constantly being stimulated with estrogen. Pregnancy allows the uterus a rest from estrogen for 7-9 months. These rest periods are important to the health of uterine tissues.

Early menarche is associated with increased incidence of uterine cancer because uterine tissues are exposed to estrogen for a longer time. (Ages 8-10 especially.) Similarly, **late menopause** is associated with increased incidence of uterine cancer because the longer a woman takes to stop menstruating, the longer her uterine tissues face exposure to estrogen.

If the endometrial biopsy is positive for cancer, the usual practice is for the affected woman to undergo a total hysterectomy to be followed by post-op treatment with either chemotherapy and/or radiation therapy.

Endometrial Cancer

Stage IA lesions of endometrial cancer (uterine cancer) are usually treated by removal of the ovaries and fallopian tubes. The reason it's important to remove the tubes and ovaries is because this cancer frequently spreads to the ovaries. Also most of the women who are affected by cancer of the uterus are postmenopausal.

Radiotherapy plays a significant role in the treatment of cancer of the uterus, in particular the stages that are not appropriate for surgery. The chemotherapeutic agents that are used in treating endometrial cancer are:

1. Cisplatin
2. Adriamycin
3. Cytoxan
4. Taxol

These are used in different combinations.

Before further treatment, the affected woman's overall health must be evaluated, to determine whether she can withstand surgery. If the uterine cancer is far advanced, then surgical intervention may not be appropriate.

If the affected woman is a good surgical candidate, then a preoperative evaluation is next. The preoperative evaluation includes CBC, blood chemistry (SMA20), urinalysis, abdominal CAT scan, barium enema, or colonoscopy, and EKG. Surgery for endometrial carcinoma is to be conducted by a gynecological surgeon.

Stage	Description
Stage 1	Tumor is confined to the uterine fundus
Stage IA	Tumor is limited to the endometrium
Stage IB	Tumor invades less than one half of the myometrial thickness
Stage IC	Tumor invades more than one half of the myometrial thickness
Stage II	The tumor extends to the cervix
Stage IIA	Cervical extension is limited to the endocervical glands
Stage IIB	Tumor invades the cervical stroma
Stage III	There is regional tumor spread
Stage IIIA	Tumor invades the uterine serosa, adnexa, or positive peritoneal
Stage IIIB	Vaginal metastases are present
Stage IIIC	Tumor has spread to pelvic or paraaortic lymph nodes

Stage IV	There is bulky pelvic disease or distant spread
Stage IVA	Tumor invades the mucosa of the bladder or rectosigmoid
Stage IVB	Distant metastases are present

(As published in 1988 by the International Federation of Gynecology and Obstetrics)

Endometriosis

Endometriosis is a gynecological problem that causes a lot of pain to women the world over. My research has shown black women to have a higher incidence of endometriosis than white women do. Endometriosis starts affecting the majority of women when they reach 30 years of age and seems to decrease by menopause. Sometimes adolescent girls suffer with endometriosis. This is often discovered when they are having difficult menstrual periods, as endometrial lesions are obstructing menstrual flow.

This disease comes from the endometrial gland's overgrowth. These growths can occur in nearby areas like the urinary tract, the gastrointestinal tract, ovaries, part of the uterine cervix and cul de sac, the sigmoid colon, and the appendix. Some of the symptoms of endometriosis include pain, dyspareunia, and dysmenorrhea (to be discussed in chapter nine). Infertility is a common side effect.

The gynecologist usually makes the diagnosis and decides on treatment. Surgical resection of the lesions (endometriomata) and hormone treatments are frequently prescribed.

Cancer of the uterus is preventable and curable if preventative measures are taken and the diagnosis is made early enough to prevent the cancer from becoming invasive. Early cancer of the uterus is curative with total abdominal hysterectomy. It is therefore important that women go to the gynecologist as soon as they notice unusual vaginal bleeding or spotting so that a thorough vaginal examination can be performed.

CANCER OF THE PANCREAS

More than 28,000 new cases of cancer of the pancreas will be diagnosed in the United States in one year; with the same number expected to die from it. About half of theses cases will be women.

Cancer of the pancreas occurs without any symptoms until it is too late. If the cancer is located in the pancreas near the common bile duct, it will be discovered early because obstruction of the common bile duct will cause a person to become jaundiced (yellow). Sometimes, the fact that the person is jaundiced may lead to saving their life because the cancer may be caught early. However, quite often, the cancer is already advanced and cure is not possible.

Usually those with cancer of the pancreas come to the physician with poor appetite, weight loss, and in advanced cases, left upper abdominal pain. The tests to evaluate cancer of the pancreas are abdominal CT scan. If a mass is documented on abdominal CAT scan, a fine needle aspiration can be done by the invasive radiologist to obtain tissue for a histological diagnosis (an examination of the organism). A gastroenterologist can do endoscopic retrograde cholangiopancreatography (ERCP) or a new procedure called endoscopic sonogram to obtain tissues to study the health of the cells. The appropriate blood tests to do when cancer of the pancreas is suspected are:

1. CBC
2. SMA 20 (blood chemistry), in particular to look at the alkaline phosphatase, the serum bilirubin, the SGOT and SGPT, LDH

Endoscopic retrograde cholangiopancreatography is an important test that can be done by a gastroenterologist with special training. During this test, if a mass is present it can be seen and material can be obtained for diagnosis. In addition, a stent can be placed to relieve the obstruction of the common bile duct to relieve the jaundice.

There are no effective cures for cancer of the pancreas. The treatments to relieve symptoms and alleviate pain are:

1. Surgical removal for early cancer
2. Radiation therapy
3. Chemotherapy

The chemotherapy combination most frequently used in cancer of the pancreas is 5FU, Adriamycin, and Mitomycin C, known as FAM.

Cancer of the pancreas behaves similarly to ovarian cancer in that it progresses with no symptoms until it is too late. If the cancer is located near the head of the pancreas, it might obstruct the common bile duct, causing the patient to become jaundiced. So, early development of jaundice due to cancer of the head of the pancreas might get a person to seek medical help. At least the patient would receive surgical intervention early on. Risk factors for cancer of the pancreas are:

1. Smoking
2. Chronic pancreatitis
3. Diabetes mellitus
4. High fat diet
5. Cirrhosis of the liver

LEUKEMIA

In 1999, more than 30,000 new cases of leukemia developed. It is expected that more than 20,000 will die of it. More than 9,000 will be women. Sixty three percent of individuals survive leukemia for fourteen years, forty three percent survive for five.

There are seven different types of leukemia:

1. Acute lymphocytic leukemia
2. Chronic lymphocytic leukemia
3. Acute myelogenic leukemia
4. Chronic myelogenic leukemia
5. Monocystic leukemia
6. Myelodysplastic syndrome
7. T-cell leukemia/lymphoma due to HTLV I and II

Symptoms of leukemia include weight loss, nosebleeds, paleness due to anemia, easy bruising due to low platelets, and hemorrhage as a result also of low platelets and abnormal coagulation. Those at risk include people with Downs Syndrome, people with AIDS, and people who have been exposed to ionizing radiation and toxic chemicals like benzene.

To diagnose leukemia it is necessary to do a complete physical examination after a history is taken. The most crucial tests are complete blood count, bone marrow aspiration, and biopsy. The bone marrow test and the blood count will identify the type(s) of leukemia present.

The most effective treatments for leukemia are chemotherapy and bone marrow transplantation. The five-year survival projection for leukemia has improved; in particular for acute lymphocytic leukemia. It has gone up from 38 percent in the 1970's to 55 percent in the 1980's for adults.

LYMPHOMA

More than 13,000 women a year are expected to die of non-Hodgkin's lymphoma. Some of the symptoms of lymphoma are enlarged lymph nodes, fever, weight loss, loss of appetite, night sweats, anemia, and sometimes diarrhea. Sometimes there is intermittent fever for several weeks—referred to as fever of unknown origin (FUO).

The best tests to do to evaluate lymphoma are:
1. Physical examination
2. Chest x-ray
3. Chest CAT scan
4. Abdominal CAT scan
5. Blood chemistry, in particular the LDH, Erythrocyte sedimentation rate (ESR), beta-2-microglobulin, CBC with differential and platelet count
6. A lymph node biopsy is the most important of these tests

The lymph node biopsy establishes the diagnosis as either non-Hodgkin's lymphoma or Hodgkin's disease.

There are excellent treatments available for Hodgkin's disease. Both radiation therapy and chemotherapy are effective depending on the cell type. Hodgkin's disease is a curable disease. Non-Hodgkin's lymphoma is also curable depending on the cell type and stage of disease. There are effective chemotherapy agents available to treat lymphomas and radiotherapy is also an effective treatment.

In 1999, there were more than 60,000 new cases of lymphoma. Included among them were more than 7,000 new cases of Hodgkin's disease and more than 50,000 cases of non-Hodgkin's lymphoma. Of these cases 27,000 individuals are expected to die of non-Hodgkin's lymphoma.

Some of the risk factors associated with lymphoma are:
1. Immunodeficiency syndrome (acquired and non-acquired)
2. Organ transplant recipients (because these individuals have to become immunodepressed in preparation for receiving a transplant)
3. Infection with HTLV I, high risk for the development of T-cell leukemia/lymphoma. HTLV I can be transmitted sexually, through needles, or blood transfusions. Frequently seen in the Caribbean, Southern Islands of Japan, northeastern South America, Central America, and New Guinea. HTLV II is associated with the development of hairy cell leukemia.
4. AIDS is associated with B cell lymphoma 90 percent of the time, usually of the large cell category. In 50 percent of these cases, the Epstein-Barr virus is a causative agent.

Other risk factors for lymphoma are:
1. Epstein-Barr virus in Burkitt's lymphoma in Africa
2. Exposure to previous chemotherapy or radiotherapy treatments
3. Gender—more men are afflicted with Hodgkin's disease than women
4. Previous infection with mononucleosis

Persons who have had infectious mononucleosis due to

115

Epstein-Barr virus are three times more likely to develop Hodgkin's disease. (Epstein-Barr virus is said to be associated with some cases of Hodgkin's disease.) Exposure to herbicides and chemicals is also associated with increased incidence of Hodgkin's disease.

MULTIPLE MYELOMA

Multiple myeloma is a cancer that comes from plasma cells. Plasma cells are cells that produce antibodies in the body to help fight infections.

Multiple myeloma is more common in blacks than whites. The five-year survival rate is 28 percent in whites and 30 percent in blacks. Despite a large difference in the incidence of multiple myeloma in white women and black women, the five-year survival rate for black women is better than for white. There exists no clear risk factor for multiple myeloma, although exposure to agricultural chemicals, radium, benzene, and radioisotopes has been mentioned in association with a higher incidence of multiple myeloma.

Some of the symptoms of multiple myeloma are bone pain; weakness; anemia; recurrent infections like pneumonia; osteoporosis; kidney failure; high serum calcium and its associated problems, including seizures. It is said that Interleukin 6 (a growth factor) is the causative protein that supports the growth of myeloma cells.

BASAL CELL CARCINOMA

The most common cancer is basal cell carcinoma (skin cancer), affecting about one million people yearly in the United States. This form of cancer appears most frequently in people of fair skin, and those constantly exposed to the sun. The most serious and malignant form of skin cancer is melanoma. Ten times more whites develop skin cancer than blacks. Other important skin cancers are Kaposi's sarcoma, seen mainly in individuals with advanced AIDS, and cutaneous T-cell lymphoma, which afflicts a small percentage of people.

Symptoms of skin cancer include a mole that has changed in size and color, usually darkly pigmented or a mole that oozes, bleeds or changes in appearance. Sometimes there is pain, tenderness, and itching. A dermatologist must quickly and immediately evaluate any skin problem that causes concern.

Risk factors to the development of skin cancer are:
1. Ultraviolet rays (exposure to the sun)
2. A fair complexion
3. Exposure to arsenic compounds
4. Exposure to radium
5. Exposure to coal tar
6. Family history of skin cancer
7. History of multiple skin moles

Melanoma

The most frequent symptoms are:
1. A sore that refuses to heal
2. Any darkly pigmented spot on the skin
3. Any mole or nodule with itchiness, oozing, and recurrent bleeding—all these should be examined and biopsied when necessary, by a dermatologist to be certain that it is not cancer

The most effective treatments for basal cell cancer are:
1. Surgical resection
2. Radiation therapy
3. Cryosurgery
4. Laser treatments

The best treatments for malignant melanoma are surgical removal with regional lymph node removal, radiation therapy, immunotherapy, and chemotherapy.

OVARIAN CANCER

In one year, it is expected that 25,000 women in the United States will develop ovarian cancer and more than 14,000 women will die of it. Ovarian cancer is hardly ever discovered early, so it is a difficult cancer to cure. A sign of cancer of the ovary is abdominal distention. The abdominal distention is due to fluid in the abdomen. By the time abdominal pain, gas, and stomach discomfort develop, the cancer is usually far advanced.

The best way to evaluate ovarian cancer is:
1. Pelvic examination
2. Abdominal examination
3. Pap smear
4. Pelvic sonogram
5. Abdominal CAT scan
6. Ca125 which is a marker for cancer of the ovary; when this blood level is elevated, it may mean that ovarian cancer is present

If an ovarian mass is found, then a laparoscopic examination should be carried out during which a biopsy can be taken for tissue evaluation. If nodes are seen, the invasive radiologist can do a biopsy. If the tissue taken is positive for cancer, then the gynecological oncologist will carry out a debulking operation while simultaneously doing a hysterectomy. In less advanced ovarian cancer, an abdominal hysterectomy with nodal dissection can be done. A complete lower bowel evaluation is always performed prior to operations for ovarian cancer, either with a barium enema or colonoscopy.

FIGO Stage Grouping for Primary Carcinoma of the Ovary (1987)

Stage	Description
Stage I	Growth limited to the ovaries
Stage IA	Growth limited to one ovary
Stage IB	Growth limited to both ovaries, no ascites, no tumor on the external surfaces, capsules intact
Stage IC	Tumor stage IA or IB but with tumor on the surface of one or both ovaries with capsule ruptured, with ascites present containing malignant cells or with positive peritoneal washing
Stage II	Growth involving one or both ovaries with pelvic extension
Stage IIA	Extension or metastases to the uterus or tubes
Stage IIB	Growth involving one or both ovaries with pelvic extension
Stage IIC	Tumor either stage IIA or IIB with tumor on the surface of one or both of the ovaries, with capsules ruptured, with ascites present containing malignant cells or with positive peritoneal washings
Stage III	Tumor involving one or both ovaries with peritoneal implants outside the pelvis or positive retroperitoneal or inguinal nodes, superficial liver metastases equal stage III; tumor limited to the true pelvis but with histologically verified malignant extension to small bowel or omentum
Stage IIIA	Tumor grossly limited to the true pelvis with negative nodes with microscopic seeding of abdominal peritoneal surfaces
Stage IIIB	Tumor of one or both ovaries
Stage IV	Growth involving one or both ovaries

Radiation therapy plays a principle role in the treatment of early ovarian cancer

Used in combination:

1. Cytoxan
2. Hexamethymelamine
3. Doxorubicin
4. Cisplatin
5. Taxol

Transvaginal ultrasound is one of the best methods of diagnosing ovarian cancer. It has a sensitivity of 81 percent and a specificity of 98.9 percent.

REVIEW

Cancer of the ovary is a very difficult cancer to treat and cure because the symptoms are almost always discovered when the cancer is far along. Women should see their gynecologists or primary care physicians yearly for pelvic examination and Pap smears. When appropriate, one should have a pelvic sonogram, so as to pick up any abnormality in the pelvis that might denote cancer in the ovary.

ORAL CAVITY AND PHARYNX CANCER (MOUTH AND THROAT)

Of more than 30,000 new cases of oral cavity and pharynx cancer, more than 8,000 can be expected to die from it. Alcohol abuse along with cigarette, cigar, and pipe smoking, and chewing smokeless tobacco are the major risks for oral cavity and pharynx cancer.

The usual symptoms of oral and throat cancer are—difficulty in swallowing, hoarseness, a sore that bleeds easily and does not heal, difficulty chewing and moving the tongue, or a white patch that will not go away. The best way to detect these cancers is by frequent examinations by an oral surgeon/dentist or frequent throat examinations by an ENT physician.

Sometimes it is necessary that a scoping of the throat be carried out, with photographs taken to identify the lesion(s) that may be cancerous. If a lesion is suspicious for cancer, then a CAT scan of the area is done to further evaluate the problem. After the above evaluations, a biopsy is usually done.

The best treatments for oral cavity and throat cancers are surgery, radiation therapy, and chemotherapy for different stages of the disease.

Abstinence from tobacco, and drinking alcohol only in moderation will go a long way toward decreasing the incidence of oral cavity and throat cancers.

BLADDER CANCER

Of more than 50,000 cases of bladder cancer expected to be diagnosed, more than twelve thousand can be expected to die from it. The most frequent symptoms are blood in the urine and increased urinary frequency.

Tobacco smoking and working with dye, rubber, and in leather industries are the most common risk factors associated with cancer of the bladder. The most effective way to diagnose cancer of the bladder is by cystoscopy (looking in the bladder with a lens fitted instrument, to visualize and biopsy lesions).

The most effective treatment for bladder cancer is surgery, immunotherapy, or chemotherapy placed directly into the bladder. When diagnosed early, in a localized state, the survival rate is 95 percent.

Much progress has been made in the detection and treatment of cancer, and many cancers are curable when detected and treated early. But much more needs to be done to understand the genetic transmission of cancer—the way cancer cells grow in the human body—so that genetic engineering can be used to prevent their growth. Society must take steps toward avoiding exposure to cancer causing agents and materials. Both government and the private sectors have a responsibility to make more money available for cancer research, cancer prevention, and treatments.

Kidney Diseases In African American Women

8

The different disorders that are associated with renal (kidney) disease in black women are:

1. Hypertension
2. Diabetes
3. Failure in black women who are hypertensive and diabetic
4. Chronic pyelonephritis
5. Sickle cell anemia
6. Polycystic kidney disease

The incidence of End Stage Renal Disease (ESRD) leading to renal failure is higher in black women than in white women.

There are sixteen million African American women in the United States and since three out of four African American women fifty-five years and older are hypertensive, it is not difficult to figure out the percentage of black women who stand the chance of getting renal disease from hypertension. About twelve million African American women have the potential of developing end stage renal disease (ESRD) if they are not treated properly for hypertension.

The reason that hypertension causes renal disease, which results in the need for dialysis, is that the kidneys have many vital

123

structures within them that are essential for their proper functions. Among those structures are the glomeruli. For a description of the functions of glomeruli, *see: The Kidney* in chapter one. The deaths of these glomeruli and other vital structures result in end stage renal disease.

In order to determine if the kidneys are sick and about to fail from years of hypertension, the physician will do a history and physical examination, as well as several blood tests, urine tests, and radiological evaluation. During this testing the physician can determine how high the blood pressure is, and examine the eye for evidence of hypertensive retinopathy.

Inside the eye is the only place a physician can see a naked blood vessel in the human body without surgery. By examining the vessel, the physician can tell if damage has occurred from untreated or poorly treated hypertension.

The Uremic Stage

In uremia, a patient may have sweet breath, flaky salty material over her skin, a swollen abdomen, swollen legs, confusion, seizures, and more. On laboratory examination, the urine may be unconcentrated with a very low specific gravity. The specific gravity is the measure of the ability of the kidneys to concentrate urine. The sicker the kidneys, the lower the specific gravity.

A kidney that's damaged by hypertension filters out plenty of protein. So by testing the urine during a routine urinalysis for proteins, the physician can be alerted as to how sick the kidneys are.

By examining the electrolytes (sodium, potassium, and chloride) in the urine of a patient with failing kidneys, the physician can tell whether a condition exists called acute **tubular necrosis** due to some sort of event such as heart attack or heavy bleeding with hypotension.

The urinary sodium testing is easy to do. One needs only to get a few milliliters of urine from the patient and send it to the lab for urinary sodium testing. In the case of acute renal failure, the urinary sodium is low. In chronic renal failure (kidneys that have been failing for a long time), the urine sodium is high. This quick and easy test is of paramount importance in the treatment of a patient who shows unexplained evidence of renal failure. When the kidneys are failing, they hold sodium in order to maintain the blood pressure and keep the body alive, but due to chronic damage a large quantity of it is allowed to pass out of the urine.

Another crucial test is the 24-hour creatinine clearance. It allows the physician to gauge how much function is left in the kidneys. The normal range of creatinine clearance in women is 125 milliliters down to about 75 milliliters per minute, and as a person gets older these numbers decrease accordingly.

In order to do this test, the serum creatinine must be measured by completely collecting all urine passed by the patient in a 24 hour time period.

The next series of essential tests are of blood electrolytes, which are comprised of sodium, potassium, chloride, bicarbonate, along with other renal function tests such as BUN (blood urea nitrogen) and serum creatinine. The reason these tests are so important is because when the kidney is failing, it is unable to filter waste materials from the blood stream properly. They accumulate in the body and result in a rise in the BUN, and serum creatinine first. As kidney failure progresses, the serum potassium will rise, while the serum bicarbonate decreases, resulting in a serious condition called **hyperkalemic acidosis**.

A serum potassium of 6 or greater is a medical emergency that must be dealt with immediately because the high serum potassium can trigger cardiac arrhythmias. These can result in death.

Blood Chemistry Tests

These are essential to the patient with kidney failure. They include the serum calcium, the serum phosphatase, the serum bilirubin, the LDH (lactic dehydrogenase), the CPK (creatinine phosphokinase), the total protein, and the serum albumin.

The blood tests necessary in evaluating the kidney failure in patients are:
- Serum sodium

- Serum potassium
- Serum bicarbonate
- Serum BUN
- Serum creatinine
- Serum phosphatase
- Serum calcium
- Serum bilirubin
- Serum protein
- Serum albumin
- Serum LDH
- Serum CPK
- CBC with differential

If the serum sodium is very high 150-160, it means that the kidney probably failed because of loss of volume (fluid) due to dehydration. Rehydrating the patient orally with water or intravenously with water and sugar (D5W), will normalize the sodium. Depending on how long the dehydration state existed the kidney function will probably return to normal.

High serum potassium is quite a bit more complex than that because there are other conditions that can cause the serum potassium to be high unrelated to renal failure. Assuming that the high potassium is due to kidney failure, the kidneys are unable to get rid of the breakdown products of proteins, which contain potassium along with potassium ingested in one's diet. The potassium accumulates in the blood, risking severe cardiac arrhythmias with potential lethal consequences if not brought down with either medications or dialysis.

Low serum bicarbonate, known as acidosis, is less crucial because the human body is made to tolerate acidosis much better than alkalosis—when the serum bicarbonate is high. Medications and/or dialysis can correct acidosis.

In alkalosis, when the serum bicarbonate is high, low potassium results, which is as serious as high potassium in causing cardiac arrhythmias that can lead to sudden death.

The high serum BUN is a reflection of the inability of the kidneys to function efficiently. They can't get rid of the breakdown products of proteins. Even though high BUN and creatinine indicate renal failure by themselves, they do not represent a threat to the life of a patient.

However, when the BUN and creatinine are high, the potassium is at the critical level of 6.5. If the phosphate is high, the serum calcium is low, the creatinine clearance is 10 ml per minute or less, and the patient feels sick, then the time has arrived for dialysis to start.

High phosphatase is a very important abnormality that must be corrected quickly because as the phosphatase goes up, the serum calcium goes down, and the low serum calcium is potentially deadly because low calcium can cause cardiac arrhythmias, seizures, tetany with muscle cramps, and twitching.

Examining the blood for possible elevation of both total and indirect bilirubins is important because in severe **hemolysis**, the kidney can acutely fail due to the clogging effect of debris from red blood cells, damaging the tubules of the kidneys.

Testing the blood for serum albumin is very important in renal failure because as the kidneys fail they allow protein to pass into the urine reducing the serum albumin. This, in turn causes fluid to pass into the extravascular compartment of the body resulting in swelling of the abdomen and lower extremities. This set of problems is referred to as **nephrotic syndrome**. In nephrotic syndrome, the patient passes three grams of protein or greater in the urine over a twenty-four hour period.

Testing the blood for total protein is very important because there are conditions such as multiple myeloma and other types of plasma cell dyscrasias in which the total protein is elevated and when protein is elevated, many complications can arise, including a condition called hyperviscosity syndrome.

If viscosity syndrome develops, the patient may experience

blurred vision, dizziness, unsteady gait, and memory loss. The acute treatment for hyperviscosity syndrome is plasma pharesis.

In multiple myeloma, renal failure occurs because light chain proteins filter out of the kidneys resulting in severe damage to the kidney tubules, which causes renal insufficiency or renal failure to develop. There is a form of myeloma called light chain myeloma in which the total protein is typically low and this is so because the light chains are passing out in the urine in large quantities and not accumulating in the blood to be reflected as elevated total protein. As the light chain proteins pass through the kidneys' tubules, the light chain proteins damage the kidneys. In fact, light chain myeloma is more frequently associated with renal failure than multiple myeloma. Multiple myeloma is much more common in black women than in white women. So it stands to reason that more black women suffer from myeloma kidney than do white women.

It is very important to test the blood for lactic dehydrogenase (LDH). An elevated LDH may be seen in a patient who has a cancer that no one knows about yet. Sometimes routine blood tests and physical examination are normal but the LDH, BUN, and serum creatinine are elevated. This could be a case of lymphoma, because in lymphoma, the cancer cells grow via the anaerobic pathway, meaning these cells grow in the absence of oxygen.

When cells grow in the absence of oxygen, lactic acid is produced as the end product of the anaerobic pathway and leads to lactic dehydrogenase (LDH). So a unilateral elevation of LDH in association with acute renal failure can mean one of several things:

1. Acute lymphoma with rapid cancer cell turnover making it difficult for the kidneys to filter out protein byproducts in the urine. The end result is acute renal failure.

2. When the LDH is unilaterally high, it could be acute hemolysis due to hemolytic anemia or any number of medical problems that cause red blood cells to hemolyze (separate from the plasma).

Once hemolysis occurs, the byproducts of the red cells will clog up the kidney tubules, which can result in acute renal failure. Black women have the propensity to hemolyze because of sickle cell disease and sickle thalassemia. If these hemolytic episodes are not handled in a proper clinical way, renal failure can result.

Elevation of serum creatinine phosphokinase (CPK) threatens the health of the kidney. It is an indicator of some trauma that caused damage to the skeletal muscles, which resulted in damage to the tubules of the kidneys. Therefore, when a patient presents with unexplained failure, testing the serum for elevation of CPK will reflect past muscle damage, and act as an important preventative measure for ongoing failure.

Doing a complete blood count in a patient is extremely important. There are three parts of the CBC that a physician caring for a patient with acute renal failure must be concerned with:
1. The white blood cell count (WBC)
2. The platelet count
3. The hematocrit

A white blood count of greater than 100,000 with **lymphocytosis** (increase in white blood cells) represents evidence of **lymphoproliferative disorder** out of control. The rapid cell turn over that occurs in this condition produces a large amount of purine, a protein byproduct that can clog the kidney tubules resulting in failure.

SICKLE CELL ANEMIA AND KIDNEY DISEASE

Another common cause of kidney disease in black women is sickle cell anemia. Sickle cell anemia damages the kidneys, as a result of both the occlusive and its inflammatory nature. Blood and oxygen flow are impaired to the glomureli of the kidneys, resulting in end-stage renal failure, requiring dialysis. The sickle cell trait often causes papillary necrosis, causing bleeding from the kidney.

When hypertension is added to sickle cell disease, the incidence of kidney failure increases. A blood pressure of 130/80 is normal in a person not suffering from sickle cell disease but in a "sickler," this is hypertension. Blood pressure is usually low in people with sickle cell disease.

The most effective treatments for renal failure are a low salt and low protein diet. Dialysis becomes necessary when renal function deteriorates to the point that the BUN and the creatinine are excessively high along with high serum potassium, high phosphatase, low calcium, and a very low creatinine clearance combined with evidence of uremia.

There are two types of dialysis that are in routine use:
1. Peritoneal dialysis
2. Hemodialysis

Different clinical situations along with the patient's preference will help to determine which type of dialysis will be used to treat the individual patient with end stage renal failure.

Kidney failure is preventable. Black women have to decrease the salt in their diet by half. Rather than eating an average of 7-8 grams of sodium per day, they should eat 3-4 grams of sodium per day.

Black women should exercise and eat a low fat and low carbohydrate diet, which will help them to lose weight. This will decrease or delay the onset of diabetes and reduce their incidence of kidney disease.

Diseases of the Stomach and Intestine in African American Women

9

Among the most frequent symptoms seen in the doctor's office are those relating to the gastrointestinal tract: Heartburn, bitter taste in the mouth, indigestion, bloating, gaseousness, increased flatus, nausea, vomiting, loss of appetite, dysphagia (pain on swallowing), pain in the stomach area, pain in the abdomen, recurrent diarrhea, rectal bleeding, pain on defecation, hemorrhoids. The list goes on.

The most common symptoms of problems with the esophagus are heartburn (dyspepsia), dysphagia, burning stomach pain, indigestion, nausea, regurgitation, and chest pain.

The reasons for these symptoms are:
1. Hiatal hernia
2. Reflux esophagitis
3. Slow motility of the esophagus
4. Esophagitis due to fungal infection of the esophagus
5. Cancer of the esophagus
6. Gastroesophageal reflux disease (GERD)

There are two different types of hiatal hernia:
1. sliding hernia
2. Paraesophageal hernia

Both types cause heartburn, regurgitation, bitter taste in the mouth, and chest pain.

131

In hiatal hernia, acid backs up toward the throat causing the symptoms as outlined above. As acid bathes the part of the esophagus that dips into the stomach, symptoms develop. Bleeding from hiatal hernia occurs frequently because of erosion in the part of the esophagus affected by the acid.

More bleeding occurs in paraesophageal hernia than in sliding hernia because in paraesophageal the affected part of the esophagus is stuck in one place. In sliding hiatal hernia the affected part slides up and down into the area containing the acid. The esophageal tissues are exposed to much less acid, reducing the incidence of bleeding.

Chronic coughing and throat irritations are frequent symptoms of GERD.

ACHALASIA

This is a serious condition that affects the esophagus. People who have AIDS frequently suffer with esophagitis (inflamed esophagus) due to fungal infection, viral infection such as cytomegalovirus, or Herpes viral infection. All cause painful swallowing.

Smoking and alcohol abuse is higher among black women than the general population and as a result, their incidence of cancer of the esophagus is higher.

A frequent contributor to stomach problems is the ingestion of contaminated foods resulting in indigestion and/or acute gastroenteritis with nausea and vomiting. Substandard foods are more likely to become contaminated, resulting in infectious gastroenteritis from bacteria such as Staphylococci bacteria, E. Coli, Salmonella, Shigella, Campylobacter, and many others. Another common reason for acute gastroenteritis is viral infection.

ULCERS

Another common stomach ailment is an ulcer. Ulcers are quite common in black women who must constantly handle discrimination. As a person faces racial bigotry, in many cases an intense anger is combined with intense fear. Both anger and fear cause the stomach to produce an excessive amount of acid and the increased level causes burning, indigestion, and eventually ulcer of the stomach. In order to cope with stress, many black women resort to alcohol and cigarettes. Both can cause severe stomach problems like peptic ulcers.

Cigarettes

Smoking puts a large amount of nicotine in the bloodstream. It sets off acid secretion, which increases symptoms of peptic dysfunction and peptic ulcer disease.

Alcohol

Peptic dysfunction is one of the common symptoms of alcohol abuse. Some of these symptoms include nausea, vomiting, retching, stomach pain, gastritis, **hematemesis** (vomiting of blood), and **Mallory-Weiss**, as a result of persistent vomiting. A Mallory-Weiss tear causes severe upper gastrointestinal bleeding, occurring as a result of forceful vomiting and retching resulting in a tear at the junction where the esophagus meets the stomach.

One of the most serious upper gastrointestinal complications of chronic alcohol abuse is **esophageal varices** (see chapter 10, Anemia in Black Women). Varices are small superficial blood vessels that develop on the surface of the esophagus. The occlusions of these vessels cause the spleen to become enlarged, which in turn causes the development of **portal hypertension**. Because the esophageal varices are superficial, they bleed easily, frequently, and profusely.

THE SMALL INTESTINE

The small intestine is attached to the lower part of the stomach and to the beginning of the large bowel. Three of the abnormalities that can affect the small intestine are:

1. Malabsorption

2. Inflammatory bowel disease (Crohn's disease)

3. Cancer of the small bowel

There are many other conditions that affect the small intestine as well.

Malabsorption

Malabsorption can occur because of **Sprue** or parasitic infestations often associated with AIDS. Fungal and viral infections of the small intestine such as **Candidiasis** and **cytomegalovirus** infection are seen in AIDS patients. It causes severe diarrhea with massive loss of minerals, electrolytes, and vitamins. Malabsorption results in general malaise, worsening the patient's condition.

One type of **Sprue** is tropical. Its cause is not known, but it is probably due to some form of microorganism, which releases a toxin into the small bowel. The result is malabsorption of iron, folic acid, vitamin B_{12} and a multitude of minerals and electrolytes. Some consequences of tropical sprue are weight loss, anorexia, diarrhea, and anemia. The treatment of choice for tropical sprue is antibiotics such as Tetracycline.

Nontropical sprue is another abnormality of the small bowel. This form caused by intolerance to gluten, a protein found in wheat. It is believed that this form of Sprue is inherited. It causes diarrhea, malabsorption, weight loss, and anorexia.

One of the common symptoms of small bowel disease is pain around the umbilicus. Others are diarrhea and rectal bleeding. Rectal bleeding can be due to **angiodysplasa**, ischemic colitis, Crohn's disease, Meckel's diverticulum, cancer, or other problems.

The lower part of the small bowel is attached to the large bowel. This organ is afflicted with the most devastating disease of the gastrointestinal tract: cancer.

THE LARGE INTESTINE AND THE COLON
Colon/Rectal Bleeding

Sometimes colon/rectal bleeding is evidence of polyps in the colon. They're precursors to cancer of the colon. Another cause of colon and rectal bleeding is diverticular disease. It's more common to people in developed countries as compared to the Third World, because developed countries eat so many processed, rich foods. Lack of roughage leads to constipation, which is associated with colon cancer.

Diverticulitis is a condition which results from an infected diverticulum (sacs inside the colon walls). Every now and then erosion due to actions of the stools works away at them. The end result is abdominal pain, fever, chills, and malaise. Diverticulitis is a very serious condition which can cause abscesses and sometimes perforation of the large bowel resulting in peritonitis and death.

Treatments of low-grade diverticulitis include antibiotics by mouth with low residue diet. For moderate diverticulitis, patients should be admitted to the hospital, fed by IV fluids, and given IV antibiotics. High-grade diverticulitis with possible abscesses also requires hospitalization.

If peritonitis is shown to be a result of perforation of the bowel resulting from diverticulitis, surgical resection of the affected part of the bowel may be necessary.

Bacterial overgrowth or **blind loop syndrome** occurs when bacteria grow in parts of the bowel where a piece of bowel is left in a pouch-like manner due to surgical repair or multiple diverticula. One of the consequences of blind loop syndrome is low B_{12} level (see chapter 2). A good indication of blind loop syndrome is a very high folic acid level in the blood in conjunction with a low serum B_{12} level. Antibiotics are used to eradicate the bacteria causing the overgrowth. After that B_{12} levels must be replenished with injections.

Colitis

Ulcerative colitis is extremely common in both men and women and the most common problem associated with it is rectal bleeding.

Ischemic colitis is seen in elderly individuals who suffer with diabetes and arteriosclerotic disease. It is associated with rectal bleeding and abdominal pain, fever, and elevated white blood cell count.

Bloody diarrhea is seen frequently in AIDS patients as a result of enterocolitis due to fungi, viruses, bacteria, protozoa, and parasites.

Constipation

Constipation can be due to many things. A diet deficient in roughage, fiber, and bulk can cause constipation. An underlying condition such as **hypothyroidism** (underactive thyroid gland) can cause constipation. Taking medications such as calcium channel blockers to treat hypertension or having angina pectoris can cause constipation because the calcium channel blocker relaxes the smooth muscles of the colon preventing contraction.

Using too many laxatives can cause constipation when the colon becomes used to the laxative effects and will not work without help. This condition is called cathartic colon. The treatment is to re-train the person in bowel habits.

Chronic constipation must always be brought to the attention of a physician because it is the first sign of cancer of the large bowel. The same can be said of chronic diarrhea.

Hemorrhoids

Hemorrhoids are found on the very end of the lower G.I. tract; namely the anus. The most frequent causes are:
1. Straining at stool due to impatience
2. Constipation
3. Obesity resulting in too much pressure being placed on the anal area
4. Weight gain during pregnancy resulting in too much pressure on the anal area
5. Driving or standing for long periods over many years
6. Obstructive colonic polyps or cancer of the colon resulting in straining at stools

If a hemorrhoid is combined with pencil-shaped stools, that usually means something is obstructing their passage. Someone suffering from this needs immediate medical attention.

The treatments for hemorrhoids are many and each person's case may be different. Conservative treatments, such as anal suppositories containing steroids, along with sitz baths or surgical removal of hemorrhoids either conventionally or with a laser are being used.

Anal Bleeding

Bleeding from the rectum is always serious and must be evaluated by a doctor. If one assumes rectal bleeding to be hemorrhoids, the time spent self-medicating destroys the chance of an early diagnosis of colon and rectal cancer. Women who are bashful have a tendency to do nothing when they see blood in their stools, and delay the diagnosis of serious problems.

Anal fissures and inflammation associated with colitis might also be the cause of rectal bleeding.

HOW TO EVALUATE GASTROINTESTINAL COMPLAINTS

The first thing a physician must do is take a careful history followed by physical examination. Next is prescribing medications along with diet modifications. Depending on the severity of the symptoms and/or the physical findings, blood tests, x-rays, or endoscopic examination might be needed.

If a patient's complaint is pain in the stomach, heartburn, hyperacididty, vomiting blood, or bleeding from the stomach, doing a CBC, serum ferritin, upper G.I. series, endoscopy examination, and abdominal sonogram are sufficient to discover most of the problems associated with the upper G.I. tract, gall bladder, and the pancreas.

An abdominal CAT scan may be needed to evaluate for pancreatic cancer. The abdominal CT is a good way to evaluate cancer of the gall bladder and the liver.

An instrument called a **sigmoidoscope** can be used to look

137

inside the lower bowel. There are two different types of sigmoidoscopes, a rigid one and a flexible one. The rigid scope can be passed up to 30 cm and the flexible scope can be passed up to 60 cm.

A **colonoscope** is a long, flexible, and hollow instrument that allows the gastroenterologist to examine the entire large bowel for abnormalities. Biopsies can be taken during these procedures and lesions such as polyps removed. When necessary, an **anoscope** can be used to look inside the rectum to evaluate local problems in that part of the bowel.

According to the recent literature, there is a microorganism that lives in the stomach of many individuals who have chronic peptic ulcer disease of the stomach. This organism is called **Helicobacter pylori.** If untreated this organism can ultimately cause cancer of the stomach. To diagnose this infection, gastric material is taken from the stomach and tested for its presence. A blood test is also available for the presence of H. pylori antibody.

HOW TO EVALUATE DISEASES OF THE GASTROINTESTINAL TRACT

The beginning of the G.I. tract is the mouth, and the best way to evaluate the mouth is by the naked eye. To evaluate the throat, a laryngoscope may be used. To evaluate the esophagus, either X-ray or endoscopy can be used.

To evaluate the stomach, an upper G.I. series or endoscopic examination makes the stomach visible. Biopsies can be done if necessary. If a gastric ulcer is detected during the upper G.I. series, then endoscopic examination must be carried out so that it can be biopsied to rule out cancer. Gastric ulcers have a high propensity to be cancerous.

The best way to evaluate the small bowel is using barium swallow with small bowel follow through. Some of the diseases found in the small bowel are Crohn's disease, cancer, malabsorption, Meckel's diverticulum, and arteriovenous malformation. To evaluate the large bowel (colon or intestine), barium enema, colonoscopy, rigid or flexible sigmoidoscopic examinations will suffice.

HOW BEST TO TREAT THE DISEASES OF THE GASTROINTESTINAL TRACT

One of the common complaints that bring patients to the physician's office is heartburn. Heartburn can be due to hiatal hernia with reflux esophagitis. Black women can suffer from this condition, especially if they are obese; obesity has a close association with hiatal hernia and heartburn. Treatments are:

1. Weight loss
2. Low fat diet
3. Decreased caffeine intake
4. Decreased alcohol consumption
5. Sleeping with head of the bed up, or placing 2-3 pillows under one's head when sleeping to prevent the free flow of acid toward the throat
6. Reglan 10 mg, 30 minutes before meals, three times a day and at bedtime

Reglan propels foods down the stomach with more ease, preventing excessive acid production. When food sits in the stomach too long, acid is over-produced. It backs up towards the upper chest causing hyperacidity, heartburn, bad taste in the mouth, bad breath and chest pain. Whenever the stomach senses food it sends a signal to the lining of the stomach where the acid producing cells are located to secrete more acid to digest the food.

H2 blockers such as Tagamet, Axid, Zantac, and Pepcid are used also in hiatal hernia with reflux with very good success. They block the production of excess acid, preventing the formation of ulcerations around the esophagus, decreasing the symptoms of heartburn.

There is no surgical procedure to repair hiatal hernia though there have been some recent claims that it can be repaired using laser. Gastroesophageal reflux disease (GERD) is being treated laproscopically, using a wraparound surgical technique that seems to be enjoying some degree of success.

Antacids such as Mylanta, Maalox, Rolaids, etc. are also helpful in relieving symptoms of heartburn and hyperacidity associated with hiatal hernia with reflux.

The best treatment available for stomach ulcers are H2 blockers, such as Tagamet, Axid, Zantac, Pepcid, and more powerful ones like Prilosec and Prevecid. These medications are usually used for two months to treat ulcers that are proven by upper G.I. series or endoscopic examination. After two months, a repeat examination is done. If the ulcer has healed, then based on symptoms, the physician may chose to continue treatment for a few more weeks or not.

If the ulcer is only partially healed then treatment with an H2 blocker can continue for two more months. If the last two months of treatment fail, a biopsy via endoscopic examination becomes mandatory to rule out cancer.

It is now accepted practice to test for H. pylori at the time of endoscopic examination using gastric tissue via biopsy to test for the presence or absence of this microorganism.

There are several ways to approach the treatment of H. pylori. One is to test the gastric tissue using a color change test (the CLO test). If the color changes from yellow to red when the tissue is placed in a medium, then it means H. pylori is present. Another way is to test the blood for the antibody of H. pylori and if the antibody is found then H. pylori is documented.

NSAIDS and Ulcers

Women with peptic ulcer disease should not take these medications because they cause gastrointestinal bleeding. The most effective and the only medication approved by the FDA to prevent bleeding from the stomach (gastric ulcer) caused by aspirin and NSAIDS is misoprostol (Cytotec). Cytotec is used at 100 mg three times per day with food. It is a prostaglandin analog and its mode of action is:

1. To increase the pH of the gastric juice

2. To increase mucous production by the stomach

3. To increase blood flow to the lining of the stomach thereby preventing erosions and ulcerations of the stomach wall

Because Cytotec is a prostaglandin analog, it can induce abortion. Therefore, women of childbearing age should not take this medication when pregnant. It can also cause deformities in a fetus.

Methotrexate, has major side effects to the liver and bone marrow so a physician must watch blood count and liver function tests.

Surgery

Surgical treatment is still used for treating ulcers of the stomach under specific circumstances. When an ulcer of the stomach fails to stop bleeding in spite of all medical treatments and in particular, when the patient who is bleeding receives too much blood; a gastrectomy is usually carried out to stop the bleeding and save the patient's life.

Gastrectomy is used when a biopsy of the stomach reveals the presence of cancer. More often than not, other treatments such as chemotherapy and/or radiotherapy are used as well.

The small intestine is frequently affected by Crohn's disease, in which case steroids with Azulfidine and added folic acid are dispensed. Surgical resection of part of the small intestine is also frequently carried out as part of the treatment as well.

Lactose Intolerance

About 60 percent of blacks suffer from lactose intolerance. In addition to abdominal cramps, flatulence, nausea, and gaseousness, lactose intolerance causes diarrhea. There is an enzyme called lactase, produced by cells in the lining of the intestine, and its role is to break lactose down into glucose and galactose.

If a person lacks lactase, ingesting dairy products results in bowel discomfort. Lactose intolerance is hereditary, but often gets worse with age. Avoiding dairy products is the mainstay of treatment. Some individuals with a mild to moderate form of this condition may benefit from taking a pill called Lactaid or drinking milk containing lactaid.

AIDS

AIDS is one of the most prevalent diseases of our time and diarrhea is one of the most severe problems that AIDS patients have to deal with. The causes of the diarrhea in AIDS patients are due to microbial, viral, and parasitic organisms. Rectal cancer or Kaposi's sarcoma can also cause rectal bleeding and diarrhea.

CMV-associated enterocolitis is quite common in AIDS patients. Herpes simplex gastroenteritis with diarrhea is common in AIDS patients.

In addition, AIDS patients frequently have gastroenteritis with diarrhea due to giardiasis, amebiasis, candidiasis, cryptosporidium, isospora belli, salmonella, and shigella.

E. Coli

Poorly cooked meats are a food source of E. Coli contamination. In the case of Staphylococcus food poisoning, the endotoxin that this organism produces is actually ingested by the individual being contaminated, resulting in symptoms eight hours later. This happens quickly because the bacterial organisms do not have to multiply in the intestine in order to produce the endotoxin.

In other situations such as, the bacteria need time to multiply in the colon to bring about the symptoms. Therefore, a person may get sick one or two days later.

INFLAMMATORY BOWEL DISEASE

No cure has been found for inflammatory bowel disease but significant progress has been made with different forms of steroid medications either in oral, intravenous, or in enema form. Medications such as Azulfidine, and Asocal have made a big difference in the majority of people suffering from inflammatory bowel disease.

There is a higher incidence of colon cancer in people suffering from inflammatory bowel disease. The reason is not all together clear, but certainly the repeated inflammatory reactions and scarring that the bowel is exposed to play a major role.

FLATULENCE

Flatulence is a condition that manifests itself by excessive passing of gas from the rectum. It is a normal biological function to pass gas from the rectum. The gas that is formed and expelled from the rectum is essentially methane. It is, however, abnormal when the gas a person passes is malodorous and when the frequency of passing gas is excessive.

When a person passes large amounts of malodorous gas too frequently, it requires medical evaluation.

MENSTRUAL PAIN

Over the centuries, women have taken aspirin to relieve menstrual pain. Women also take nonsteroidal anti-inflammatory drugs. These medications are anti-prostaglandin. By blocking the effects of prostaglandins, the uterine muscle relaxes while the medication relieves uterine pain.

GASTROENTERITIS

Infectious gastroenteritis requires treatment in the hospital with IV fluid, IV electrolyte replacement, and IV antibiotics. The IV fluid must contain dextrose with sodium chloride. The purpose of the dextrose is to maintain the affected patient in an anabolic state to hasten recovery. In this setting, even a diabetic patient can be given dextrose with added regular insulin. The patient can also be treated at home with oral medication.

Acute gastroenteritis can be due to viruses. Viral gastroenteritis is quite common and can be very severe if not treated prompt-ly and properly. Its complications include electrolyte imbalance, cardiac arrhythmia, renal failure, and DIC, depending on underly-ing chronic medical problems and the age of the individuals affected.

Treatments are by fluid IV or by mouth to prevent dehydra-tion. Electrolyte replacement is accomplished with soups, sodas, juices, or IV. Antipyretics such as Advil and Tylenol are important to bring fevers down. Antidiarrhea and anti-nausea medications as described above are helpful as well.

Differentiating bacterial, viral, fungal, or parasitic gastroen-teritis is left to the physician.

INTESTINAL PARASITES

People who originate or travel to the tropics, or who live in the rural parts of the southern United States can suffer from intesti-nal parasites. Intestinal parasitism is commonly seen in people who migrated to the United States from Southeast Asia and other third world countries where poor sanitation and poverty are prevalent. Examples of intestinal parasites are **Necator Americanus, Trichuris trichiuria, Schistosoma mansoni, Tenia saginata, Tenia solium, Ascaris, lumbricoides, pin-worm** and **hookworm.**

The symptoms of intestinal parasitic infection can manifest as nausea, vomiting, constipation, diarrhea, weakness, dizziness, headache, chronic cough, skin rash, and general itchiness. In recent years, there has been a greater increase in intestinal para-sitism brought about by the AIDS epidemic. People who are immunosuppressed are more prone to be infested by parasites.

Medications such as Mebendazole, Pryantel pamoate, Piperazine citrate, and Flagyl can be used to treat different types of parasitic infection. Parasitic infestations afflict more black women than white because parasitism is associated with poverty and poor sanitary conditions due to substandard housing. Among the conditions that facilitate parasitic infestations are the absence of toilets and running water.

Fecal materials permit parasites to enter into people's bloodstream and if no water is available to wash hands after bowel movements, people's hands are soiled with parasite contaminated stools which provide an entry point for intestinal parasitism.

INGUINAL HERNIA

Inguinal hernia can be associated with colorectal cancer. An obstructing mass within the large bowel inevitably causes the person harboring the mass to generate a great deal of pressure in the muscle of the lower abdomen. This tears the intraabdominal muscle causing the development of inguinal hernia.

It is therefore very important to investigate an individual who is in the 45 and older age group, who spontaneously develops an inguinal hernia. Any patient who fits this profile ought to have a lower G.I. evaluation with either a barium enema or colonoscopy before he or she undergoes an inguinal hernia repair.

It is crucial that black women pay close attention to the multitude of factors outlined in this chapter to keep from falling victim to preventable diseases that will hurt their chances of survival.

Anemia In African American Women

10

Anemia is a condition in which the human body has too little blood. Why is too little blood harmful? It carries oxygen to all the organs for proper functioning. When an individual is anemic, the organs are deprived. The condition is called **anoxia**, and an anoxic organ can die as a result of oxygen deficiency.

Anemia is common in women because they lose a significant amount of blood through menstruation. Added to menstrual blood loss is that lost during childbirth, combined with iron loss during breastfeeding. The more children a woman has, the more she loses. In the aggregate, black women tend to lose more blood than their white counterparts because of a heavier menstrual flow. This heavier flow is due to a higher incidence of uterine fibroids. Uterine fibroids cause very heavy menstrual blood loss with heavy clot formation, which tends to result in chronic iron deficiency anemia. Furthermore, black women tend to have more children than white women.

The average menstrual blood loss is between 45 and 50 cc of blood per month. The average blood loss for each delivery varies. During a normal delivery with natural childbirth, a woman can lose anywhere from 200 cc to 600 cc of blood. The period of bleeding can continue for one to two weeks after delivery. In a difficult delivery requiring episiotomy or a caesarian section, the skill of the doctor and the hemostatic status of the woman determine the amount of blood she will lose. The average iron loss during each normal pregnancy is 750 mg, which is the equivalent of 3 units of blood.

Another reason many black women tend to be more anemic than many white women is because many live in poverty or substandard conditions such as subsidized housing. Subsidized housing conditions are often rife with carcinogens. Lead paint on walls can result in lead poisoning anemia at an early age.

Impoverished black women eat a diet deficient in iron. The incidence of alcohol abuse is very common in black women in America; this too results in anemia. Black women are more afflicted with a condition called **pica** (ingesting unusual materials), which is associated with iron deficiency anemia. Black women pass on hereditary anemia. They also have a higher incidence of gastrointestinal cancer often associated with bleeding and hence may develop secondary anemia.

Hemoglobin

Red blood cells contain a substance called hemoglobin. Its function is to bind with oxygen and to carry it to the places the body needs. The **Oxygen Dissociation Curve** is medicine's way of determining whether the right amount of oxygen is present in the blood. It portrays the level of oxygen as a curve. When something happens that results in an oxygen deficiency state, then the curve moves to the left. Ordinarily, the curve moves to the right as to allow red blood cells to discharge their content of oxygen to the tissues for proper functioning. The Oxygen Dissociation Curve is influenced by the pH of the blood. The inability of the red cells to discharge their content of oxygen to body tissues results in improper perfusion of these tissues; the tissues get no nourishment to survive.

What are some of the symptoms of anemia? It depends on how long the person has been anemic and how severe it is. A normal hemoglobin and hemotocrit in a woman is 13–14.5 grams hemoglobin and 38 to 42 percent hematocrit. The more acute the blood loss, the less able the individual is to tolerate it. Younger patients

148

are better off than older ones. The elderly may have underlying medical problems such as heart or kidney disease, hardening of brain arteries, etc., which complicates anemia.

A person who has been anemic for many years, as with some black women, tolerate the condition because, over time, they become adjusted to the anemic state. But gradually vital organs—the heart, brain, and kidneys are affected by an anemic state.

The most common symptoms of anemia are: weakness, malaise, headaches, shortness of breath, tiredness, irritability, depression, chest pain, menstrual irregularity, infertility, insomnia, and so on.

SIGNS OF ANEMIA

Before anemia can occur, a person must be bleeding or have recently bled. They must be hemolyzing red blood cells (breaking up red blood cells in the body). Bone marrow will have stopped producing red blood cells because it fails or the bone marrow cavity is filled with mutated cells (like cancer cells) leaving little or no room for red blood cells to be made. Fibrous tissues (myelofibrosis) or any combination of the above conditions may also replace the bone marrow.

There are many physical signs of anemia; dependent upon the type of anemia the person is suffering.

Bleeding from the vagina, the rectum, vomiting blood from an upper gastrointestinal wound, or from the urinary tract (kidney stone, sickle cell disease, cancer of the bladder, kidney or uterus), resulting in 1800 cc of blood loss or more will cause a drop in the blood pressure and anemia.

Another frequent sign of anemia is rapid heart rate. The rate speeds up because the heart is trying to make up depleted oxygen by increasing cardiac output. If anemia goes untreated for many years, the heart may fail from **high output failure**.

Paleness of the skin, nail beds, and conjunctivae are all chronic signs of anemia. By looking at the conjunctivae (the white of the eye) a physician can see blood vessels with the naked eyes and can tell if these vessels are pale, indicating chronic blood loss. An eye exam will also catch degrees of icterus (yellowish tint) if the patient is hemolyzing. There are many other conditions having nothing to do with hemolytic anemia that can bring on the yellowing, so it's not a definite sign.

Less obvious signs of anemia include rapid breathing and certain heart murmurs referred to as slow murmurs. Both are a function of the thinness of the blood as it passes through the heart valves.

TYPES OF ANEMIA

The most common anemia in black women is iron-deficiency anemia. The second is sickle cell disease. Sickle cell disease, as discussed here, takes six forms. They are **sickle cell anemia (SS), sickle cell trait (AS), sickle cell C (SC), sickle cell thalassemia, sickle cell thalassemia trait,** and **homozygous hemoglobin C.** A large section of this chapter will be devoted to sickle cell anemia. First I'd like to discuss how anemia has evolved in the African American culture.

A fairly common cause of anemia in black women is **lead poisoning-associated anemia.** They can be exposed to lead as youngsters without their knowledge and continue to suffer with this problem throughout adulthood.

Also common to black women is **nutritional deficiency anemia.** Poor nutrition begins at an early age for many black youngsters who may go to school without breakfast. The first meal of their day may be the school lunch, whose quality varies depending on the community. In many cases, it is merely a prototype of fast foods, neither healthy nor nutritious.

It is possible for a combination of anemias to affect a black woman, making her anemic state much more difficult to diagnose and treat. Anemia seems to have a predilection for young black women. **Autoimmune hemolytic anemia** is quite common in black women as a whole.

Black women who migrated to the United States from tropical

countries like Haiti, South America, Latin America, Central America, the Caribbean, and Africa where the incidence of parasitic infestation is high also suffer from iron deficiency anemia. Their blood loss is due to worms sucking blood from their intestines, which is then lost in the stool. This parasitic infestation is problematic because most recent immigrants are surviving on a meager diet to begin with.

Hereditary hemolytic anemias are seen in black women. Varied genetic abnormalities cause them, and the degree of severity depends on that abnormality.

Sickle Cell Anemia

The severest anemia is sickle cell anemia. The sickle cell gene (sickle cell trait) is carried by 8.5 percent of the African American population. The same goes for Hispanic and Caribbean blacks.

About 50,000 African Americans actually have **homozygous** sickle cell anemia (full blown sickle cell disease). At birth, more than 1,600 African American babies born are expected to develop sickle cell disease.

It was research into sickle cell disease that led to Dr. Linus Pauling's study and his first Nobel Prize. His work gave birth to the entire field of molecular biology. Without his study the world of biological science and chemical science would not be what it is today.

Dr. James Herrick, a cardiologist from Chicago, first discovered sickle cell disease in a young black dental student from the island of Grenada in 1910. It causes the red blood cell to become sticky, deformed, and develop into a half moon or banana shape as compared to its normal disc shape.

These abnormalities in the membranes interfere with red blood cells passing through small vessels, to deliver oxygen to tissues of the body, like the heart, brain, spleen, etc. Lack of oxygen delivery to these organs is responsible for many problems associated with sickle cell disease.

Historically, the sickle cell gene can be traced to three areas of Africa. The most prevalent sickle cell gene came from Benin near

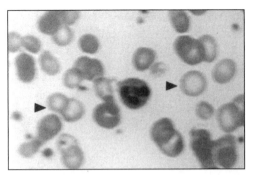

Figure 10.1: Peripherial blood smear showing hypochromic pale red cell showing lack of hemoglobin. (Arrow head) Arrow showing microcytic red cell (small red cell) due to lack of hemoglobin.

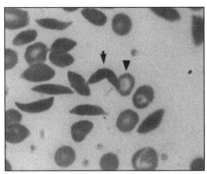

Figure 10.2: Arrow showing sickle cell (banana-shaped cell), Arrow head showing a target cell in a patient with sickle cell anemia, with thalassemia combined. (sickle thalassemia)

Nigeria in Central Africa. Another came from Senegal on the West Coast. The third came from the Bantu-speaking area of Central Africa.

The same three genes can be found within North American blacks and in the Caribbean. African slaves brought these sickle cell genes to the American continent. Since slavery started, the sickle cell gene has had time to penetrate the North American black race, leaving much pain, suffering, despair, and death in its wake.

As early as 1670, there is evidence that clinical sickle cell disease existed in a Ghanaian family. Sickle cell disease also affects Indians, Italians, and Arabs.

How to Prevent It

Sickle cell disease is preventable. If carriers educate themselves about how it's inherited, they can save lives. Here's what they need to know.

- If a non-carrier and a carrier decide to have children, 50% will be born without the sickle cell gene and 50% will carry it.
- If both parents carry the sickle cell trait, 25% of their children will be born normal, 25% will be born with the full-blown

sickle cell disease (SS) and 50% will carry the sickle cell trait.
• If one parent has full-blown sickle cell disease and the other is normal, all children will carry the sickle cell trait (AS).
• If one is carrying the trait and the other has full blown sickle cell disease, 50% of the children will be born with the sickle cell trait and 50% will be born with full blown sickle cell disease.
• If both of these individuals have full blown sickle cell disease, all children will be born with full-blown sickle cell disease.

What makes sickle cell so deadly is the inability of the hemoglobin to carry oxygen to the different tissues and organs of the body for proper functioning. Basically, sickle cell hemoglobin gels where there is lack of oxygen. This process is called **polymerization**.

Because of polymerization the red cell becomes stiff, sticky, and unable to pass freely through small vessels. Venules, arterioles, capillaries, and other medium-sized vessels become blocked.

Sickle cell disease is a multisystem disease. It affects every organ in the human body from the skin on. Lower extremities develop ulcers due to skin breakdown. If the brain of a sickle cell patient is damaged early and severely so, it can suffer stroke in someone 4 to 6 years old.

How does sickle cell disease cause stroke? The misshapen sticky red cells clog small vessels preventing oxygen to the brain. Ischemia follows, which causes the stroke. Sickle cell induced stroke in a child causes loss of vision, usually in one eye, and aphasia (inability to speak), sometimes permanently.

Difficulty swallowing is quite common and sometimes turns into recurrent aspiration pneumonia, which may lead to lung abscesses, bronchiectasis, or pulmonary death. Another frequent complication of stroke is seizures. They can be quite troublesome even with anti-seizure medication.

Pulmonary problems such as pneumonia, pulmonary embolism, and **congestive heart failure** (fluid in the lungs), constrict breathing. Severe **hypoxia** (lack of oxygen) results.

As potentially lethal as these conditions are, acute chest syndrome is the most deadly. In acute chest syndrome the sickle cell patient suffers chest pain, tachycardia, fever, and a high white blood cell count, together with a drop in the hematocrit and increased platelet count. Because the acute chest syndrome is so severe, it is recommended that antibiotics be added to the treatment regimen. If the patient can tolerate it, a transfusion with red blood cells is recommended to try to save their life.

Acute chest syndrome is said to be associated with multiple fat emboli (the pushing/growing of one part into another). These microemboli are due to fat breakdown. Fat byproducts cause damage to small vessels. The syndrome can be detected by chest x-ray. There is also a blood test available called activated phospho lipase A-2 that results from the breakdown of fat products.

Effects On the Brain and Bones

Sickle cell disease frequently affects the bone and brain of individuals suffering from it.

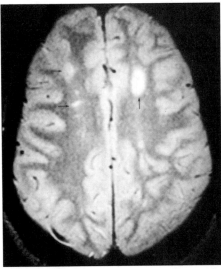

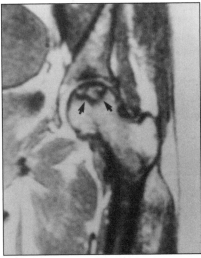

Figure 10.3: Arrows showing multiple infarcts (stroke) in the brain of a patient with sickle cell disease as documented by a brain MRI.

Figure 10.4: MRI of femoral head of hip of patient with sickle cell disease. Arrows showing avascularnecrosis.

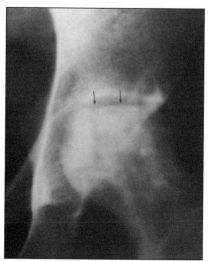

Figure 10.5: Arrows showing a vascular necrosis (lack of blood flow to bone) of femoral head with flattening necrosis of head bone in a patient with sickle cell disease.

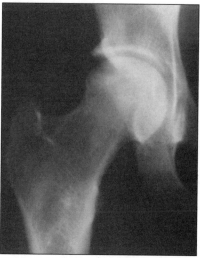

Figure 10.6: X-ray of a normal hip.

The Heart and Sickle Cell Anemia

The heart is always affected in a rather severe way by sickle cell disease. The vessels that allow blood to flow to the heart delivering oxygen are different sizes. The smaller they are, the easier it is for them to clog with sticky misshapen sickle cells. The red cells just cannot pass through vessels easily, and the heart muscles suffer ischemia. This sets off the substance called kinins, released by tissues once they've become **ischemic** (starved for oxygen).

Kinins mentioned earlier were in connection with chest pain. The substance is also at the root of painful sickle cell crisis, the most common sickle cell disease. The ischemia that occurs with sickle cell disease is just as detrimental to the heart as any other ischemia. It leads to muscle scarring. If one or more of the coronary arteries become blocked because of scarring, myocardial infarction results.

A patient with sickle cell disease constantly hemolyzes. Homolysis deposits lots of iron in the blood stream. This is a serious condition called **hemochromatosis** (See chapter 5, Diabetes Mellitus in African American Women).

Hemochromatosis causes high serum ferritin. This storage iron gets deposited mostly in heart muscles, liver, pancreas, and joints. Once it accumulates in the heart muscles, it causes the heart to become enlarged (a condition called cardiomyopathy). When the iron breaks down, it releases free radicals, which damage myocardial tissues.

The two most effective treatments are Phlebotomy—removing one unit of blood—(500 cc) from the body at a time—and Desferol. Desferol chelates the iron, removing it from the body and passing it out in the urine, decreasing toxic levels.

The ischemic myocardial disease from which patients with sickle cell suffer makes red cells hemolyze consistently. The constant hemolysis deposits iron in the bloodstream. It accumulates in, and damages the heart muscle, enlarging the heart. The working of the heart becomes so sluggish that blood stagnates within its chambers. Clots are taken to organs as emboli.

All of this leads to congestive heart failure and cardiac arrhythmias. The most worrisome aspect of these conditions in the presence of sickle cell disease is their propensity to develop embolus. The brain is particularly vulnerable to this situation. If an embolus gets loose and becomes lodged there, it will cause a massive stroke. Patients with enlarged hearts are frequently treated with Coumadin, a blood thinner.

Emboli can also disrupt the kidney, which leads to permanent damage. It can be recognized as harsh lower abdominal pain. The circulation of the large bowel disrupted by emboli can lead to **ischemic colitis** (the colon breaks down from lack of oxygen), if not taken care of right away. It in turn leads to a lethal condition called dead bowel syndrome.

When sickle cell enlarges the atrium (the smallest chamber of the heart), it holds onto the blood clots. It then contracts and sends the clot to an organ, where the real problems begin. But many atrial fibrillation sufferers live perfectly normal lives as long as they're on medication.

People who suffer from sickle cell disease (SS), sickle thalassemia, and sickle cell C disease also suffer the following:
1. Painful sickle cell crises
2. Hemolytic crises
3. Hypoplastic crises
4. Acute chest syndrome
5. A combination of acute painful crises and hemolytic crises

It is not always clear what triggers sickle cell crises. Stress, infection—particularly viral infection—brings on hemolytic crisis. Other risk factors include bacterial or fungal infections. Cold weather causes vasoconstriction, preventing oxygen delivery to tissues in sufficient amounts, causing ischemia and pain.

An acute hypoplastic crisis can be brought on by suppression of the bone marrow due to these different infections. They shut down the bone marrow preventing it from producing red blood cells, white blood cells, and platelets.

A form of crisis seen in the pediatric age group is the sequestration crisis. It is brought on by an acute hemolytic episode causing a massive shift of blood into the spleen resulting in shock. If not recognized and treated promptly, the infant or young child is likely to die.

What Happens When Sickle Cell Episodes Hit

The small vessels in the body are clogged by the misshapen, sticky red cells. Oxygen is not properly perfused through the tissues. The lack of oxygen delivery results in tissue anoxia. The **anoxic tissues** (tissues deprived of oxygen) secrete kinins, which cause burning pain.

This pain can be quite severe. The body of the sickle cell patient is under stress from whatever induced the episode, which raises the pulse rate. It needs more oxygen delivery to tissues and when that need cannot be met, it further aggravates the anoxia. A painful crisis is thus triggered.

Hemolysis

Hemolysis can happen quickly. The person's urine becomes dark and their eyes turn as yellow as a lemon even though they were fine just the day before. If such symptoms appear so drasticlly overnight, they must be brought to the hospital.

Recent studies have found that vessel damage is responsible for the occlusive nature of sickle cell disease. The sickled red cells cause damage to the inner lining of blood vessels. The lining then produces a series of adhesion proteins. Proteins produced by white blood cells and platelets bring on sickle cell crisis.

Patients with sickle cell disease hemolyse all the time. The half-life of the sickle cell patient's red cell is ten to twenty days, as compared to the 120 day half-life of a regular red cell. Under the stress of an infection, patients can begin to hemolyze to the point of severe anemia.

Shortness of breath, chest pain, drop in blood pressure with shock, congestive heart failure, and heart attack can occur as a result of this severe drop in hematocrit. It must be recognized quickly so the person can get help. In addition to a very low hematocrit, high bilirubin, high LDH, and reticulocyte count also occur during hemolytic crisis.

A high dose of folic acid must also be given when the patient is hemolyzing. The recommended dose of folic acid in patients with chronic hemolytic disease such as sickle cell is as much as 25 mg of folic acid per day. Everybody that is hemolyzing is, by definition, folate deficient.

New Treatments

Along with these new concepts and mechanisms in sickle cell disease, there are proposed newer treatments. It is believed that hydroxy urea works in sickle cell disease not only by raising Hemoglobin F, which is an excellent carrier of oxygen, but also by decreasing the level of white blood cells and platelets, to improve the disease's symptoms. So sickle cell patients on hydroxy urea benefit even if their hemoglobin F level does not go up, because of the decreased white cells and platelets. It also enables oxygen to permeate tissues preventing ischemia. The end result is less pain and fewer symptoms of sickle cell disease.

Other proposed treatments include inhalation of nitric oxide gas to dilate blood vessels, allowing for better tissue perfusion. Low dose aspirin works as an anti-inflammatory against the effects of the adhesion proteins. Aspirin also works to prevent platelet aggregation resulting in better blood flow through vessels, and decreases the incidence of sickle cell crises. It's bad enough for a person to have anemia without having to fight their medicine. Morphine sulfate is a much better pain medication.

Fresh packed red cells are essential to a blood transfusion for a chronically anemic patient. Anemia can be made worse if the patient is transfused with old packed red cells. As blood sits in the blood bank, the level of 2,3, DPG constantly decreases. Blood that is depleted when infused in an already anemic person, shifts the oxygen dissociation curve further to the left making it much more difficult for oxygen to be delivered to the tissues. Cells should be less than a week old.

Sodium butyrate has been shown to increase the hemoglobin F level. Recombinant human erythropoietin is being used in combination with hydroxy urea today.

Gallbladder Disease and Sickle Cell Anemia

Gallbladder disease shows up as abdominal pain, nausea, and vomiting. This collection of symptoms is called **acute cholecystitis**. Because people with sickle cell disease and other chronic hemolytic diseases hemolyze constantly, they dump large amounts of bilirubin pigments into the blood stream. Bilirubin containing gallbladder stones begin to form.

Over time, stones cause the gallbladder to become inflamed and sometimes infected. The diagnosis and treatment of gallbladder disease is described in chapter 9.

Other problems that people with sickle cell disease have to cope with are:
1. Sickle cell retinopathy (bleeding into the eyes)
2. Leg ulcers

3. Priapism (male)—a painful erection with engorgement that can lead to sexual impotence or necrosis of the penis

4. Aseptic necrosis of the bones

5. Microscopic or gross hematuria that is due to papillary necrosis, predominant in left kidney

6. Infected with capsular bacterial organisms such as pneumococci and hemophilus influenzae; bone infection with Salmonella bacteria resulting in osteomyelitis

7. Spleen destroyed by the time young patients become teenagers due to the recurrent insults of the sickling phenomena to the splenic circulation. It is recommended that these patients get vaccinated with Pneumococcal vaccine about every three years or so

8. Sickle hepatopathy (sickle cell liver disease), engorgement of the liver, symptom is right upper abdominal pain

A Cure

Despite millions of research dollars, no cure has been found. Bone marrow transplantation is being tried but it is in its infancy. As for the future, gene therapy holds some promise in helping people with sickle cell disease.

Genetic counseling still remains the most worthwhile approach for those who are affected with the sickle cell disease. By maintaining a consistent medical checkup schedule, potential parents can know for sure if they are afflicted. They must be aware of the odds I've described in this chapter, to determine their children's chances of carrying and inheriting the trait.

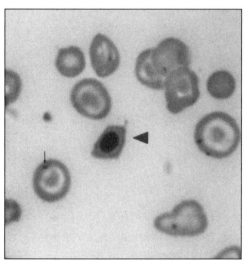

Figure 10.7: Thalassemia (Arrow head) showing nucleated red cell, small arrow showing howel jolly body. Big arrow target cell.

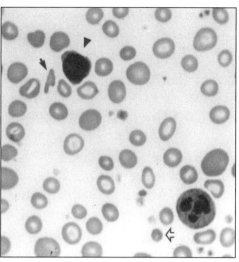

Figure 10.8: Hemolytic anemia (Arrow head) showing nucleated red cell. Arrow showing schistocyte (fragment of red blood cell). Open arrow showing spherocyte (very small red cell full of hemoglobin).

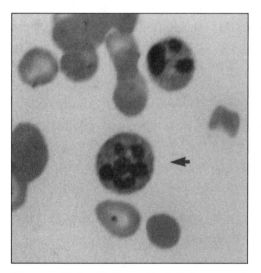

Figure 10.9: Folic acid deficiency and alcoholism. (Big arrow showing segmented polynucleated white cell with 7 lobes, typically of microcytic anemia. Small arrow showing macrosyte. Large immature red blood cells).

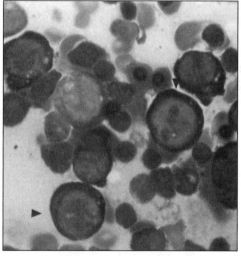

Figure 10.10: Bone marrow as piration smear (arrow heads) showing megaloblastic red cells (Very large immature red cell and pernicious anemia due to B_{12} deficiency).

Beta Thalassemia

This is another anemia common to black women. Sometimes it is seen in conjunction with sickle cell trait, resulting in sickle thalassemia.

In North America, thalassemia is seen in those of Greek and Italian descent in addition to blacks and a multitude of people who migrated to the North American continent from other parts of the world. The gene for **alpha thalassemia** is also extremely common among African Americans.

Although alpha thalassemia kills many in Southeast Asia, China, Thailand, and certain parts of the eastern Saudi-Arabian peninsula, it does not cause disease in blacks. Both alpha thalassemia and beta thalassemia genes have their origin in West Africa, however black people don't get sick from alpha thalassemia. A black person missing one alpha globulin gene is a silent carrier and not anemic.

Not only do blacks not get sick from alpha thalassemia, but if they have sickle cell disease and carry the alpha thalassemia gene, it becomes less severe by decreasing the total number of sickle cells in the blood stream.

Millions of black people with sickle cell trait that live in malaria infected areas of Africa survive because of the sickle cell trait. Sickle cells infected with malaria get taken out of their body quickly by the spleen, decreasing the number of malarial organisms in the blood stream.

How does someone know if they have thalassemia or not? Infants born with thalassemia get sick very early on in life. They get weak because they are anemic.

How can one tell what type of thalassemia it is without doing expensive tests in the laboratory? After taking a history and doing a physical examination a CBC is done. If microcytosis is identified, (red cells that are too small) and erythrocytosis is noted, (too many red cells) the diagnosis is thalassemia trait, thalassemia minor, or thalassemia major.

A quantitative hemoglobin electrophoresis can be done. It costs about twenty-four dollars. There are two classic patterns that can be seen in the hemoglobin electrophoresis as it relates to thalassemia. One picture is high hemoglobin A2 beta thalassemia with normal hemoglobin F, and the other is normal A2 beta thalassemia with high hemoglobin F.

The hemoglobin electrophoresis is also able to determine if the person is carrying sickle cell hemoglobin, hemoglobin C, and many other abnormal types of hemoglobin, many of which cause severe anemic diseases.

All the abnormal hemoglobins discussed above can be diagnosed in utero by doing amniocentesis. Genetic counseling is also available to help prospective parents understand the medical implications of these abnormal hemoglobins.

Complications

Another very serious complication of thalassemia is iron overload, known as hemochromatosis, discussed earlier in the section on sickle cell disease. The hemochromatosis seen in the individual who suffers from hemoglobinopathies is the secondary type, as compared to idiopathic or primary hemochromatosis.

In secondary hemochromatosis, the result of hemoglobinopathies, iron gets dumped into the blood stream as a result of shortened red cell lives, resulting in hemolysis.

The best way to determine if someone has hemochromatosis is to do a serum ferritin. It costs about fifty-six dollars. It's indispensable as an evaluation of total body iron. A serum ferritin of 500 or greater establishes a diagnosis of hemochromatosis. During a woman's menstrual period the iron level will read low.

When looking at this patient's complete blood count, at a glance they can be said to have thalassemia of some sort. Occasionally, a patient who suffers from polycythemia vera becomes iron deficient.

Autoimmune Hemolytic Anemia

Autoimmune hemolytic anemia has multiple causes. It is seen in black women in association with diseases such as (SLE) lupus, lymphomas, other cancers, and collagen vascular diseases of different types. The treatment of autoimmune hemolytic anemia usually requires treating the associated disease along with steroid, cytotoxic agent, and folic acid.

Alcohol abuse, hemolytic anemia and poor nutrition, among other things, cause folic acid deficiency. To evaluate a person for folic acid deficiency, it is often necessary to measure serum folate level in red blood cells folate level (red blood cells' folate level is more accurate than serum folate level, but it is not routinely available). The serum folate level reflects the last folate containing meal that the person ate before the testing was carried out.

In true folate deficiency the homocytein level is elevated, so measuring homocytein level is a more accurate way to diagnose folate deficiency. In folate deficiency, the blood smear shows large red blood cells (macrocytes) and hyper-segmented polys, and the bone marrow is B_{12} deficient. The treatment of folate deficiency is 1 mg of folic acid by mouth or IV daily.

Another form of anemia frequently seen in black women is B_{12} deficiency anemia, (Megaloblastic anemia). B_{12} and Folate is required for the production of red blood cells. The deficiency of either of them causes an arrest in maturation of red cells, resulting in macrocytosis. The list of things that can cause B_{12} deficiency is quite long:

1. Atrophic gastritis
2. Gastrectomy
3. Blind loop syndrome
4. Fish tapeworm infection
5. Malabsorption
6. Malnutrition
7. B_{12} deficiency of the elderly
8. Pernicious anemia
9. Nitrous oxide gas abuse

Pernicious Anemia

To diagnose B_{12} deficiency, a serum B_{12} level is done. The normal serum B_{12} level is 200-900 PG/ml. A B_{12} deficiency state is damaging, no matter what the cause. One B_{12} deficiency state is called pernicious anemia.

When a low B_{12} level is discovered, a clinical search must be undertaken to find the cause. Before starting an evaluation for pernicious anemia, several weeks of B_{12} treatment intramuscularly must be given to correct the malabsorption. Following this procedure, a schilling test determines if the low B_{12} has caused pernicious anemia.

To diagnose pernicious anemia, a person is given 1000 mcg of B_{12} IM to saturate the B_{12} receptor sites. Then a capsule of B_{12}, which contains a nuclear tracer, is given to the person by mouth. Urine is collected and B_{12} is measured in that urine sample. If the level in the urine sample is normal, it completes the first part of the schilling test and this patient has no B_{12} absorption problems.

If the B_{12} level in the urine sample is low, then another dose of nuclear tracer containing B_{12}, along with intrinsic factor is given by mouth and urine is again collected for twenty-four hours, then the level of B_{12} examined. If the B_{12} is now elevated, then the person can be said to have pernicious anemia.

If the B_{12} remains low in spite of the addition of the intrinsic factor, this means the patient has malabsorption; they cannot absorb B_{12}. It is very important to establish a diagnosis of pernicious anemia because it is associated with gastrointestinal malignancy. Pernicious anemia is also associated with hypo- or hyperthyroidism and vitiligo.

Treatment of Pernicious Anemia

The treatments for pernicious anemia and other form of B_{12} deficiencies include 1 mg of B_{12} injection monthly after appropriate loading doses have been given. Failure to treat B_{12} deficiency leads to combined system disease, organic brain syndrome, psychosis or mental illness. After five years the damage is irreversible.

How To Prevent Pernicious Anemia

1. Since most blood and iron are lost during menstruation,

black women must be evaluated and treated for any dysfunctional vaginal bleeding that can be the result of uterine fibroids or other problems, as to minimize blood and iron loss.

2. Black women from Third World countries and African American women who reside in the rural south must have their stool tested for parasites.

3. In the United States, some black women are afflicted with pica; in particular those who reside in the South. Eating clay or starch binds iron as it goes to the stomach, preventing its absorption. Pica is a psychological problem and very hard to stop. It is ingrained as part of the culture in certain parts of the black community and has been going on for hundreds of years. It is very difficult to eradicate but must be dealt with.

4. Don't drink tea with a meal. The best way for a woman to drink tea is on an empty stomach, or three to four hours after eating iron-containing foods.

BIRTH RATES AND ANEMIA

Black women worldwide have a higher pregnancy rate than white women. The reasons are many—cultural preferences, religious beliefs, poverty, lack of formal education, lack of professional status, and psychosocial and psychoracial circumstances.

There are reasons African women have many children. Traditionally the family needs children to tend the farm; religious beliefs deny birth control (in many regions); and some men see many children as proof of virility, masculinity and prowess.

These beliefs permeate the society of the Americas and the Caribbean Basin communities. Black and Hispanic minorities in America often maintain values rooted in the African culture. It's a culture well imprinted in the genes.

ALCOHOL AND ANEMIA

Alcohol abuse is associated with many conditions that cause iron deficiency anemia. For instance, gastritis. The blood lost as a result of gastritis can lead to iron deficiency anemia if it's recurrent. This is often the case.

Alcohol abuse also causes **esophageal** (as said previously, the esophagus connects the throat to the stomach) **varices** (like varicose vein) with recurrent bleeding. We're all familiar with liver damage from alcohol (cirrhosis of the liver). It can bring on breakthrough vaginal bleeding. Both conditions are at the root of iron deficiency anemia. The incidence of colon cancer is quite high in black women in the United States and one of the most common signs of colon cancer is—you guessed it—iron deficiency

IRON DEFICIENCY AND DIET

Many black women suffer from a condition called **pica**, an appetite for unnatural foods such as chalk or paste. All the picas are associated with iron deficiency anemia. The most common picas are eating starch, clay, and ice.

Drinking tea with food in the stomach can prevent absorption of iron, making iron deficiency anemia worse. Tea contains tannic acid, which binds to iron in the food. So drinking tea is okay but it's best drunk on an empty stomach.

TOO MUCH IRON

The organs most affected by iron deposits are the heart, liver, endocrine organs (like adrenal glands), the pituitary gland, gonads, and the pancreas.

Iron deposits into the pancreas often result in diabetes mellitus Type II (see chapter five, Diabetes Mellitus in African American Women) because the beta cells within the pancreas get damaged, then destroyed. Osteoarthritis is a common disease in people affected by hemochromatosis. Many black women are particularly afflicted because of lower economic status. Many do heavy work to earn a living, which places their bone and musculoskeletal structure under stress. With iron deposits added to the condition, osteoarthritis is made worse.

Iron deposits cause damage to tissues and organs because they release free radicals. These are extremely toxic to human tissues. They cause: cardiomyopathy resulting in heart failure or liver damage resulting in cirrhosis, scarring and eventually hepatocellular carcinoma. One of the best ways to diagnose iron deposits in the liver is by doing an MRI. If it's positive for iron deposits it shows a starry sky-type picture.

Iron deposits also affect the joints. The free radicals released from the byproducts of iron deposits in the joint spaces cause inflammation. This ultimately destroys the joints, causing severe arthritis.

Most people don't know that they have hemochromatosis. The worst-case scenario is that they carry abnormal hemoglobin which predisposes them to constant hemolysis with iron deposits dumped in their body. At the same time, they carry the hemochromatosis gene, which makes them over absorb iron.

Another organ affected by hemochromatosis is the skin, the largest organ in the human body. In primary hemochromatosis the skin has a bronze color to it. The easiest and best treatment for hemochromatosis is phlebotomy—removing blood from the body (if the person is not anemic).

During the procedure 500 ml of blood is removed, and along with it 250 mg of iron. It is important that a physician examines the individual whose blood is being removed, to be sure they're not anemic. Cardiac contraindicates the removal of that much blood too.

The only other treatment is a chelating agent called desferol, which excretes iron through the kidneys, into the urine. Desferol is given with 100 to 200 mg of vitamin C. The vitamin C helps mobilizes iron in the tissues making it easier for the chelating agent to remove the iron from the body. This is why it can be dangerous for someone to take vitamin C unless it is prescribed by a physician.

ANEMIA AND WOMEN

If a woman loses 50 cc of blood during her menstrual period, she loses 25 mg of iron. Multiplied by twelve months, it adds up to 300 mg of iron; slightly more than 1 unit of blood lost every year. It's easy to see why so many women have iron deficiency or **ery-thropoesis**.

Breast milk contains iron. Mothers lose iron in their breast milk. Breastfeeding worldwide is more common in black women than Caucasian women.

Long before iron deficiency anemia comes about, the loss of blood and iron has begun. The first iron a person loses when bleeding is from storage, as reflected by serum ferritin. Iron is stored as ferritin in the bone marrow.

When a person's iron store is absent, they feel tired all the time, can't concentrate well, become irritable easily, and feel general malaise. An adult woman usually has about 1 gram of iron in her total iron store. That's the equivalent of 4 units of blood. About 1.5 grams of iron is located in her circulating blood, which is the equivalent of 6 units of blood. Once she loses the entire iron store, she begins to use up the circulating iron meant for the production of red cells.

As the level of the circulating iron decreases, iron deficiency anemia sets in and gets worse over time. Iron is an integral component of blood, and ferritin should be looked at as a scale, in that the level of ferritin going down represents blood being lost slowly, for reasons ranging from excessive vaginal bleeding to cancer.

In the case of cancer of the gastrointestinal tract, the decreased level of serum ferritin can be detected as many as four years prior to the person becoming anemic. It can alert someone very early to the presence of colon cancer.

There is a new test called the **soluble serum transferrin receptor level**, which is much more sensitive to diagnose iron deficiency anemia. Infection or inflammation does not affect this test. Iron is attached to the receptors in the transferrin protein to be carried to the early red blood cells in the bone marrow to produce new red blood cells. When there is no iron, these receptor sites remain unoccupied and their level is elevated. This is where the test picks up the problem.

Replacing Iron

The last iron that is replaced is the iron in store. Circulating iron is replaced first. It takes almost two years to fully replace iron in a menstruating woman. One must take about 180 mg per day to be able to absorb about 60 mg of it. Doctors prescribe, for example, ferrous sulfate 325 mg three times a day to replace iron. Each 325 mg of ferrous sulfate contains only 60 mg of elemental iron and when one multiples that by three it equals 180 mg. That is where that figure comes from. There is a product called Chromagen which contains 200 mg of elemental iron plus some vitamin C. It costs more, but it is more convenient and is better tolerated.

BLOOD TRANSFUSIONS

Blood and blood product transfusions must be given with informed consent, because of the possibility of the transmission of AIDS or HIV (Type I and HIV Type II). Since 1987 the chances of getting HIV (Type I) is anywhere from 1:50,000 to 1:150,000 blood transfusions. Other infectious diseases, such as HTLV I, THLV II, Hepatitis A, B, C, and also CMV virus can be transfused with blood products. The transfusion will provide sufficient oxygen for the tissues.

DETERMINING THE CAUSE OF THE ANEMIA

If the person is throwing up blood, the bleeding is from the upper gastrointestinal tract. If they are passing large amounts of red blood per rectum, they are bleeding from the lower GI tract. But, sometimes it's not that simple.

Just because a person is anemic does not mean that he or she is bleeding. Anemia can be the result of (1) bleeding (2) hemolysis (3) failure to make sufficient red blood cells, or a combination of all three. Since she has been anemic for a long time there is no reason to rush into just any treatment. What should be hurried is the evaluation to determine the cause.

Frequently, it's a lesion in the GI tract; cancer; diverticulosis; polyps; inflammatory bowel disease; gastritis, or other small bowel, stomach, or large bowel disease that can be causing them to bleed. If it is cancer that invades the bone marrow (preventing red cell production) it will require chemotherapy or radiotherapy.

Anemia is a serious disease. A hematologist who is an expert in blood diseases should be brought in to evaluate it properly.

Gynecological and Obstetrical Diseases In African American Women

11

Among the most troublesome gynecological problems affecting black women are sexually transmitted diseases (STD). The following is a list of the most common sexually transmitted diseases:

1. Genital herpes
2. Gonorrhea
3. Bacterial vaginosis
4. Trichomonas vaginitis
5. Human papilloma virus infection (HPV)
6. Venereal warts
7. HIV infection
8. Lymphogranuloma venerum
9. Chancroid
10. Granuloma inguinale
11. Condylomata acuminata
12. Molluscum contagiosum
13. Pelvic inflammatory disease (PID)
14. Tubo-ovarian abscess

GENITAL HERPES

About one million people become infected every year with Herpes Simplex Type I and, Herpes Simplex Type II, genital herpes.

Genital herpes is most often transmitted during sexual intercourse or oral sex with an infected partner. It can be transmitted from a buttock or lip lesion. The first symptoms of genital herpes infection appear within seven days of exposure.

The first symptom is a burning, tingling or itching in the perineal (in between genitals and anus) area. The second is a crop of small, water-filled lesions, which are quite itchy. There may be a low-grade fever.

The pain in the vulvar area may be quite severe with extreme tenderness. Once the lesions break open, the area may become infected. Passing urine becomes a major task because of the irritation of the groin. Some urinary retention can occur.

Lymph node enlargement in the inguinal area is common and quite painful. In women who have AIDS, these herpatic lesions accelerate in a disabling manner all the way to the perianal area. Hospitalization for intravenous medications and intramuscular pain medications helps. A person infected with herpes simplex may be able to infect a sexual partner even though he or she has no open herpatic sores.

The incidence of genital herpes is quite high in black females, but is seen in every ethnic group and socioeconomic status. Any woman who is sexually active can become infected with the herpes virus. This is particularly so if they are having sexual intercourse without a condom.

Examination

On examination, the physician is likely to see small versicles over the labia majora, labia minora, and the skin of the perineal area and the vulva. The cervix may be infected with the herpes virus. It's painless because the cervical tissues are not manifesting the pain. The patient may have a mucous discharge because of the inflammation in the vagina.

Diagnosis can be made by taking a culture from the infected areas, or by rupturing the vesicles and culturing the fluid within them.

Herpes infections are recurrent. Stressful situations will

induce an outbreak. Some of the stresses are common cold, menstruation, examinations, and indigestion—basically physical/psychological stress from everyday situations. These situations increase adrenaline, which stresses the immune system and allows dormant herpes to appear.

Pregnancy complicates herpes infection of the genitalia. Women who are infected with genital herpes while pregnant frequently have spontaneous abortion or premature birth. Almost 60 percent of babies born to women who have active genital herpes infection are infected themselves. A cesarean section must be performed to prevent the infant's mucous membrane from coming in contact with the infected birth canal. This prevents problems such as blindness.

Infants born to herpes simplex infected mothers can start having problems three to four days after birth. As many as 60 percent die during the neonatal period. Forty to 50 percent of survivors develop problems such as mental retardation, microcephaly, microphthalmos and seizures.

Treatment of Herpes Infection

If the herpes is localized, the treatment is acyclovir by mouth and acyclovir cream to relieve symptoms. Oral medication is needed too. The question is, how long to treat? The breakdown is as follows:

• Primarily, genital herpes should be treated with acyclovir 200 mg by mouth, 5 times a day for 10 days, or Valtrex 1000 mg by mouth, 2 times per day for 10 days.

• Treatment for recurrent genital herpes is Valtrex 500 mg by mouth, 2 times per day for 5 days; or acyclovir 400 mg by mouth, 3 times per day; or Famvir 125 mg by mouth, 2 times per day for 5 days.

• For suppression of chronic genital herpes, Famvir 250 mg by mouth, 2 times per day, or Valtrex 500 mg by mouth daily, or acyclovir 400 mg 2 times per day. This treatment must be continued indefinitely.

This virus is very difficult to treat because it is slow growing, has a thick capsule, and the ability to hide for a very long time in the human body. It flares up intermittently, causing discomfort to those who are infected.

GONORRHEA

Gonorrheal infection is more prevalent in younger women who have many sexual partners in adolescence. The bacterium responsible for causing the gonorrheal infection is a **gram-negative intracellular diplococci** (Neisseria gonorrhea).

A woman gets gonorrhea during sexual intercourse with a man who is infected with gonorrhea. A man's symptoms include purulent discharge from the penis. Sometimes however, a man may be carrying the gonorrheal virus with no symptoms. During unprotected sexual intercourse, the man deposits the infected ejaculate into the woman's vagina, infecting her.

Once infected, several things can happen to the woman. Five days to a week after being infected, the woman may notice a foul smelling vaginal discharge with pain and irritation in the vaginal area. If she does not seek medical care right away, the symptoms increase as the infection travels up into her tubes causing inflammation.

The infection can also get into the cervix and body of the uterus and infects them. If the ovaries become infected then tubo-ovarian infection—which can lead to abscesses—becomes a problem, too. At this point the woman has what is called acute pelvic inflammatory disease (PID) secondary to gonorrhea.

Complications

The gonorrheal infection can continue into the bloodstream causing gonococcal septicemia. In different joints, it causes acute gonococcal arthritis with the potential for destroying the affected joints. It is absolutely critical to tap the joint fluid and send it to the lab for gram stain, cell count, and culture, should the disease progress in this manner. Treatment of gonococcal arthritis must be started immediately to prevent the destruction of affected joints.

The organs infected by gonorrhea stick to each other and wrap around the bowels or liver on the right side of the abdomen. It shows up as pain in that area and is referred to as **Fitz-Hugh-Curtis Syndrome** with violin-like adhesive bands pulling on the liver capsule. Until these bands are surgically lysed, pain in the right part of the abdomen persists.

How to Diagnose Gonorrhea in Women

A good history of the woman's sexual habits and symptoms will be taken. The last menstrual period must be recorded because the tissues in the gynecological organs are swollen, making it easier for both a freshly acquired infection to spread or a chronic infection to flare up.

The next thing to be done is a good pelvic examination, looking for a foul smelling vaginal discharge and cervical tenderness. Then a special gonococcal culture of the vaginal discharge is sent to the lab. The same specimen can be cultured for chlamydia.

Treatment of Gonorrhea

The approach is guided by the symptoms. If a woman knows she has just been sexually exposed to a man with gonorrhea or suspects gonorrhea, the treatment is Ceftriaxone 250 mg in one dose with Doxycycline 100 mg 2x per day for 7 days, and Flagyl 250 mg by mouth twice per day for 4 days.

Alternatively, the patient can be treated with Floxin 800 mg by mouth, one dose along with Doxycycline 100 mg 2 times per day for 7 days, plus Flagyl 250 mg 2 times per day for 2 days.

Ceftriaxone is a penicillin-like medicne and the best medication available to treat uncomplicated or suspected gonorrhea, intramuscular in the office or clinic. Ceftriaxone, however, will not treat chlamydia. Since it is often impossible to tell gonorrhea from chlamydia, it is wise to treat both with Doxycycline or Floxin. The rationale for using Flagyl in conjunction with these other medications is because **Trichomonas** (parasite) is frequently found along with the other infections.

For women allergic to penicillin, Floxin can be used. Pregnant women who became exposed sexually to gonorrhea while pregnant must be treated properly to prevent spontaneous abortion. There is also a higher incidence of pre-term labor in pregnant women infected with gonorrhea.

Treatment During Pregnancy

If a woman is infected with uncomplicated gonorrhea and is pregnant (and not allergic to penicillin), the treatment of choice is Ceftriaxone 250 mg IM, one dose, and Erythromycin 250 mg 4 times per day for one week to cover for possible chlamydia infection. Spectinomycin can be used instead of Ceftriaxone in a pregnant penicillin-allergic woman infected with uncomplicated gonorrhea.

Tetracycline cannot be used in pregnancy, particularly in the first trimester. It will stain the bones of the fetus. Nowadays, tetracycline is rarely used to treat gonorrhea because the organism may be resistant to it.

If the fetus becomes infected with gonorrhea it may develop sepsis, infection of the eyes, the scalp, arthritis, and more. The newborn will require intravenous antibiotics.

In-Hospital Treatment of Gonorrhea

- Ceftriaxone—2 grams IV every 12 hours
- Doxycycline—100 mg p.o. or IV every 12 hours until symptoms subside, then Doxycycline to complete 10-14 days
- Clindamycin—900 mg IV every 8 hours in addition to Gentamycin—2 mg/KG IM or IV. Once the patient is improved, Doxycycline—100 mg by mouth every 12 hours to complete a 14-day course. Add Flagyl 500 mg every 6 hours during the acute phase of the infection for accompanying Trichomonas infection and anaerobic organisms that may be playing a role in the infectious process.
- Patients who cannot tolerate Doxycycline or who are allergic to penicillin can be treated with Norfloxin 400 mg IV every

12 hours.

Prevention of Gonorrheal Infection
1. Abstinence
2. Responsible sexual intercourse
3. Monogamy
4. Use a condom

The high incidence of gonorrhea reported among black women as compared to white women in the United States is due in part to their poorer socioeconomic status and higher incidence of drug abuse, which leads to destructive behavior. When people are high they inevitably become careless.

The incidence of STD among working- and middle-class black women in the United States is no higher than it is among white women of the same socioeconomic level.

By the eleventh grade, 70 percent of teenagers have had sexual intercourse and 40 percent have had four or more sexual partners. This group is at great risk for STDs.

CHLAMYDIA INFECTION

It is believed that four million people are infected with chlamydia annually. Women become infected with chlamydia through unprotected sexual intercourse. Men pass the infection to women in their ejaculates causing a mucopurulent endocervical discharge.

The infection can then work its way up the woman's genital tract, infecting the uterus and the fallopian tubes. PID (pelvic inflammatory disease) can result, causing chronic pelvic pain. Ectopic pregnancies and infertility occur frequently as a result of untreated chlamydial infection.

Following a good history with lower abdominal and pelvic examination, a culture of vaginal discharge should be taken, placed in a special culture medium and sent to the microbiology laboratory for culture.

Treatment of Chlamydia

- Doxycycline—100 mg. two times per day for 7 days
- Floxin—300 mg two times per day for 7 days
- Erythromycin—500mg four times per day for 10 days
- Azithromycin—single dose of 1 gram by mouth
- Amoxicillin—500mg three times per day for 10 days
- Either Erythromycin, Amoxicillin, or Azithromycin can be used during pregnancy

SYPHILIS

Syphilis is one of the most common STDs to afflict mankind and has been in the New World since 1494 when Columbus and his men came to America.

Syphilis is usually transmitted sexually. Once the organism is deposited into the human tissue it takes anywhere from 14 to 21 days for primary syphilis to develop. In women, the part of their genitalia first affected by early syphilis is the labia, fourchette, or cervix.

The first manifestation of primary syphilis is a chancre, (painless sore). The chancre may be seen in the mouth, lips, arms, rectum, nipples, or navel. After 4 to 8 weeks the chancre heals. Untreated syphilis spreads via the lymphatic system to disseminate throughout the body, causing secondary syphilis.

The first manifestation of secondary syphilis is usually a rash on the palms of the hands and sometimes the soles of the feet. It is often scaly, smooth, and may be itchy. Because secondary syphilis is a systemic disease, it can cause sore throat, headache, fever, weight loss, with aches and pains. There may be swollen glands in the neck, under the arms and elsewhere in the body.

The physician has to be suspicious enough to order a blood test for syphilis. A scraping from the rash can be studied via dark field technique, which might show the spirochetes treponoma pallidum wiggling around under the microscope. Similarly, scraping material taken from the primary syphilis chancre can be seen on a slide.

Secondary syphilis may bring on arthritis, hepatitis, condyloma, uveitis, iritis, otitis, CVA, kidney problems, hepatitis, weight loss, poor appetite, memory loss, seizure, or meningitis.

If the syphilis remains untreated after the primary and secondary stage (about 12 weeks), then it enters into the latent stage. Many suffer symptoms and don't recognize them. In about two years untreated syphilis enters into the tertiary stage.

Tertiary syphilis is an advanced stage that affects the heart, liver, brain, and other vital organs. The involvement of vital organs in untreated syphilis will end in death. Syphilis can cause paralysis, seizures, and even insanity due to changes in the brain.

The Tuskegee Study

The Tuskegee study took place from 1932-1974 in Tuskegee, Alabama under the control of the United States Public Health Service. The reason given by them for the study was to determine effects of untreated syphilis on the human body. It was as cruel, inhuman, barbaric, and racist as any study done in Nazi Germany, and it took place right here in America.

In fact, another study—the Oslo study—had already shown what untreated syphilis could do to the human body. It was the first syphilis study between 1891 and 1951, and included 2000 patients.

Nonetheless, from 1932 to 1974 during the Tuskegee study, black men were injected with live syphilis organisms to examine the effects on their bodies. These men did not consent to the study and didn't know they were being injected with syphilis. Penicillin had not yet been discovered, so there was no way to treat them.

The United States government, organized medicine, physicians—some white, some black—and hospital administrators stood by while these men suffered and died. A lesson we can all learn from this is how dangerous it is to neglect our roles in society as watchdogs. We must always speak against those who claim to be the authority when they commit unspeakable acts of exploitation against oppressed people. What happens to one of us, happens to us all.

Treatment for Different Stages of Syphilis

- Primary syphilis—chancre stage (if not allergic to penicillin)—1.2 million units of Benzathine penicillin in each buttock, IM.
- Secondary syphilis—(if not allergic to penicillin)—1.2 million units of Benzathine penicillin in each buttock IM weekly, times three weeks in sequence.
- Latent syphilis—(if not allergic to penicillin)—1.2 million units of Benzathine in each buttock IM weekly times three weeks in sequence.
- Tertiary syphilis—(if not allergic to penicillin)—1.2 million units of Benzathine penicillin in each buttock IM weekly, times three weeks in sequence.
- Neuro syphilis—(if not allergic to penicillin)—spinal tap; send CSF for VDRL and FTA-ABS testing. If positive, admit patient to the hospital and treat with 12 to 24 million units per day of aqueous penicillin g IV for ten days or 600,000 units daily of procaine penicillin IM daily for 14 days. The IM treatment can be carried out on an outpatient basis.

Any person who is HIV positive and VDRL and FTA positive must be assumed to have neurosyphilis. A spinal tap must be done and the CSF study for syphilis. An additional weekly dose of benzathine penicillin for three weeks is also required.

If a person is allergic to penicillin and has early stages of syphilis, the treatment of choice is erythromycin or tetracycline 500 mg by mouth, four times a day, for 15 days. For more advanced stages of syphilis, including neurosyphilis. The treatment of choice is erythromycin or tetracycline 500 mg by mouth four times a day for 30 days.

It is very important to do follow-up VDRL after treating a person for syphilis. Every three months a repeat should be done to show that the VDRL titer has gone down. Sometimes it remains high even though adequate treatment was given. This situation can be quite confusing because it's possible to become re-infected.

Again, it is absolutely crucial that pregnant syphilitic women not be treated with Tetracycline in the first trimester of pregnancy. It will stain the bones of the fetus.

STD AND VAGINAL INFECTIONS AND HOW TO TREAT THEM

Chancroid is an STD caused by a bacterial organism called **hemophilus ducreye**. Its symptoms occur three to five days after a woman has sexual intercourse with an infected man. They include pain and tenderness in the vulvae, ulcer formation in the area with foul odor and large inguinal nodes on both sides of the groin, which are quite tender and painful with subsequent formation of buboes (necrotic tissue).

The diagnosis is made by gram stain, culture, or biopsy of a bulbo or necrotic tissue from the vulvae. Treatment is usually Erythromycin 500 mg by mouth 4 times per day for 7 days or Ceftrioxone 250 mg intramuscularly one time.

Mucopurulent cervicitis and bacterial vaginosis are STDs caused by bacterial organisms. Common symptoms are foul smelling vaginal discharge, and burning and itching in the vaginal area. The diagnosis is made under the microscope. The usual treatment is Flagyl 500 mg 2 times per day for 7 days and ampicillin 500 mg 4 times per day for 7 days, or tetracycline 500 mg 4 times per day for 7 days. It is imperative that the woman's sexual partner gets treated, to prevent re-infection during sexual intercourse.

Candidiasis vulvo-vaginitis, a candidal infection of the vulva and vaginal areas of the reproductive organs, is one of the most common infections in women. There are several predisposing conditions to this infection. Among them are:

    1. Diabetes mellitus
    2. Antibiotic use
    3. The use of birth control pills
    4. Pregnancy

A fungus called *Candidiasis albican* causes vaginal candiasis. Diabetes is highly associated with vulvo-vaginitis because the fungus grows best in the presence of sugar. If a woman is diabetic and her blood sugar is too high, her vaginal secretions also have too much sugar, thus feeding *Candidiasis albican*. In fact, the first indication that a woman is diabetic is when she contracts recurrent fungal vaginal infections.

Antibiotics and Yeast Infections

How does antibiotic use cause **fungal vaginitis** (yeast infections)? Many different types of bacteria plus *Candidiasis albican* live in the vagina. When a woman is treated with antibiotics, the bacteria are decreased by the effect of the antibiotic. The balance between bacterial flora and fungal flora is changed in favor of the fungus. Fungal overgrowth results in fungal vaginitis.

It is ill advised to assume vaginal infection when a woman develops discharge. Over-the-counter vaginal creams are dangerous, because there are many serious diseases that first manifest as a yeast infection. If woman develops vaginal discharge she should go for a proper pelvic examination.

Many women cannot afford a doctor and fall back on self-treatment. Sometimes they use home remedies. This is highly discouraged.

Lympho-Granuloma Venerum (LGV) is an STD caused by chlamydia. It appears one to four weeks after unprotected sexual intercourse with an infected individual. Symptoms such as fever and headache develop along with painless ulcer in the vulva and vaginal areas. The infection spreads via the lymphatic system into the anus and rectum resulting in ulcers, recto-vaginal fistulas and abscesses. If left untreated, rectal stenosis can occur.

Diagnosis is made by a Frei test. Treatment is tetracycline or erythromycin 500 mg 4 times a day for 3 weeks or doxycycline 100 mg for 3 weeks.

Granuloma Inguinale is an STD caused by the bacterial organism *Donovania granulomatis*. Small papules develop around the vagina one to twelve weeks after sexual intercourse with an infected person. These papules quickly develop into ulcers, which spread to the anus, vagina, perineum, and cervix. If left untreated, fibrosis and scarring develop along with keloid formation, due to destruction of the lymphatic system in the general pelvic area.

To make the diagnosis, tissue from the infected ulcers is stained with either Giemsa or Wright stain and examined under the microscope. Treatment is usually with tetracycline 500 mg, 4 times per day for 3 weeks.

Condyloma acuminata (venereal warts) is an extremely contagious STD, transmitted by skin-to-skin contact during sexual intercourse. Venereal wart infection is frequently associated with other STDs such as trichomonas vaginosis infection and bacterial vaginitis.

The organism responsible for venereal warts is human papilloma virus. These lesions proliferate more in women who are diabetic, on birth control pills, pregnant, or immunosuppressed.

Venereal warts can involve the perivaginal area, the vulva, and the perianal area. They appear in a cauliflower formation and frequently bleed. They are very difficult to treat.

Pregnant women whose perivaginal and vulva areas are infected should undergo a cesarean section to prevent the baby from coming into contact with the virus.

Treatments include 25 percent trichloracitic acid, salicyclic acid in Collodion, or podophyllin resin, weekly. Sometimes, laser treatments, electrosurgery, or cryosurgery with liquid nitrogen are used to remove the warts.

Molluscum contagiosum is an STD whose cause is a contagious virus that affects the vulva and perineal areas. It is quite contagious and transmitted by skin contact. The treatment is electrosurgery.

Hepatitis C and **Hepatitis B** are blood borne infections transmitted by needle or blood transfusions. Both are found in vaginal secretions and semen, and therefore can be transmitted sexually.

There is a vaccine for Hepatitis B, which is given in a three-stage manner. There is no vaccine available for Hepatitis C. Alpha interferon injection is used in conjunction with Ribaverin when it affects the liver. According to the most recent literature, Hepatitis A can also be transmitted via blood products, transfusion, and therefore via sexual intercourse as well.

Toxic shock syndrome is usually caused by tampons. The causative organism is Staphylococcus. The usual symptoms vary from flu-like to lower abdominal cramps with fever and excessive vaginal bleeding. Once recognized, treatment with IV antibiotics against Staphylocci is effective and curative.

GYNECOLOGICAL BASICS—MENSTRUATION

Premenstrual syndrome, known as PMS, is a complex of symptoms that occur seven to ten days before the onset of menstrual blood flow. It has been around since Hippocrates. We all know the most common symptoms, but some are kept under wraps because they seem so extreme. They are:

• Depression
• Crying spells
• Suicide contemplation
• Decreased libido

It's important for women to understand that these are natural feelings that will pass when the body balances again. Healthy diet and a good attitude will help buffer these symptoms.

Many theories have been postulated regarding the causes of PMS. Among them are abnormal levels of hormones such as estrogen, progesterone, cortisone, and androgens. Overload of antidiuretic hormone, deficiencies in the levels of vitamins A, B, B_6, decreased levels of magnesium, melatonin, reactive hypoglycemia, abnormal menstrual stress, and psychosocial problems all contribute to PMS.

Ovulation seems to play a major role in PMS, because it doesn't occur before puberty or after menopause. Symptoms seem to be improved by Vitamin B_6. Some women respond to hypnosis. The most grounded approach is dietary management. Low fat, low carbohydrates, and reduced caffeine ingestion are a good rule of thumb.

If a hysterectomy has been performed to treat problems like uterine fibroids, the symptoms of PMS dissipate. NSAIDS (non-steroidal anti-inflammatory drugs) and birth control pills with progesterone seem to help. Sleeping pills or relaxants are discouraged due to their addictive potential.

Dysmenorrhea (cramps) is common to women the world over. There are primary and secondary dysmenorrheas. Usually symptoms of dysmenorrhea show up six to twelve months after a young girl starts her period (menarche).

Dysmenorrhea is attributed to uterine contractions. During the secretory phase of the menstrual cycle the level of prostaglandins seems highest. The interplay between prostaglandins and blood flow to the uterus result in cramping and pain.

Some women actually black out from the intensity of the pain and can't function for a day or two. Diarrhea, nausea, vomiting, headache, and extreme fatigue are the symptoms that some women experience during their menstrual period.

Secondary dysmenorrhea is associated with such conditions as chronic PID, endometriosis, uterine fibroids, or intrauterine contraception devices (IUD). Treatment includes NSAIDS, with recommended dosages being different for each kind. For Motrin, 600 mg 4 times per day. Naprosyn, 250 mg 3 times per day. Anaprox, 275 mg 3 times per day. Advil 2 tablets 4 times per day. Aleve 2 tablets 3 times per day, or Aspirin 325 mg 1 tablet 3 times per day.

Birth control pills also ease the symptoms of Dysmenorrhea by reducing menstrual blood flow and inhibiting ovulation. Some women use both birth control pills and NSAIDS for relief.

Treatments for secondary dysmenorrhea are essentially based on treating the underlying causes like endometriosis, uterine fibroids, PID, removing IUD, uterine polyps, uterine malformations, and cervical stenosis. Some say symptoms lessen once they start having children. Women are encouraged to see their gynecologists for guidance.

FIBROID TUMORS

Fibroid tumors of the uterus are extremely common in women and can cause minor or major complications. About 20 percent of women develop uterine fibroids by the time they reach forty. Fibroid tumors are 3 to 4 times more common in black women than in their white counterparts.

Fibroids develop from smooth muscles in the wall of the uterus. Estrogen facilitates their growth. Women who take estrogen for menopausal symptoms or osteoporosis have an increased chance of having their fibroids increase in size, even though they are no longer menstruating.

It is speculative to say why black women have such a high incidence of uterine fibroids but Negroid genes tend to have a high propensity toward keloids when cutting or abrasion traumatizes the skin. The constant shedding of the lining of the uterus might be causing keloids.

The symptoms of uterine fibroids are many:
1. Abdominal mass causing lower abdominal pressure
2. Lower back pain
3. Constipation
4. Urinary frequency
5. Abdominal pain
6. Pain on intercourse
7. Urinary retention
8. Vaginal bleeding between periods
9. Heavy and prolonged vaginal bleeding forming clots
10. Secondary iron deficiency anemia as a result of chronic vaginal blood loss
11. Weakness and lassitude as a result of iron deficiency

Uterine fibroids affect fertility. Also large uterine fibroids make it very hard for women to carry a fetus to term because they crowd out the fetus and prevent it from growing. The result is spontaneous abortion. Fibroids have to be removed via **myomectomy** in order to carry a pregnancy to term. Some women prefer myomectomy to hysterectomy because they keep their uterus.

Black women's ideas of womanhood are in large measure, similar to those of other races, but there are some differences. Many women are reluctant to have hysterectomies because of the notion that when a woman loses her womb she is no longer sexually desirable. Removing a woman's uterus for her own safety does not diminish her sexuality.

Pelvic ultrasound is the best radiological test to diagnose uterine fibroids along with the pelvic examination. An endocervical mass (large fibroid) requires a more extensive evaluation to make sure that the woman is not suffering from cancer. This abdominal mass can cause pain, nausea, vomiting, constipation, bloating, poor appetite, urinary incontinence, and urinary tract infections.

If a woman of childbearing age has fibroids and wishes to have a child, the gynecologist may decide to do a myomectomy to remove some of the fibroids. Sometimes, a D&C is done to stop vaginal bleeding. Lupron is given intramuscularly to decrease the size of uterine fibroids for several weeks before surgically removing fibroids. A new procedure embolizes the blood flow to the fibroids so as to prevent their growth and avoids major abdominal surgery.

Women forty-five years old or older who are no longer interested in having children should consider removal of ovaries and tubes, eliminating chances of future cancer of the ovaries and tubes. The development of osteoporosis as a result of removal of the ovaries is possible but black women have a very low incidence of osteoporosis.

IRREGULAR BLEEDING

Excessive vaginal bleeding is one of the most common signs of uterine cancer. Cervical Pap smear and endometrial biopsy are two of the tests used to diagnose it. Women should see the gynecologist for a pelvic examination, Pap smear and, if necessary, an endometrial biopsy. It is always abnormal for a woman to bleed heavily in between menstrual cycles, and if she is, she should see a gynecologist immediately.

Uterine cancer is more common in African American women than white American women. Once again, we have to consider obesity. It is closely related to uterine cancer because fat cells can be converted to estrogen by the ovarian and the adrenal glands. The higher level of estrogen is cancerous. For greater detail, review chapter 7, Cancer in African American Women.

The second most common cancer of female reproductive organs is cancer of the ovary. Pelvic examination, pelvic ultrasound, abdominal CAT scan, and a blood test called Ca125 are the tests that are available to diagnose it. Women with one member of their immediate family affected by ovarian cancer have two to four times the risk of developing it.

Evidence from recent literature shows that part of the problem is in the examination of the female pelvis. Bi-annual examination missed 36 percent of fibroids and 70 percent of abnormalities in the adnexa in women. (*American Journal of Obstetrics and Gynecology*, 1996; 175: 1189-1194). This is an alarming finding considering that managed care companies are often reluctant to pay for tests, and many African American women can't afford to pay for a pelvic ultrasound to pick up early ovarian cancer.

Birth control pills seem to decrease the chances of getting ovarian cancer. This occurs apparently because birth control pills suppress ovulation and interfere with ovarian functions.

The usual treatment for ovarian cancer is total hysterectomy with removal of the ovaries, fallopian tubes, and the uterus, as well as treatment with chemotherapy, radiation therapy, or a combination of both.

The more men a woman has had sexual intercourse with, the more irritation the women's cervix is exposed to. Men have different sized penises. The larger the penis the more potential it has to irritate the cervix, which sits right in the center of the vagina. It's within easy reach of even the smallest adult male penis.

Another gynecological issue is male hygiene. An unclean man introduces irritating materials to a woman's cervix. Bacteria, viruses, fungi, and smegma from under the man's penis or foreskin complicate the delicate balance of bacteria in the vagina. There are many bacteria, both grams negative and positive, and fungi, such as Candidiasis, that inhabit the vagina as a natural habitat, to keep the vaginal tissues properly moist and healthy. For more information, review yeast infections in this chapter.

Microorganisms become imbalanced due to douches that women use to treat a legitimate bacterial infection somewhere in the body. Killing the bacterial flora only allows the fungi to grow, resulting in a fungal vaginitis. Black women, in particular, have habits of douching with corrosive douches such as vinegar, Lysol, etc. The solutions are quite irritating to the cervical tissues, can cause dysplasia, and in extreme cases can be deadly. Imbalances brought about by infections or chemicals predispose women to cancer of the cervix.

Black men from the Third World are often uncircumcised. The penile foreskin is prone to phimosis, paraphimosis, and balanitis. The foreskin's smegma can cause cells of the cervix to become dysplastic. Black women have a higher incidence of cervical cancer in part because of uncircumcised partners. Proper hygiene minimizes the transference of smegma. The woman's vagina produces it too but in the labia minora, away from the cervix.

Women infected with the HIV Type I or Type II viruses are prone to develop an invasive and aggressive form of cervical cancer because of human papilloma virus. African-American and Hispanic women in the United States are particularly affected by this problem. Their rate of HIV infection is high due to drug use among them and their male sexual partners.

THE PAP SMEAR

The Pap smear is classified as:

Class I	Normal
Class II	Inflammatory atypia
Class III	Dysplasia
Class IV	Carcinoma in situ
Class V	Invasive carcinoma

What to do with the Results

Sexually active women should have a Pap smear every year. Women 60 and older who are not sexually active and who have had two to three negative Pap smears in sequence can probably have a Pap smear every three to five years. False positive Pap smears happen 20 percent of the time. This finding is troubling but if a colposcopic biopsy is done, the true diagnosis can be made.

The colposcope is a type of microscope with low magnification which is used by a gynecologist to visualize a woman's cervix, looking for abnormalities. A camera may be attached to the colposcope to allow for pictures to be taken of tissues of the cervix, which can be re-photographed later as a follow-up.

Laparoscopic examination is used frequently in examining the pelvis, to evaluate abnormalities seen on pelvic examination and CAT scan. A small incision is made around the umbilicus to introduce the instrument so that the gynecologist can carry out the procedure in a minimally invasive way.

CERVICAL CANCER

Vaginal bleeding is the most frequent symptom of invasive carcinoma of the cervix. The bleeding may occur as:

1. Post-sexual intercourse bleeding
2. Excessive and prolonged menstrual bleeding
3. Bleeding between periods
4. Post-menopausal bleeding

Cryosurgery, laser, electrocoagulation, loop electro diathemy excision, and cervical cone biopsy are used to treat early cervical cancer. Hysterectomy is used to treat more advanced stages. Radiation therapy is effective for some stages to alleviate vaginal bleeding. Cancer of the cervix is a curable disease if diagnosed early and treated early.

PREGNANCY

When women are pregnant, more often than not, it goes well but the process is serious and should not be taken for granted for reasons that will be discussed later in the chapter. Many things can go wrong with expecting mothers and their infants. Pregnancy is a serious medical situation.

Toxemia

One of the most common and potentially deadly conditions that affect pregnant women is toxemia of pregnancy. It can be a threat to the life of both mother and unborn fetus and must be treated quickly.

The American College of Obstetrics and Gynecology classifies hypertensive disorder in pregnancy this way:
1. Preeclampsia eclampsia (hypertension peculiar to pregnancy)
2. Chronic hypertension
3. Chronic hypertension with superimposed preeclampsia
4. Late or transient hypertension

Mild preeclampsia occurs most frequently in young women during their first pregnancies. For more information, review *Toxemia* in chapter 1.

Severe preeclampsia occurs when the blood pressure is greater than 160/110 and urinary protein is greater than five grams for twenty-four hours. A woman may become oliguric (excrete less than 400 mg of urine in a 24-hour period), and suffer headache, blurry vision, altered consciousness, cyanosis or pulmonary edema, and pain in the upper stomach.

The second stage of hypertension associated with pregnancy is eclampsia, when all of the above problems crescendo into grand mal seizure. No one knows what causes this condition. One theory is that utero-placental ischemia causes production of vaso-constrictive substances which lead to the development of a substance called aldosterone. It in turn causes salt retention and water retention with elevation of blood pressure.

Another frequent complication of pregnancy is gestational diabetes. About 0.5 percent of pregnant women develop gestational diabetes. The screening for gestational diabetes usually begins between the 24th and 28th week of pregnancy. For more information, review gestational diabetes in Chapter 5.

Autoimmune Disease and Pregnancy

Rheumatoid arthritis is an autoimmune disease which causes inflammation of the joints. It can also affect many other organs. During pregnancy flare-up can occur. Many medications treat the symptoms of rheumatoid arthritis but most cannot be used during pregnancy. Aspirin is allowed.

Salicylates, which are the main ingredient in aspirin, do cross the placenta, which means that side effects like bleeding are possible. In addition, the woman might bleed excessively at the time of delivery. NSAIDS are very good to treat arthritis but should be taken with caution. Their side effects might present problems both for the fetus and neonate.

Systemic lupus erythematosis (SLE) is an autoimmune disease more common in woman than men and is seen quite frequently in African American women of childbearing age. SLE affects all organs in the human body. A pregnancy induced flare-up causes serious medical problems with possible deadly consequences. It's a bad idea for any woman with SLE to get pregnant.

For more information on arthritis and SLE see Chapter 13, Arthritis in African American Women.

When **Idiopathic thrombocytopenic purpura** is seen in pregnancy, both the welfare of the mother and fetus must be carefully monitored. Fetal hemorrhage is the biggest problem. If platelet count is less than 50,000, Caesarean section should be done to prevent brain hemorrhage in the fetus as a result of birth canal trauma.

MENOPAUSE

Menopause is a well-known condition to women the world over. Women reach menopause when they stop menstruating. They are born with about 1.5 million eggs (ova) and by menarche (the beginning of menstruation) have 450,000 left. Women use up one egg per menstrual cycle. Pituitary gonadotropins, hormones which the pituitary gland produces, control the function of the ovaries to produce estrogen and progesterone. Both hormones dictate the menstrual cycle.

As a woman gets older, the ability for the ovaries to produce those hormones lessens and lack of estrogen in her bloodstream brings about menopause. Its symptoms include hot flashes, sweating, dizziness, heart palpitation, insomnia, lethargy, depression, and crying spells.

Dryness of the vagina and of the urethral meatus can result in urinary tract infection. Sexual intercourse may hurt. If women start to avoid sex because of pain, a lubricant is the simplest remedy.

The negative aspects of increased estrogen production in obese black women are, higher incidence of both breast cancer and cancer of the uterus. High estrogen levels overstimulate these tissues and they develop cancer much more easily.

Estrogen replacement is one option. Among the complications of estrogen replacement treatments are:
1. Deep vein thrombophlebitis
2. Pulmonary embolism
3. Strokes
4. Salt retention
5. Fluid retention
6. Rise in high blood pressure

When an individual takes estrogen replacement treatment, there is a substance in the human body called antithrombin III, which keeps blood thinners properly balanced. When the level of antithrombin is low the blood becomes too thick, resulting in slower movement inside the blood vessels. Clot formation causes **pulmonary embolism** (clots in the lungs), strokes, and clots to other areas such as kidney, heart, and abdomen.

Estrogen replacement in Caucasians has been shown to decrease coronary artery disease and heart attacks. However, these results cannot always be applied to black women because of their particular risk factors:

1. Obesity
2. Hypertension as a result of salt sensitivity
3. Hyperlipidemia due to poor dietary habits and poverty
4. Higher propensity toward breast cancer due in part to obesity
5. Higher propensity toward uterine cancer due in part to obesity
6. Higher propensity toward arteriosclerotic heart disease

Rather than taking a chance on estrogen replacement with all its side effects, small doses of sedative and anti-anxiety medications may help black women through the difficult periods of menopause.

AIDS In African American Women

AIDS stands for Acquired Immune Deficiency Syndrome (as opposed to Inborn Immune Deficiency Syndrome). The virus, the HIV Type I or Type II, a retrovirus, enters the human body and attacks and kills the T helper lymphocyte. A decrease in their number results in immunodeficiency.

The **T helper lymphocytes** are in the body to keep it healthy, while the **T suppressor lymphocytes** (also called CD8) are in the body to cause it to be sick, when their numbers are increased. Therefore, in AIDS, the number of T helper lymphocytes is lower than the number of the T suppressor lymphocytes.

How does the AIDS virus cause the immunosuppression? The virus enters the blood stream and then into the T cell or lymphocytes. Once inside the lymphocyte, the virus multiplies. It can generate as many as several billion copies per day, until the body gradually becomes immunosuppressed, leading ultimately to full-blown AIDS.

A HISTORICAL PERSPECTIVE

The first reported cases of AIDS appeared in an article published in June 1981 in *The New England Journal of Medicine* in which a group of homosexual men were found to be sick with pneumocystis carinii pneumonia.

Further evaluation revealed that they were immunosuppressed, and that state predisposed them to the development of pneumocystis carinii pneumonia (PCP).

The AIDS epidemic was underway. Subsequently it was published that a young man living in the streets of St. Louis who had had frequent contacts with homosexual men died of an unknown disease associated with fever, weight loss, and pulmonary infection. This was in the early 1960s.

An autopsy on the St. Louis man was performed with tissue and plasma samples that were frozen. In the 1980s after the AIDS epidemic was well underway, the pathologist who had frozen the samples tested them for the AIDS virus and found them teeming with it.

So in retrospect, the AIDS virus had been around the United States, since the early 1960s.

As a doctor training in the inner city of New York, I saw many drug addicts with febrile illness associated with large lymph nodes, and had no idea what they had. Their blood contained lymphocytic hyperplasia and we used to think materials used to cut cocaine or heroin were responsible for its presence, little realizing that these people probably had AIDS.

So, one does not have to go to Africa, Haiti, and other Third World countries to look for a scapegoat for the origin of the AIDS virus. The AIDS virus developed in inner cities long before 1981.

AIDS has now spread worldwide and knows no racial boundaries. It spares no social class or sex. It is the largest epidemic that mankind has ever known. Every few seconds someone in the world is being infected with the AIDS virus, mainly through sexual intercourse.

In 1999, 2.6 million individuals died of AIDS in the world; 2.1 million of them were adults, 1.1 million were women, and 470,000 were children. Of the 16.3 million deaths from AIDS, 13.7 million have occurred in Sub-Saharan Africa. Sub-Saharan Africa is home to 23.3 million cases of HIV/AIDS. (See Tables 12A and 12B.)

Table 12A: (As published by MNAIDS/WHO, December 1999)

Region	Epidemic Started	Adults & Children Living w/ HIV/AIDS	Adults & Children Newly Infected w/ HIV	Adult Prevalence Rate[1]	Percent of HIV Positive Adults Who Are Women	Main Mode(s) of Transmission[2] for Adults Living with HIV/AIDS
Sub-Saharan Africa	Late '70s-Early '80's	23.3 million	3.8 million	8.0%	55%	Hetero
N. Africa & Middle East	Late '80's	220,000	19,000	0.13%	20%	IDU, Hetero
South & Southeast Asia	Late '80's	6 million	1.3 million	0.69%	30%	Hetero
East Asia & Pacific	Late '80's	530,000	120,000	0.068%	15%	IDU, Hetero, MSM
Latin America	Late '70s-Early '80's	1.3 million	150,000	0.57%	20%	MSM, IDU, Hetero
Caribbean	Late '70s-Early '80's	360,000	57,000	1.96%	35%	Hetero, MSM
Eastern Europe & Central Asia	Early '90's	360,000	95,000	0.14%	20%	IDU, MSM
Western Europe	Late '70s-Early '80's	520,000	30,000	0.25%	20%	MSM, IDU
North America	Late '70s-Early '80's	920,000	44,000	0.56%	20%	MSM, IDU, Hetero
Australia & New Zealand	Late '70s-Early '80's	12,000	500	0.1%	10%	MSM, IDU
Total		33.6 million	5.6 million	1.1%	46%	

[1] The proportion of all adults (15-49 years of age) living with HIV/AIDS in 1999, using 1998 population numbers.

[2] MSM (Sexual transmission among men who have sex with men), IDU (transmission through intravenous drug use), Hetero (transmission through heterosexual sex).

More black women are infected with the AIDS virus in the United States than white women. More Hispanic women are infected than white women also, but the number of black women who are infected surpasses both Hispanic women and white women combined.

TABLE 12B:
GLOBAL SUMMARY OF THE HIV/AIDS EPIDEMIC DECEMBER 1999

People newly infected with HIV in 1999	**Total**	**5.6 million**
	Adults	5 million
	Women	2.3 million
	Children <15 years	570,000
Number of people living with HIV/AIDS	**Total**	**33.6 million**
	Adults	32.4 million
	Women	14.8 million
	Children <15 years	1.2 million
AIDS deaths in 1999	**Total**	**2.6 million**
	Adults	2.1 million
	Women	1.1 million
	Children <15 years	470,000
Total number of AIDS deaths since the beginning of the epidemic	**Total**	**16.3 million**
	Adults	12.7 million
	Women	6.2 million
	Children <15 years	3.6 million

As published by MNAIDS/WHO, December, 1999

Why is AIDS so much more prevalent among black women as compared to white women? More black women are using intravenous drugs than white women in America. Also, more black men are using intravenous drugs than white men. Once the men become infected they pass it on to their sexual partners.

Of the 129,190 AIDS cases in women reported in the United States in the year 2000, 74,331 were African Americans, 27,889 were white, and 25,680 were hispanic.[1] About 62 percent were African American women. More than two and a half times more black women get AIDS from using IV drugs than white women and more than two times the number of black women get AIDS from sexual contact than white females.

To make the situation even worse, many of these AIDS-infected women become pregnant and give birth to babies who are infected. The total number of pediatric AIDS cases as of December 1996 were 7,621. The breakdown is as follows:

White	1,369
Hispanic	1,770
Black	4,409

There are more than twice the number of black babies with AIDS than white and Hispanic babies put together. This is because more black women of childbearing age are infected with the AIDS virus than either white women or Hispanic women.

About 40 percent of babies born to mothers who are infected with the AIDS virus are not infected. Infected women who take the medication AZT from the first trimester of pregnancy give birth to more babies who test HIV negative at birth and remain that way.

The states and cities with the largest numbers of AIDS cases are[1]:

California	98,157
Florida	58,911
New Jersey	32,226
New York	106,897
Texas	39,871

***

Atlanta	12,121
Chicago	16,139

Houston	14,293
Los Angeles	34,643
Miami	18,292
New York	91,799
Newark	13,213
Philadelphia	13,325
San Francisco	24,272
San Juan	11,639
Washington, D.C.	16,787

In 1993, according to the AMA, AIDS was the fourth leading cause of death among women ages twenty-five to forty-five in the United States. In June 2000, the total number of cases was 753,907. As of June 2000, 36,616 black women have died from AIDS.

Getting Infected

The following can infect a person:

1. A man having unprotected sexual intercourse with another man
2. A man having unprotected sexual intercourse with both men and women
3. A man or woman injecting IV drugs
4. A woman having unprotected sexual intercourse with men who use IV drugs
5. A woman having unprotected sexual intercourse with bisexual men
6. An individual receiving blood or blood products contaminated with the HIV virus
7. Being a baby born to a mother infected with the HIV virus
8. Being accidentally stuck with needles contaminated with the HIV virus (most common among healthcare workers)
9. Being bitten by a person with AIDS
10. Engaging in passionate kissing with a person with AIDS
11. Engaging in oral sex with a person with AIDS

Some of the high-risk behaviors that can lead to the transmission of the AIDS virus from one person to another are:

1. Anal intercourse
2. Intravenous drug use
3. Prostitution
4. Having multiple sex partners
5. Having unprotected sexual intercourse with strangers

In order for a person to become infected with the AIDS virus, the virus must enter their bloodstream.

A woman can become infected with the AIDS virus while having intravaginal intercourse with an infected man because the natural vaginal milieu of a woman has a high pH that allows for growth and multiplication of the HIV virus.

During sexual intercourse, there is also microtrauma of the capillaries that occurs naturally. This gives HIV an opportunity to enter into a woman's blood stream. The virus is in the semen deposited during intercourse. Open sores, such as genital herpes, syphilitic sores, and other venereal chancres, increase her chances of infection severalfold. There is a very high correlation between STD and HIV infection.

When HIV enters the bloodsteam the virus goes into the T helper lymphocyte and multiplies. Within two to four weeks the newly infected person develops fever, aches and chills, runny nose, and cough. These symptoms then disappear and the person feels fine.

The HIV virus continues to multiply in the blood stream and within the nodes of the body. This is the infection stage.

Testing

In the next ten days to two weeks the **antigen T24** is elevated and can be measured. The **ELISA** test becomes positive after the window period, which is six to twelve weeks after infection. During the window period both the ELISA for the HIV, the P24 antigen, and the HIVI DNA PCR will be positive if the person is infected with the AIDS virus.

The HIVI DNA PCR is the earliest test to become positive if a person becomes infected with the HIV virus. It becomes positive seven to ten days after infection. A Western Blot test is done to confirm whether the ELISA test is truly positive. The Western Blot test is an actual electrophoresis of the protein contained within the body of the virus itself.

One problem with the ELISA test is that it can be falsely positive; another is that during the window period, the HIV test could be falsely negative. To deal with this problem, the P24 antigen test can be done because it shows up positive within a minimum of ten days after the virus enters the body. The HIV DNA PCR test can be done to confirm the HIV test as well.

To recap the tests available to diagnose AIDS are:

1. ELISA Test
2. Western Blot Test
3. HIV1 DNA PCR test
4. HIV1 RNA PCR test
5. P24

Health professionals who get stuck with needles contaminated with blood from AIDS patients are treated with triple therapy of AZT, 3TC, and a protease inhibitor. They get their blood taken for baseline HIV and hepatitis and VDRL. They are retested for a few months. As soon as the incident happens it is reported to appropriate authorities where the person works.

PROGRESSION OF AIDS

As the HIV viruses continue to multiply, the number of T4 lymphocytes decreases while the number of suppressor lymphocytes increases. This triggers the immunosuppressive states that occur in AIDS.

The HIV infection moves from the HIV infected stage to ARC stage and then to the AIDS stage. The HIV stage may be completely silent, except for some patients who may develop thrombocytopenia (low platelet count) with or without enlarged nodes.

During the ARC (AIDS Related Complex) stage the patient will start to lose weight, suffer widespread lymph node enlargement, develop thrush, diarrhea, fever, headache, oral hair leukoplakia, shingles, thrombocytopenia, molluscum contagiosum, recurrent herpes simplex, aphthous ulcer, and condyloma.

Some individuals take many years to progress from these stages to full-blown AIDS. The mode of infection and the stage of HIV infection in the infector may play a role in how fast one develops AIDS.

Chemokine receptors CCR5 and CX4 seem to play a role in when the HIV virus progresses to full-blown AIDS. For that matter, certain people with chemokine receptors may be resistant to the HIV infection. This is a new concept and has yet to be proven.

One of the important factors governing a patient's survival is the overall makeup of the infected individual in terms of his or her immune strength, his or her ability to pay for medical care, to pay for anti-HIV medication, and to afford good nutrition.

In order to say that a person has AIDS, clinically established criteria have to be met, as defined by the Center for Disease Control (CDC). For example, a person with HIV infection whose CD4 count drops below 200 can be said to meet one criteria for AIDS.

The list of AIDS-defining illnesses include the following:

TABLE 12C:
Diseases diagnosed definitively, without confirmation of HIV
Infection in patients without other causes of immunodeficiency

> Candidiasis of the esophagus, trachea, bronchi, or lungs
>
> Cryptococcoses, extra pulmonary
>
> Cryptosporidiosis > 1 month's duration
>
> Cytomegalovirus infection of any organ except the liver, spleen, or lymph nodes in patients > 1 month old
>
> Herpes simplex infection, mucocutaneous (> 1 month's duration) or of the bronchi, lungs, or esophagus in patients of 1 month's duration
>
> Kaposi's sarcoma in patients < 60 years old
>
> Primary CNS lymphoma in patients < 60 years old
>
> Lymphoid interstitial pneumonitis (LIP) and/or pulmonar lymphoid hyperplasia (PLH) in patients < 13 years old

Mycobacterium avium complex of Mycobacterium kansasii
disseminated

Pneumocystis carinii pneumonia

Progressive multifocal leukoencephalopathy

Toxoplasmosis of the brain in patients > 1 month old

Diseases diagnosed definitively with confirmation of HIV infection

Multiple or recurrent pyogenic bacterial infections in patients
< 13 years old

Coccidioidomycosis, disseminated

Histoplasmosis, disseminated

Isosporiasis > 1 month duration

Kaposi's sarcoma, any age

Primary CNS lymphoma, any age

Non-Hodgkin's lymphoma (small, noncleaved lymphoma;
Burkitt or non-Burkitt type; or immunoblastic sarcoma)

Mycobacterial disease other than Mycobacterium tuberculosis, disseminated

M. Tuberculosis, extra pulmonary

Salmonella septicemia, recurrent

Disease diagnosed presumptively with confirmation of HIV infection

Candidiasis of the esophagus

CMV retinitis

Kaposi's sarcoma

LIP/PLH in patients < 13 years old

Disseminated mycobacterial disease (not cultured)

P. Carinii pneumonia

Toxoplasmosis of the brain in patients > 1 month old

HIV encephalopathy

HIV wasting syndrome

Center for Disease Control—Definition of AIDS

AIDS is a multisystem disease in that it affects all systems in
the body in one form or another, to one degree or another; leading eventually to death.

The first system affected with the AIDS virus is the immune system resulting in immunosuppression. The immune system has three parts to it:

1. Cell mediated
2. Humoral mediated
3. The complement system

As outlined in the book *AIDS The Expanding Epidemic; What the Public Needs to Know - A MultiCultural Overview*, V. Alcena, M.D., 1994.

Cell mediated immunity.

Dominated mainly by T-lymphocytes, macrophages also play a role in this system. There are different types of T lymphocytes such as CD4, T helper lymphocytes, CD8, T-suppressor lymphocytes, CD4 or T helper lymphocytes. They are necessary to antigens (substance that stimulates production of antibodies).

A D4 or T helper lymphocyte is necessary to help the body maintain a normally functioning immune system. A decrease in the total T helper lymphocytes leads to immune deficiency, be it congenital or acquired. When the level of CD4 goes down, the level of CD8 or T suppressor goes up, leading to further suppression of the immune system.

These systems are major players in the fight against infections and in maintaining good health while infected with the AIDS virus:

Humoral mediated immune system is dominated by B lymphocytes. These B lymphocytes give rise to plasma cells, which then produce antibodies. They have many functions, but paramount among them, is the protection of the body from infections. When the level of antibody producing B lymphocytes goes down, as occurs in AIDS, all sorts of infections can attack.

The **complement system** is the third immune system that plays a major role in the fight against infection in the human body. The complement system is divided into the classical pathway and the alternate pathway. These components work with other immunoglobulins to lyse microorganisms such as bacteria and viruses. They kill them, preventing them from killing the human organism.

When there is a decrease in the level of complement in the human body it can lead to a state of Immunodeficiency. If not corrected, it can lead to bacterial, viral, fungal, and parasitic infections creating many problems for the human organism and ultimately its death.

Hemapoietic System (The Blood)

The routine blood system includes the white blood cells, red blood cells, platelets, and the coagulation system. The two earliest affected cells are the white blood cells and the platelets.

The first indication that someone is HIV infected is low platelet count, known as **thrombocytopenia**. In this situation, the HIV virus directly infects the megakyryocytes, the cells that produce the platelets.

Leukopenia, a low white cell count, is due to a combination of HIV infection plus the medications that people with HIV infection are treated with.

ANEMIA AND HIV

The red blood cells are low (anemia) due to different reasons. One is that the HIV virus enters into the earliest red cells (erythroblasts) and infects them. The infection prevents them from maturing. This results in anemia.

HIV infection is frequently associated with pavo virus B #19. The pavo virus enters early red blood cells resulting in pure red cells aplasia and anemia.

Another cause of anemia in HIV infected individuals (AIDS) is low levels of erythropoietin, the protein made by the kidneys, whose job it is to stimulate the production of red blood cells. AIDS patients with an erythropoietin less than 500 usually respond to erythropoietin injections (to treat anemia), combined with AZT (for AIDS).

HIV infected individuals become anemic from chronic gastrointestinal blood loss, fungal gastritis, esophagitis, and viral or other infections of the GI tract. Patients with AIDS frequently have folate deficiency and at times B_{12} deficiency. B_{12} deficiency results in anemia.

Poor nutrition in patients causes a low protein anemia. The state of chronic infection causes a cytokines-associated anemia of chronic diseases. The pulmonary system in patients with full-blown AIDS is affected by infection. Pneumocystis caranii pneumonia (PCP) is often seen.

Other pulmonary infections seen in AIDS patients are pneumococcal infections, H. Influenzae infections, pseudomonas infections, and fungal infections.

VIRUSES

Among the viruses that infect AIDS patients are herpes simplex and cytomegalovirus (CMV); both infect the organs.

INFECTIONS

A multitude of fungi can cause infections in AIDS patients. The most common ones are toxoplasma and histoplasma which cause the brain become infected with different microorganisms.

NEUROLOGICAL DISEASES IN AIDS PATIENTS
Opportunistic infections
Toxoplasmosis
Cryptococcosis
Progressive multifocal leukoencephalopathy
Cytomegalovirus
Syphilis
Mycobacterium tuberculosis
HTLV-1 infection
Neoplasms
Primary CNS lymphoma
Kaposi's sarcoma

Result of HIV-1 infection
Aseptic meningitis
AIDS dementia complex (HIV encephalopathy)
Myelopathy
    Vacuolar myelopathy
    Pure sensory ataxia
    Paresthesia/dysesthesia
Peripheral neuropathy
    Acute demyelinating polyneuropathy
    Mononeuritis multiplex
    Distal symmetric polyneuropathy
Myopathy

TABLE 12D:

Disease	Clinical Features	Characteristic CSF Findings	Characteristic Radiologic Findings
HIV enecephalopathy (AIDS dementia complex)	Personality changes, dementia, unsteady gait, seizures	Nonspecific increases in cells and protein	Cortical atrophy, ventricular dilation, spots on T2-weighted MRI
Toxoplasmosis	Fever, headache, focal neurological deficits, seizures, + antibodies in 95%	Nonspecific	Single or multiple ring-enhancing lesions in multiple locations
Cryptococcal meningitis	Fever, nausea, vomiting, confusion, headache	Elevated protein, low glucose, positive cryptococcal antigen or culture	Nonspecific
Progressive multifocal leukoencephalopathy	Multiple focal deficits without changes in level of consciousness	Nonspecific	Multiple white matter lesions on T2-weighted MRI images
Neurosyphilis	Meningitis, neuroretinitis, deafness, focal neurologic deficits	Positive VDRL, elevated protein, increase in cells	Nonspecific
Lymphoma	Seizure, focal neurologic deficits, headache	Nonspecific in primary CNS lymphoma; malignant cells in systemic lymphoma	Single or few ring-enhancing lesions
Tuberculosis meningitis	Fever, headache, confusion, meningitis, cough	Elevated protein, low glucose, pleocytosis, positive smear/culture for acid-fast bacilli (AFB)	Mass lesions in approximately 50%, abnormal chest X-ray

As outlined in *Harrison's Principles of Internal Medicine, 14th Edition.*

MANAGEMENT OF HIV INFECTION

The decision as to when to start treatment in a person who becomes HIV positive is quite controversial. Most clinicians, however, start patients who are HIV positive on AZT and to prevent resistance, add 3TC (Epivair). The same regimen is continued in the ARC stage of HIV infection along with antifungal medications, such as Ketoconazole.

Seizure is seen in patients with AIDS, due to either fungal infection of the brain, lymphoma of the brain or Progressive multifocal leukoencephalopathy (PML). Once the patient has full-blown AIDS, then treatment is dictated by their illness.

Toward the end of full-blown AIDS, a wasting stage sets in. Few, if any, ever recover from this stage despite expensive treatment and good nutrition. While there is no cure and no vaccine yet available for people infected with AIDS, there are many medications.

MEDICATIONS

The first AIDS medications were reverse transcriptase inhibitors. Examples of reverse transcriptase inhibitors are Zidovudine (AZT), didanosine (ddi), zalcitabine (ddc), and stavudine (D4T). AZT, ddi, and ddc can be used as combination or mono therapy in early HIV disease. D4T is best used in people with advanced AIDS who are not able to tolerate the other medications.

Lamivudine (Epivair, 3TC) is used in combination with AZT to treat HIV infections. The importance of this combination is that HIV virus becomes resistant to AZT reasonably fast. When 3CT is added to the AZT or the DDI or the DDC it enhances the sensitivity of the reverse transcriptase that is used along with it to kill the HIV virus. By itself, 3TC has very little effect against the HIV virus.

A new drug for the treatment of HIV was just approved by the FDA. It is a combination of AZT and 3TC named **Combivir**.

Triple Therapy

The key component of the triple therapy is the addition of a protease inhibitor. The protease inhibitors in use are Saquinavir, Ritonavir, Indinovir, and Nelsinavir. The so-called AIDS cocktail is usually made of a reverse transcriptase inhibitor, such as AZT, with 3TC, and a protease inhibitor such as Indinovir.

The turnover of the HIV virus in an infected person is tremendous. In any one day about 10 billion viral particles are produced and cleared from the HIV infected person. About 2 billion CD4 lymphocytes are produced and destroyed from the HIV infected person daily.

CANCER AND HIV

Cancer is one of the complications that afflict the HIV infected person. Among the cancers that HIV infected people have to contend with is Kaposi's sarcoma, found mostly in male homosexual patients with full-blown AIDS, and said to be caused by herpes virus #8. Women infected with HIV are prone to the development of invasive cervical cancer. Large cell lymphoma is quite common in AIDS patients as well.

REVIEW:

The takehome lesson for black women is to change high-risk behaviors like using IV drugs and having sexual intercourse without the protection of a condom. These changes in behavior will go a long way toward decreasing the incidence of HIV infection in black women and all women who are engaged in high-risk behavior.

Arthritis In African American Women

13

Arthritis is an inflammatory condition that affects joints. Its symptoms are swelling, pain, restriction of movement, and ultimately, deformity of the joints. Chronic bony destruction and edematous destruction also occur. Certain types of arthritis affect organs such as the heart, the lungs, the kidneys, and the blood system.

TYPES OF ARTHRITIS

The most common forms of arthritis are:
1. Osteoarthritis
2. Rheumatoid arthritis
3. Gouty arthritis
4. Ankylosing spondylitis
5. Psoriatic arthritis
6. Reiter's Syndrome with arthritis
7. Systemic lupus erythematosus associated with arthritis
8. Polymyalgia rheumatica
9. Infectious arthritis
10. Lyme disease associated with arthritis
11. Sickle cell disease associated with arthritis

Osteoarthritis

Osteoarthritis is the most common form. Worldwide about 60 percent of the population, age sixty to seventy have osteoarthritis of one joint or another. Certain ethnic groups seem to be affected by arthritis in different ways. For example, Africans and southern Chinese women have less arthritis in their hip joints.

The knees seem to be the joint most frequently affected by osteoarthritis in all ethnic groups. The aging process plays a major role in the development of osteoarthritis. It is classified as primary or secondary (See Table 1).

TABLE 1
CLASSIFICATION OF OSTEOARTHRITIS

I. Primary-Idiopathic
  A. Localized
    1. Hip—superolateral, superomedial, medial, inferoposterior
    2. Knee—medial, lateral patellofemoral
    3. Spinal apophyseal
    4. Hand—interphalangeal, base of thumb
    5. Foot—first metatarsophalangeal joint, midfoot, hindfoot
    6. Other—shoulders, elbows, wrists, ankles
  B. Generalized
    1. Hands—Heberden's nodes
    2. Hands and knees; spinal apophyseal generalized osteoarthritis

II. Secondary
  A. Dysplastic
    1. Chondrodysplasia
    2. Epiphyseal dysplasias
    3. Congenital joint displacement
    4. Developmental disorders Perthes' disease, epiphysiolysis
  B. Post-traumatic
    1. Acute
    2. Repetitive
    3. Postoperative

C. Structural failure
 1. Osteonecrosis
 2. Osteochondritis
D. Postinflammatory
 1. Infection
 2. Inflammatory arthropathies
E. Endocrine and metabolic
 1. Acromegaly
 2. Ochronosis
 3. Hemochromatosis
 4. Crystal deposition disorders
F. Connective tissue
 1. Hypermobility syndromes
 2. Mucopolysaccharidoses
G. Etiology obscure
 1. Kashin-Beck disease
 As outlined in the literature

Primary osteoarthritis occurs as part of the aging process. Secondary is due to some abnormality that misaligns the joint. Sometimes these changes are the result of joint injuries or repeated stress, as in job related carpal tunnel. Stress or injury can turn into arthritis. If a joint becomes infected and the infection is not treated quickly, then that joint can develop post-inflammatory arthritic damage.

Hemochromatosis is a condition that causes iron to be deposited in joints and breaks down into free radicals within the joints. Free radicals cause breakdown of the tissues and the bones in the joints. The end result is arthritis.

Blacks have a high percentage of secondary hemochromatosis as a result of diseases like sickle cell anemia that causes a large amount of iron to be deposited in the blood stream from hemolyzed red blood cells.

Blacks and other individuals who suffer from sickle cell disease develop arthritis as a result of aseptic necrosis (tissue death) of joints such as the hips, shoulders, and elbows because the sickling phenomenon impedes the ready flow of blood with oxygen to them.

Obesity is a major predisposing factor in the development of arthritis. The knees are most prone to the development of arthritis because of the stresses placed on them by the excess weight.

The chances of someone developing osteoarthritis can be determined by the body mass index of that person. The greater the body mass index, the greater the extent of the osteoarthritic changes that a person is likely to develop. (See Table 2, Body Mass Index.)

TABLE 2
DETERMINING BODY MASS INDEX (BMI) FROM HEIGHT AND WEIGHT

Body Mass Index* (kg/m2)

Height (in)	19	20	21	22	23	24	25	26	27	28	29	30	35
58	91	96	100	105	110	115	119	124	129	134	138	143	167
59	94	99	104	109	114	119	124	128	133	138	143	148	173
60	97	102	107	112	118	123	128	133	138	143	148	153	179
61	100	106	111	116	122	127	132	137	143	148	153	158	185
62	104	109	115	120	126	131	136	142	147	153	158	164	191
63	107	113	118	124	130	135	141	146	152	158	163	169	197
64	110	116	122	128	134	140	145	151	157	163	169	174	204
65	114	120	126	132	138	144	150	156	162	168	171	180	210
66	118	124	130	136	142	148	155	161	167	173	179	186	215
67	121	127	134	140	146	153	159	166	172	178	185	191	223
68	125	131	138	144	151	158	164	171	177	184	190	197	230
69	128	135	142	149	155	162	169	176	182	189	196	203	236
70	132	138	146	153	160	167	174	181	188	195	202	207	243
71	136	143	150	157	165	172	179	186	193	200	208	215	250
72	140	147	154	162	169	177	184	191	199	206	213	221	258
73	144	151	159	166	174	182	189	197	204	212	219	227	265
74	148	155	163	171	179	186	194	202	210	218	225	233	272
75	152	160	168	176	184	192	200	208	216	224	232	240	279
76	156	164	172	180	189	197	205	213	221	230	238	246	287

As published by The American Diabetes Association

Body mass index or BMI, is the measurement of choice to determine obesity. BMI is a formula that takes into account both a person's height and weight. BMI is a person's weight in kilograms divided by height in meters squared (BMI=kg/m2). The table printed above has already done the conversions. To use the table, find the appropriate height in the left-hand column. Move across the row to the given weight. The number at the top of the column is the BMI for that height and weight.

In general, a person age 35 or older is obese if he or she has a BMI of 27 or greater. For people age 34 or younger, a BMI ≥ 25 or more indicates obesity. Obesity is an indication for further clinical evaluation.

The BMI measurement poses some of the same problems as weight-for-height tables. BMI does not provide information on a person's age or body fat or take into consideration the person's body fat distribution.

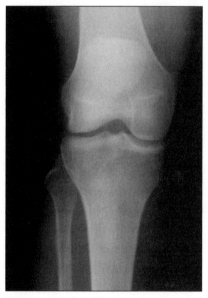

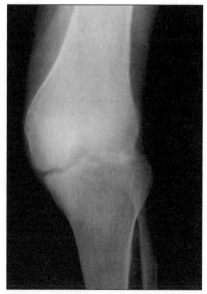

Figure 13.1: X-ray of a normal knee.

Figure 13.2: X-ray of a knee affected with osteoarthritis.

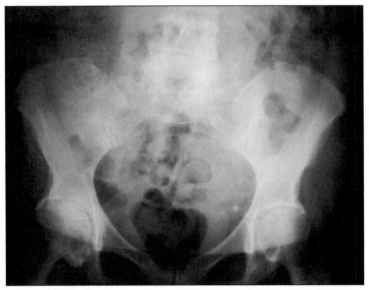

Figure 13.3: X-ray of hip joint affected with osteoarthritis.

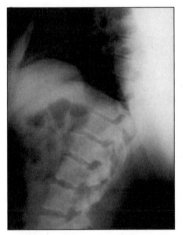

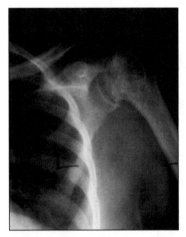

Figure 13.4: X-ray of lumbar spine affected with osteoarthritis.

Figure 13.5: X-ray of shoulder joint showing aseptic necrosis in a patient with sickle cell anemia.

Osteoarthritis can be painful and disabling. In many cases the affected joint must be surgically replaced after conservative management, like medication and physical therapy, has failed.

Medical management consists mainly of nonsteroidal antiinflammatory drugs such as aspirin, Indocin, Motrin, Aleve, Naprosyn, Relefan, Daypro, Anaprox, Vioxx, and Celebrex to relieve the pain and stiffness associated with the disease. These medications ease inflammation in the joints, thereby easing the pain.

Physical therapy works by relieving the stiffness and by strengthening the affected joint or joints, so it's obviously the most ambitious treatment. Should physical therapy fail, surgical replacement of hips, knees, and other joints is a common alternative—provided the individual is not too obese. If a person's weight is properly managed, physical therapy has a much better chance to succeed.

Before a decision can be made to replace a joint, X-rays, CAT scan, or MRI have to be done to properly evaluate the extent of the osteoarthritic changes. (See Figures 1-4 above.)

Osteoarthritis is so common in black women because many have jobs requiring physical labor. These jobs require a lot of physical activity which places the sort of chronic stress on the joints of the fingers, shoulders, elbows, knees, lumbar spine, cervical spine, and the hip joints that causes arthritic injury. Osteoarthritis—as a disease—is quite commonly seen in athletes, it's the same sort of repeated stress.

Preventive measures such as eating a proper diet to maintain an ideal weight and wearing proper sports equipment during demanding physical activity decrease the incidence of osteoarthritis.

Rheumatoid Arthritis

About one percent of the population suffers from rheumatoid arthritis. It is a chronic inflammatory disease of the joints that causes chronic deformity of the bones with destruction of the joints. Even with treatment, a person suffering with rheumatoid arthritis may develop joint deformities.

The joints frequently affected by rheumatoid arthritis are the feet, hands, fingers, elbows, wrists, shoulders, and hips. The cause of rheumatoid arthritis is unknown. Although many theories have been proposed, none have been proven. Women are affected much more than men. It is a multisystem disease, but the joints, bones, muscles, skin, and blood system are affected the most. The cardiovascular and pulmonary systems are affected, too. In the beginning, the symptoms of rheumatoid arthritis can be insidious and difficult to discern. General malaise, weakness, minor aches and pains, and morning stiffness don't really make many suffers think they're afflicted, because moving around diminishes the signs.

As the disease progresses, then the signs of synovitis with swelling of the joints with pain and warmth become evident. (See Table 3.)

TABLE 3
CLASSIFICATION OF RHEUMATOID ARTHRITIS REVISED
(As Published by the American College of Rheumatology)

1. *Guidelines for classification*
   a. Four of seven criteria are required to classify a patient as having rheumatoid arthritis.
   b. Patients with two or more clinical diagnoses are not excluded.

2. *Criteria**
   a. Morning stiffness: Stiffness in and around the joints lasting 1 hour before maximum improvement.
   b. Arthritis of three of more joint areas: At least three joint areas, observed by a physician simultaneously, have soft tissue swelling or joint effusions, not just bony overgrowth. The 14 possible joint areas involved are right or left proximal interphalangeal, metacarpophalangeal, wrist, elbow, knee, ankle, and metatarsophalangeal joints.
   c. Arthritis of hand joints: Arthritis of wrist, metacarpophalangeal

joint, or proximal interphalangeal joint.

d. Symmetric arthritis: Simultaneous involvement of the same joint areas on both sides of the body.

e. Rheumatoid nodules: Subcutaneous nodules over bony prominences, extensor surfaces, or juxtaarticular regions observed by a physician.

f. Serum rheumatoid factor: Demonstration of abnormal amounts of serum rheumatoid factor by any method for which the result has been positive in less than 5 percent of normal control subjects.

g. Radiographic changes: Typical changes of RA on posteroanterior hand and wrist radiographs which must include erosions or unequivocal bony decalcification localized in or most marked adjacent to the involved joints.

Criteria a thru d must be present for at least 6 weeks. A physician must observe criteria b thru e.

A history is crucial in a person in whom the physician suspects rheumatoid arthritis. If other immediate members of the family have it, that knowledge is relevant. Rheumatoid arthritis runs in families.

No one test is diagnostic of rheumatoid arthritis, but a series of blood tests together with x-ray should do the trick. X-rays of the proximal interphalangeal, metacarpal phalangeal, and metatarsal phalangeal (finger joints), have distinct characteristics that are seen mainly in rheumatoid arthritis. Changes of the hands and wrists resulting in swan neck deformities is classic for rheumatoid arthritis but show up much later. (See Figures 13.5 and 13.6.)

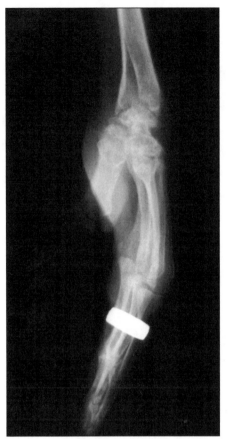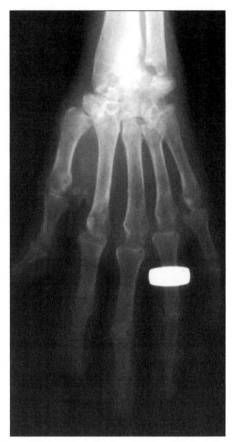

Figures 13.6 and 13.7: X-ray of the wrist and hand joint showing arthritic changes in a patient with rheumatoid arthritis.

Other systemic involvements of rheumatoid arthritis are:

1. Vasculitis involving medium sized vessels.

2. Shortness of breath and diffuse interstitial fibrosis may develop resulting in chronic lung disease.

3. The eyes are afflicted with **keratoconjunctivitis sicca**, (also known as Sjoren's Syndrome) causing dry eyes.

4. In about 10 percent of individuals with rheumatoid arthritis the spleen is enlarged. Frequently, when the spleen is enlarged in rheumatoid arthritis, the white blood cell count is also low. (This is called Felty's Syndrome.)

5. Still's disease (also seen in children) with fever spike, polyarthralgia, myalgia, a maculopapular rash, pericarditis, pneu-

monitis, sore throat, large spleen, lymphadenopathy, and pain in the abdomen.

6. The heart can become involved and pericarditis can occur. Aortic regurgitation and conduction abnormalities of the rhythm of the heart.

Damage to Other Systems

Neurological problems may result when, as a result of tenosynovitis of the wrists, compression of the median nerve occurs. This is what causes carpal tunnel syndrome.

The hematopoietic system (blood system) is markedly affected by rheumatoid arthritis. Anemia is the most serious and most common blood abnormality that complicates it. The anemia seen in rheumatoid arthritis is **normochromic, normocytic** (meaning the sizes and the hemoglobin contents of the red cells are normal but there are not enough red cells produced, resulting in anemia).

Although there is plenty of iron in the body, anemia exists because there is an abnormality involving the release mechanism of the iron. It accumulates in the cells. The failure to release iron ends up as anemia. In effect, the rheumatoid person suffers from iron deficiency anemia because he or she has the inability to use the iron in the body (iron deficient dyserythropoiesis).

Recent findings suggest that some cytokines play a major role in this process of anemia of chronic disease (now also referred to as anemia of inflammatory diseases).

Leukopenia (low white blood cell) is frequently seen in rheumatoid arthritis and in particular when there is splenomegaly (known as Felty's Syndrome).

Other abnormal blood tests in rheumatoid arthritis are:
1. Elevated ESR (erythrocyte sedimentation rate)
2. Elevated rheumatoid factor (latex fixation)
3. ANA (antinuclear antibodies) elevated in up to sixty percent of patients with rheumatoid arthritis

Rheumatoid afflicted individuals whose life circumstances place them in poor working conditions have a hard row to hoe.

Earning a living using stiff, painful and swollen hands, elbows, shoulders, knees, feet; and lower back is very stressful. Stress and illness engage in a vicious downward spiral for many frustrated black women.

Treatment

There is no cure for this disease. Rheumatoid arthritis is primarily treated with:

1. Aspirin, 2 tablets t.i.d. with food to prevent stomach irritation.
2. Endocin 25 mg t.i.d. or q.i.d., again with food in the stomach.
3. Nonsteroidal antiinflammatory drugs (NSAIDS) such as Motrin, Naprosyn, etc.

People with kidney disease, such as renal insufficiency, ought not to take NSAIDS because these medications themselves can not only cause kidney disease, they can also make it worse. They should be monitored by a physician for blood counts, liver function, and kidney function.

When medications no longer work or the side effects become clinically unacceptable, then a new family of drugs can be used. The most effective is Methotrexate (see chapter 9, *Diseases of the Stomach and Intestine in African American Women* for warnings). Recently a medication called minocycline has proved to be effective. Steroids, such as prednisone, calm down flare-ups. Its long-term use ought to be avoided because it has major side effects.

There is a family of medications referred to as disease-modifying anti-rheumatic drugs (DMRDs) that have been used in rheumatoid arthritis when all else fails. Among these drugs are:

1. Gold
2. D-penicillamine
3. Chloroquine and sulfazalozine

Arava (Leflunomide) is one of a new family of medications used in the treatment of rheumatoid arthritis. The usual dose of Arava after a loading dose is 20 mg daily by mouth. These medications, too, have major side effects and should be used very carefully by physicians familiar with their use.

Physical Therapy

Physical therapy fights weakness, contractures, atrophy, and other assorted problems affecting the joints of people suffering with rheumatoid arthritis.

Systemic lupus erythematosus (SLE)

Systemic lupus erythematosus (SLE) is an autoimmune disease of unknown cause that affects women of childbearing age, though a small percentage of men can also be affected. This disease is most common in black women.

Morning stiffness with swelling and pain in the joints is a symptom of SLE. The musculoskeletal system may be affected by myalgias, arthralgias, polyarthritis with bony erosions, deformities of the hands, myositis, myopathy, and ischemic necrosis of bones.

The skin may be affected with a malar rash over the cheeks, a discoid rash, photosensitivity, ulcers of the mouth, maculopapular rash, urticarial rash, bullous rash, alopecia, or vasculitis.

The hematopoietic system (blood system) may be affected with anemia, both chronic and hemolytic; leukopenia (low white blood cell count); thrombocytopenia with circulating anticoagulant; large spleen; and lymphadenopathy (large lymph nodes).

SLE affects the neurological system. Among the symptoms in patients with SLE are memory loss, acute psychosis, seizures, peripheral neuropathy, vasculitis and stroke, and so on.

The lungs are frequently affected in patients with SLE. Patients can develop pleurisy, pleural effusion, pneumonitis, interstitial fibrosis, pulmonary hypertension, and ARDS (adult respiratory distress syndrome).

Among the problems that affect the heart are:
1. Pericarditis
2. Myocarditis
3. Endocarditis

The kidneys are frequently affected in patients with SLE, which can ultimately result in renal failure. Syndromes occur, with associated thrombosis of organs, such as the brain, lungs, vascular system, and placenta in pregnant women, which results in spontaneous abortion. Any woman who has had frequent spontaneous abortions should be evaluated for the anticardiolipin/antiphospholipid syndromes.

Treatment of SLE

Prednisone is the main drug used to treat lupus and its multitude of complications. Cyclophosphamide (Cytoxan) and azathioprine are also quite effective in treating SLE. Lupus has no cure but can be treated and managed for a very long time. Some patients go on to develop renal failure requiring chronic dialysis.

SARCOIDOSIS

Sarcoidosis is a disease of unknown cause which is most common among blacks. The affected person may have fever, malaise, and anorexia with weight loss. The vast majority of individuals who develop sarcoidosis are younger than forty. The lungs are the most frequently affected organs. Patients with pulmonary sarcoid often have shortness of breath, cough, and sometimes chest pain. The chest x-ray in sarcoidosis often shows bilateral hila adenopathy in association with pain in the joints.

Other organs affected by Sarcoidosis are:
1. Skin
2. Eyes
3. Upper respiratory tract
4. Bone marrow
5. Spleen
6. Liver
7. Kidney
8. Heart
9. Endocrine system
10. Nervous system
11. Musculoskeletal system
12. Exocrine system

Lymph node, cervical, inguinal and axillary node enlargement is quite common in sarcoidosis. Biopsy of any of these peripheral nodes is likely to show the classic lesions seen in sarcoidosis. Other skin lesions that can be seen include a maculopapular rash, subcutaneous nodes, and lupus pernio (indurated blue/purple, swollen lesion on the nose, cheeks, lips, ears, fingers, etc.).

How to Diagnose Sarcoidosis

X-rays will show bilateral hila adenopathy. If the presenting symptoms refer to the eye, then an eye examination is important, uveitis is a frequent finding in patients with sarcoidosis with eye symptoms.

Laboratory tests that are helpful are the CBC, the chemistry profile, the ESR, and most important of all, is the angiotensin I converting enzyme, which is elevated in about 2/3 of patients with sarcoidosis. The gold standard for sarcoidosis however, is the finding of non-caseating granuloma on lymph node or other tissue biopsy.

If the complex of symptoms fits the profile; the angiotensin-converting enzyme is elevated and the tissue biopsy shows non-caseating granuloma, then the patient most probably has sarcoidosis.

How to Treat Sarcoidosis

Steroid treatment is the treatment of choice for sarcoidosis. Prednisone interferes with the cellular process in the affected tissues thereby decreasing the inflammation. In up to 50 percent of cases, the disease resolves spontaneously, but it is not wise to take a chance. The disease can cause permanent damage to vital organs such as the eyes, the heart, and the lungs.

Sarcoidosis is a disease of unknown origin that affects blacks more than whites, women more than men. Sarcoidosis is not curable, but treatable.

Psuedo-gout

Another condition that causes acute and chronic pain in

joints is pseudo-gout. Pseudo-gout occurs more in women than men and in much older individuals than seen in regular gout.

The inflammatory reaction that occurs in pseudo-gout is due to calcium pyrophosphate dihydrate crystals. The blood test that is elevated in gouty arthritis, is uric acid. The uric acid test is part of a routine chemistry profile ordered when testing a person's blood routinely for chemistries. The higher the level of uric acid in the blood, the more likely that it will accumulate in joints causing inflammation. The repeated inflammation will eventually destroy the joints.

When someone has a swollen, hot, and painful joint, there are really three major considerations:
1. Gout
2. Pseudo-gout
3. Septic arthritis

Septic arthritis can occur as a result of bacteria in the blood settling into a joint, causing inflammation to occur. There are a multitude of clinical conditions that can be associated with septic arthritis:
1. Gonorrheal infection (probably the most common in a sexually active group)
2. Pneumonia with bacteremia
3. Sub-acute bacterial endocarditis (SBE) (as seen frequently in IV drug abusing individuals or any non-IV drug addict with SBE)
4. Penetrating traumatic wound in a joint

To differentiate gouty arthritis in the joint from septic arthritis, one must tap synovial fluid off the joint and send it to the laboratory for evaluation.

To treat gouty arthritis the physician has to determine the extent and severity of the symptoms. The most effective treatment is intravenous colchicine. Once the attack has been brought under control, Allopurinol 300 mg per day is given to lower the level of uric acid in the blood, along with Colchicine 0.6 mg two times per day.

NSAIDS or Indocin may be given to prevent acute attacks. For reasons that are not quite clear, acute gouty arthritic attacks seem to occur in spite of the fact that the patient is on a good dose of prophylactic medications.

Both gout and pseudo-gout can lead to markedly deformed joints with chronic arthritic pain. It is said that sweetbread, shellfish, and red wine can all contribute to bring about acute attacks of gout.[1] Therefore, dietary management with a decreased intake of protein seems a reasonable approach in its management.

Arthritis is a common disease. Although there are no cures for these different arthritic conditions, there are many treatments that are available to relieve the symptoms. Therefore, it is important that black women be responsive to symptoms and seek medical attention as quickly as possible.

Eye Diseases In African American Women

14

Eye disease and blindness is more common in black women than their white counterparts. Many diseases predispose the development of eye problems. For example, hypertension, diabetes, and glaucoma are much more common in black women than white. The incidence of glaucoma is five times higher.

GLAUCOMA

Glaucoma is the number one cause of blindness among black women, and runs in families. What makes glaucoma so dangerous is the fact that it causes no pain. So a person whose intraocular pressure is high—the first stage—will not know it. This undermines the best medications and medical procedures.

There are basically four different types of glaucoma:
1. Primary open angle glaucoma
2. Secondary glaucoma
3. Angle closure glaucoma
4. Congenital glaucoma

One fourth of all cases of glaucoma are present at birth and are congenital. According to the Center for Health Statistics, in Bethesda, Maryland, 1.2 persons out of every 100 individuals have some form of eye disease. Although this is a high percentage, it's

even worse among the black population. This is because of:
1. The high incidence of glaucoma in blacks.
2. The higher incidence of hypertension, leading to hypertensive retinopathy with hemorrhage inside the eyes.
3. The higher incidence of diabetes in blacks and obese black women leads to diabetic retinopathy with bleeding inside the eyes.
4. The high incidence of trauma to the eye in blacks in injury-plagued jobs.

Besides glaucoma, diabetes, and hypertension, other diseases that affect the eyes include cataracts, syphilis, sarcoidosis, sickle cell disease, AIDS, temporal arteritis, vitamin deficiency, and malignant tumor. The incidence of blindness as a result of glaucoma is up to eight times higher in blacks than whites.

Open Angle Glaucoma

The reason for open angle glaucoma is an inherited defect in the function of the cells inside the eyes. The end result is twofold; increased production of aqueous humor fluid and failure of drainage of the aqueous humor. Fluid increases pressure inside the eyes. While an intraocular pressure of 13 - 20 mm/Hg is normal for whites, it is not necessarily normal for blacks. Glaucoma is a much more aggressive disease in blacks. An intraocular pressure above 14 in a black person much be watched closely and evaluated more often.

When the pressure inside the eyes is elevated it damages the optic nerve. The optic nerve is the nerve that allows the eye to see, so once damaged, it's very serious.

The test used to evaluate the optic nerve is called a visual field. Elevated intraocular pressure does not always mean glaucoma. An opthamologist is essential to picking up on this disease because the patient *will not* feel it.

Open angle glaucoma is responsible for more than 90 percent of blindness due to glaucoma. The first sign that a person has glaucoma is loss of peripheral vision.

Three things happen in open angle glaucoma:
1. Intraocular pressure of 24 mm/Hg or greater
2. Cupping of the optic disc
3. Visual field loss

Typically, the first treatment is eyedrop medication. Some are:
1. Pilocarpine
2. Timoptic
3. Ocupress
4. Trusopt
5. Carbochal
6. Phystignine salicylate
7. Demecromium bromide (Humorsol)
8. Acetozolamide (Diamox)
9. Isopurphate (Floropryl)
10. Btaxololhydrochloride (Betoptic)
11. Optipranolol
12. Propine
13. Latanoprox solution (Xalatan)
14. Betagan

If eyedrop treatment fails to bring the intraocular pressure down and visual field abnormality starts to develop, then laser treatment is used. This surgery facilitates drainage of aqueous humor fluid from the eye, thereby reducing the intraocular pressure.

Angle Closure Glaucoma

This mostly affects farsighted people over the age of fifty-five. About 5 percent of the immediate family of those with angle closure glaucoma are affected with the same condition.

There are three different stages of angle closure glaucoma:
1. Sub-acute angle closure glaucoma
2. Acute angle closure glaucoma
3. Chronic angle closure glaucoma

Sub-acute vs. Acute Angle Closure Glaucoma

In sub-acute angle closure glaucoma, fluid is draining ever so slightly. It's an insidious disease because the patient's eyes find ways to compensate, maintaining intermittently normal intraocular pressure. But in acute angle closure glaucoma, pressure rises, resulting in a painful red eye with reduced sight. The eyeball is rock hard and quite painful. Next to trauma to the eye, acute angle closure glaucoma is the severest emergency seen in the field of ophthalmology.

The first step in the treatment of acute angle glaucoma is to try to bring the intraocular pressure down quickly. A doctor is likely to treat the eye with pilocarpine eyedrops for five minutes. Later 0.5% Timolol solution is placed in the affected eye. If this does not work then 500 mg of Diamox IV is given to bring the pressure down.

If the intraocular pressure fails to come down in spite of these treatments, surgery is necessary to save the eye. The aqueous humor fluid is drained, bringing the intraocular pressure down. After surgery, eyedrops are used to maintain a normal pressure.

Angle closure glaucoma affects both eyes, they must receive immediate treatment with 0.5% - 1% pilocarpine followed by Timolol or other beta-blocker-like drops.

Other forms of glaucoma include:
1. Low tension glaucoma
2. Congenital glaucoma
3. Secondary glaucoma from using iridocyclites, steroid treatment for long periods of time

REVIEW:

Glaucoma occurs in black women at a younger age than white women and is more aggressive. It leads to blindness more rapidly than in white women. The most important prevention is a regular eye examination, this is the only way to know if the pressure is elevated. Taking appropriate measures prevent progression to blindness.

CATARACTS

Another common disease of the eye is cataracts. The most common are age-related cataracts or senile cataracts. They are basically an opacification of the lens of the eyes.

The second form of cataracts is a congenital cataract, usually the result of maternal rubella or cytomegalovirus infection during the first trimester of pregnancy. Cataracts can result from diabetes, steroid abuse, myotonic dystrophy, uveitis, cigarette smoking, heavy alcohol consumption, and more.

Physical trauma to the eye can cause cataracts. Traumatic cataract is seen in many black women because of harsh economic circumstances that expose many black women to lifestyle and work related trauma.

The first sign of cataracts is blurry vision, which progresses over months and years with no pain or redness. There is obvious clouding of the lens of the eyes when examined with the ophthalmoscope. There are three types of cataracts:

1. Posterior subcapsular cataracts
2. Cortical cataracts
3. Mixed cataracts

Treatment of Cataracts

Once the diagnosis of cataracts is established, the first mode of treatment is glasses to improve vision. This is the conservative response. If this treatment fails, then surgical removal of the cataract is recommended. There are two types of cataract removal procedures:

1. Extracapsular cataract removal with implantation of an intraocular lens
2. Intracapsular cataract removal

The second type of surgical procedure is much less popular since the advent of microsurgery. Cataract removal surgery is carried out in the operating room with the patient able to go home in a few hours after the operation has been completed. The patient is fully awake during the time of the surgery. Only the eye being operated on is anesthetized.

HYPERTENSION AND THE EYES

Hypertension, if left untreated, will affect many organs. Hypertension increases pressure within the vessels of the eye that causes damage within the lumen of the vessels, just as it does to vessels all over the body. The damaged vessels then trap platelets and materials from the blood on the inner surface vessels, starting a nidus, which leads to plaque formation. (For further explanation, review Chapter 1, on Hypertension.)

It is also said that fatty material leaks from these damaged vessels, making the situation more complicated.[1] Over time this causes vascular abnormalities resulting in **hypertensive retinopathy**.

Severity of Hypertensive retinopathy is graded as 1, 2, 3, and 4, depending on the vascular abnormalities.

- Grade 1 shows arteriolar narrowing
- Grade 2 shows arterio-venous nicking, some exudate and hemorrhages
- Grade 3 shows retinal edema, hemorrhage and cotton wool spots
- Grade 4 shows a combination of Grade 3 plus papilledema

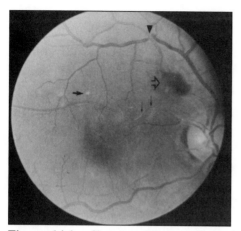

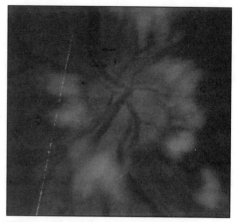

Figure 14.1: Showing different types of abnormalities in the eye of a hypertensive patient (hypertensive retinopathy). Small arrow showing silver wiring. Big arrow showing hard yellow exudates. Open arrow head showing blot hemorrhage. Arrow head showing A-V nicking.

Figure 14.2: Showing different types of abnormalities in the eye of a hypertensive patient (hypertensive retinopathy) Small arrows showing early papilledema. One big arrow pointing to vein engorgement (larger vessel). The other big arrow pointing to arterial attenuation (smaller vessel); open arrow showing cotton wool exudates.

If proper treatment is not provided for these abnormalities, the patient often develops blindness.

Water pills (diuretics) are the most appropriate, and the most effective medication available to treat hypertension in blacks. According to a recent report in the *Internal Medicine News* (February 15, 1998), it costs about $73 to treat a black patient with a diuretic, as compared with an Ace inhibitor and calcium channel blocker which costs about $1000 per year.

The end result is that they are getting the wrong treatment. Their poorly controlled blood pressure causes end organ damage because it persists as if the patient never sought care. The eyes are one of the end organs.

Even if the right medication is prescribed, in many cases, it is too expensive. It's not difficult to see why there is such a high incidence of glaucoma and other hypertension-associated lesions in the eyes of black women and men. (Refer to Figure 14.1 and 14.2.)

DIABETIC RETINOPATHY

Diabetic retinopathy is a very serious disease, which causes blindness in a significant number of blacks. Needless to say, the same is true for any individuals who suffer from diabetes. Some of the lesions that can be seen in patients who are suffering from diabetes are:

1. Micro aneurysm
2. Arteriolar narrowing
3. Retinal edema
4. Hard exudates
5. Venous abnormalities
6. Soft exudates
7. Vitrous hemorrhages
8. Retinal hemorrhages
9. Retinal detachment, etc.

Once the patient is diagnosed with diabetes, the treating physician should refer the patient to an eye doctor for evaluation to prevent unnecessary blindness. It is very important that black women with diabetes understand that if they go to the eye doctor early enough, keep their blood sugar under tight control, and remain under constant care of a qualified ophthalmologist they can prevent blindness secondary to the effects of diabetes.

DIABETES AND ISCHEMIC DISEASE

Diabetes causes ischemia due to plaque deposits, in the same way that it affects the vessels of the legs. Plaque fills the vessels of the eyes. When these very delicate vessels within the eyes have plaque within their lumens, and lipid material leaks out, platelet deposition and plaque deposition take place. Gradually the vessels become blocked.

SICKLE CELL AND EYE DISEASE

Sickle cell disease is the number one abnormal hemoglobin disease that affects the eye. Three different types of sickle cell disease cause retinopathy:

1. Sickle cell disease retinopathy (SS)
2. Sickle Cell-C retinopathy (SC)
3. Sickle thalassemia retinopathy

The most severe among these is Sickle Cell-C disease. There are two types of retinopathies here: the proliferative type and the non-proliferative type. Proliferative is more common in SC disease and sickle thalassemia than in SS disease.

AIDS AND EYE DISEASE

As a viral illness, AIDS frequently affects the eyes. The most common infection is cytomegalovirus (CMV). CMV causes retinitis. Black women are affected more than white women with AIDS-associated CMV retinitis because the percentage of black women with AIDS is much higher than that of white women (See chapter 12 on AIDS).

CMV retinitis in AIDS is quite difficult to treat and eradicate. The most effective medication is Ganciclovir. This medication has serious side effects and must be treated by IV in the hospital setting.

TEMPORAL ARTERITIS AND EYE DISEASE

Temporal arteritis (giant cell arteritis) is a condition seen in middle-aged to elderly men or women. The diagnosis cannot be missed, and, in fact must not be, for the end result is permanent blindness in the affected eye. Usually, the patient comes in with headache and general malaise, visual abnormality, and low-grade fever. Following a physical examination, a diagnosis can quickly be established by doing an erythrocyte sedimentation rate (ESR).

If the SED rate is very high (normal ESR is from 10-20 ml/hr) then the diagnosis of temporal arteritis is likely. The next step is to admit the patient to the hospital for treatment with high dose IV steroids. The ophthalmologist always must be brought in to carry out a thorough eye examination.

The next step is a temporal artery biopsy. This is a surgical procedure. It is not necessary to wait for the biopsy before starting steroid treatment. If the physician waits for the results of the biopsy, it may be too late to save the eyes.

A negative temporal artery biopsy does not rule out the diagnosis of temporal arteritis because this disease is often a segmental disease. A normal segment of artery could easily have been biopsied and the abnormal skipped over.

VITAMIN DEFICIENCY AND EYE DISEASE

A vitamin B_6 deficiency from alcoholism can lead to Werneke's disease, associated with nystagmus, ptosis, retinal hemorrhage, diplopia, and internal strabismus. Treatment consists of injection of thiamine to replete stores, followed by B complex vitamins by mouth, which contains all the B vitamins, combined with abstinence from alcohol. Thiamine by mouth can also be given to counteract repletion of the stores.

MALIGNANT TUMOR

Malignant tumors, such as primary melanoma and tumors of the eyelid (associated with xeroderma pigmentosum) can affect the eye. It is also affected by sarcoma, malignant and melanoma. Malignant melanoma is a particularly troublesome disease that must be diagnosed quickly and treated immediately.

Metastatic cancer may first show up in the eye. This is believed to be due to autoimmune phenomenon (the body reacting to the cancer as a foreign agent). It produces an antibody against it, causing inflammation.

SYPHILIS AND EYE PROBLEMS

In the latter stage of syphilis, a variety of eye problems can occur. One problem may be small, irregular pupils that still react to light. Another problem might be the Argyle-Robertson pupils (the result of atrophy of the iris), which are seen in neurosyphilis.

The incidence of syphilis is many times more common in blacks than in whites. Neurosyphilis is twice as common in men as in women.

According to The Center for Disease Control and Prevention (CDC) guidelines, treatment for neurosyphilis must include blood VDRL, FTA-ABS. A lumbar puncture should be done to obtain the cerebrospinal fluid (CSF). The CSF fluid must be sent for VDRL and FTA-ABS.

If it is positive, then treatment for neurosyphilis must be started by giving 10 to 20 million units of aqueous penicillin daily by IV for ten days. In addition, a three weeks course of 2.4 million units of bicillin must be given. If the patient has HIV infection (AIDS) and a positive VDRL, FTA-ABS in the blood—even if the CSF is negative or the patient refuses a lumbar puncture—the same thing should be done.

Neurosyphilis is quite prevalent in individuals with AIDS. If a person is allergic to penicillin then erythromycin 2 grams by mouth daily for 30 days or tetracycline 2 grams daily for 30 days should be prescribed to treat it.

THE DIFFERENCE BETWEEN OPTHAMOLOGISTS, OPTOMETRISTS, AND OPTICIANS

An ophthalmologist is a person who went to medical school, studied medicine, and underwent several years of training in the field of ophthalmology. This physician is a trained and experienced specialist in diseases of the eyes.

The optometrist is a specialist trained to deal with eyeglasses, including filling out prescriptions written by the ophthalmologist.

The optician is a specialist trained to deal with matters of optics, including the making of eyeglasses. Opticians can also fill prescriptions prescribed by the ophthalmologist.

As you can see, there is a big difference between these three specialists. If your eyes have not been examined by an ophthalmologist (the physician) then your eyes really have not had a thorough examination. You may have had your eyeglasses constructed and adjusted, you may have been evaluated for visual acuity and your prescription filled, but a real eye examination that can detect many serious diseases of the eyes must still be carried out.

A person may be going too long to the wrong specialist without knowing it and by the time it is realized, serious conditions may have gone undetected.

The overall economic and educational situations of African American women will have to be improved drastically if one expects to really fight the accelerated rate of blindness from which black men and women are suffering.

15

Depression In African American Women

Depression is one of the most common diseases that afflict mankind. It is said that in the United States depression is as widespread as the common cold. There are different types of depression.

1. Transient situational depression
2. Permanent or chronic situational depression
3. Depression associated with taking medications for a medical condition
4. Depression associated with alcohol abuse or drug abuse
5. Minor classical depression
6. Major classical depression
7. Depression associated with anxiety reaction and panic attacks
8. Manic depression

Blacks and Hispanics experience as much depression, anxiety, and panic attacks as whites. The difference is in the cultural expression of these symptoms and the cultural conditioning and reluctance to express the symptoms of these illnesses for fear of being ostracized by their communities.

In many African ancestral societies, mental illness is taboo because it is seen as a sign of weakness. A failure to endure whatever it is society can dish out and live long enough to tell the tale is an essential part of the indigenous black culture. Many black and Hispanic people see mental illness as a label that can be used to further discriminate against them. Because many people are afraid of having mental illness on their records they hide their symptoms of depression and suffer in silence or they do not tell a physician/therapist about their mental illness unless they absolutely have to.

Some of the symptoms of major depression:
- depressed
- loss of interest, pleasure
- feels sad or empty
- significant weight loss or weight gain
- insomnia or hypersomnia every day
- psychomotor agitation or retardation (unnatural slowness) nearly every day—observable by others
- Fatigue or loss of energy every day
- Feelings of worthlessness, excessive or inappropriate guilt
- Diminished ability to think or concentrate, or indecisiveness, nearly every day
- Recurrent thoughts of death (not just fear of dying)

Note: Five (or more) of the following symptoms have been present during the same 2 week period and represent a change from previous functioning.

Classical minor depression is defined as three or four depressive symptoms for two weeks or longer. Major depression is defined as five or more depressive symptoms for 2 weeks or longer.

Some symptoms of minor depression:
- A distinct period of abnormally and persistently elevated, expansive or irritable mood, lasting at least 1 week (or any duration if hospitalization is necessary).
  1. Inflated self-esteem or grandiosity
  2. Decreased need for sleep (e.g., feels rested after only 3 hours of sleep)

3. More talkative than usual or feels pressure to keep talking

4. Flight of ideas or subjective experience that thoughts are racing

5. Distractibility (i.e., attention too easily drawn to unimportant or irrelevant external stimuli)

6. Increase in goal-directed activity (either socially, at work or school, or sexually), psychomotor agitation

7. Excessive involvement in pleasurable activities that have a high potential for painful consequences (e.g., unrestrained buying sprees, sexual indiscretions, or foolish business investments)

The most common forms of depression seen in black men and women are:

1. A mixed form of depression associated with anxiety and panic attacks

2. Transient and permanent situational depression

3. Depression associated with alcohol abuse and drug abuse

Often when a person of African ancestry is troubled by a mood disorder, he or she goes to an elder or group of family members for advice. This is a tradition that continues to manifest itself in many African American families.

Because of racism and the distrust that it causes, many blacks in America are understandably reluctant to talk to Caucasian therapists. Why should they go to a therapist to expose their private lives, when the white world has been responsible for much of their anxiety to begin with?

When blacks are evaluated for mental illness by a non-minority psychiatrist/therapist, often times the diagnosis is often wrong. There are documented cases of blacks diagnosed as schizophrenics, when in fact they were not. A great deal of subjectivity is involved in the diagnosis of mental illnesses, and a white therapist has no empirical knowledge of the black experience.

Transient situational depression occurs in all groups regardless of ethnic background. Isolated sadness often lasts longer in African American women because there exists a mental fragility born out of constant exposure to racial injustice. It's difficult not to cross the line to a more permanent depressive state.

Permanent and chronic situational depression in a black person (man or woman) in America, can be a condition of constant exposure to racial discrimination. It does not matter if they are a sanitation worker or a judge in a court of law; here they are black before they are anything else.

Many black people feel a sense of constant persecution. This causes anger, paranoia, and stress. Some blacks in America have developed coping mechanisms that can be very hard on the body. For instance black professionals often say something to the effect of, "You may not like the color of my skin and many other things about me, but I dare you to doubt my ability to beat you at your own game and do my work with excellence." Many know they must generally work twice as hard to break even.

Many black men, women, and children have allowed their anger and despair to cause them to fall into the trap of substance abuse, which has totally taken them over. This causes them to commit unspeakable crimes against their neighbors and their communities. (See Chapters 16 and 17 on drug abuse and alcohol abuse.)

ANXIETY ATTACKS

Depression, associated with anxiety and panic attacks, is extremely common in black women. In fact, this type of depression is much more common in black women than white based on the fact that black women often have additional reasons to be anxious that white women don't have, and additional reason to be panicky.

Black women face racism. Compounding the problem, many face poor education, joblessness, lower economic status, single parenthood, and so much more. All this creates a sense of uncertainty. The end result too often is anxiety, panic attacks, and depression. Educated and professional black women facing depression are beginning to seek help and are receiving psychological treatment as they learn to change their attitudes toward professional help.

Some of the most common symptoms of depression and mania

Depression
- Persistent sad, anxious, or "empty" mood
- Loss of interest or pleasure in activities, including sex
- Feelings of hopelessness, pessimism
- Feelings of guilt, worthlessness, helplessness
- Sleeping too much or too little, early morning awakening
- Appetite and/or weight loss or overeating and weight gain
- Decreased energy, fatigue, feeling "slowed down"
- Thoughts of death or suicide, or suicide attempts
- Restlessness, irritability
- Difficulty concentrating, remembering, or making decisions
- Persistent physical symptoms that do not respond to treatment, such as headaches, digestive disorders, and chronic pain

Mania
- Abnormally elevated mood
- Irritability
- Severe insomnia
- Grandiose notions
- Increased talking
- Racing thoughts
- Increased activity, including sexual activity
- Markedly increased energy
- Poor judgment that leads to risk-taking behavior
- Inappropriate social behavior

A thorough diagnostic evaluation is needed if five or more of these symptoms persist for more than two weeks, or if they interfere with work or family life. An evaluation involves a complete

physical checkup and information gathering on family health history.
(As published by the National Institute of Mental Health)

Some of the symptoms of panic attack:
1. Palpitations, pounding of heart, or accelerated heart rate
2. Sweating
3. Trembling or shaking
4. Sensation of shortness of breath or smothering
5. Feeling of choking
6. Chest pain or discomfort
7. Nausea or abdominal distress
8. Feeling dizzy, lightheaded, or faint
9. derealization (feelings of unreality) or depersonalization (being detached from oneself)
10. Fear of losing control or going crazy
11. Fear of dying
12. paresthesias (numbness or tingling sensation)
13. Chills or hot flashes
14. Abdominal pain
15. Diarrhea
16. Black out spells
17. Urinary frequency
18. Hyperventilation
19. Leg cramps
20. Insomnia
[Partially modified from DSM IV]

EVALUATION

In the black community, the primary care physician is likely to be the one to see depression because black women seek their help before seeing a specialist, and definitely before seeing a therapist. They may not know they are depressed and must be handled with the greatest of care and sensitivity.

The first step in evaluating someone with depression includes a complete history and physical examination. The next step is a series of laboratory tests such as:

1. CBC
2. Chemistry profile (SMA 18)
3. Thyroid profile – T4, TSH
4. Urinalysis
5. Serum ferritin
6. Serum B_{12}
7. Chest X-ray
8. EKG
9. Mammogram, if the woman is forty and up, younger if a mass is felt in the breast or if there is a family history of breast cancer.
10. A CAT scan of the brain or MRI of the brain, if there is headache, dizziness, forgetfulness, or signs of neurological symptoms during the history and physical examination. In fact, it may be important to do a CAT scan anyway, even with no obvious neurological symptoms.

Other blood tests may become necessary based on the physician's assessment of the case.

Approaching the patient in this way allows the physician to ascertain whether the patient's symptoms of depression, anxiety, or panic attacks are organic (defined as nothing physical can explain her symptoms).

Diseases like diabetes; hyper thyroidism; hypothyroidism; cancer; iron deficiency anemia; kidney failure; heart disease such as mitral valve prolapse, atherosclerotic heart disease with angina pectoris, congestive heart failure with low cardiac output; and poor brain perfusion; and B_{12} deficiency, can all cause depression.

It is not unusual to find a patient permanently committed in a psychiatric hospital as a result of B_{12} deficiency that was either not diagnosed at all, or diagnosed too late, resulting in permanent neurological and mental disease.

A brain tumor may show symptoms of mental disease. It is

necessary for a person who manifests symptoms of depression to undergo a thorough medical evaluation by a primary care physician before any definite statement can be made.

Prior to starting any psychotropic medications, a CBC, liver function test, and EKG should be done. Psychotropic medications have side effects that cause the white blood cell count, the platelets, the red blood cell count, as well as the EKG and liver function test to be abnormal.

Some of these medications can affect the rhythm of the heart, so a baseline EKG must be done before starting them. Lithium, for instance, can cause the kidneys to malfunction, it can bring the number of white blood cells down, and it can interfere with thyroid function.

TREATMENTS

Depression is treated usually with medications, psychotherapy, and, at times, with ECT. Some of the medications used to treat depression are:
(These are serotonin-specific reuptake inhibitors)
1. Zoloft
2. Paxil
3. Prozac
(These are serotonin non-selective reuptake inhibitors)
4. Effexor
5. Wellbutrin
6. Ludiomil, which is basically a Dopamine active medication
7. Norpramin
8. Pamelor
9. Desyrel
10. Asendin
11. Buspar
12. Klonopin
13. Xanax
14. Lithium

(These are called tertiary amine)
15. Elavil
16. Tofranil
17. Anofranil
18. Sinequan
(These are called MAOIs (monoamine oxidase inhibitors):
19. Parnate

The usual dosages and side effects of these medications are:

1.   Zoloft

The initial dose is 50 mg per day; this dose can be increased up to a total of 200 mg per day. There are several tolerable side effects of Zoloft such as palpitations, leg cramps, dry skin, itching. Liver function tests and EKG must be closely monitored along with blood levels while the patient is on Zoloft.

2.   Paxil

The usual starting dose of Paxil is 20 mg per day and can be increased up to a total of 50 mg per day for those who fail to respond to the 20 mg dose. Paxil can cause several tolerable side effects such as dizziness, blurred vision, dried mouth, etc. Liver function tests and EKG must be monitored along with Paxil blood level.

3.   Prozac

The usual dose of Prozac is 20 mg per day. If a patient fails to respond to 20 mg per day, the dose can be increased up to a total of 80 mg per day. Prozac has several side effects such as increased appetite, bruising, leg cramps, etc. Liver function tests and EKG needs to be monitored along with the blood level of Prozac.

4.   Effexor

The usual starting dose of Effexor is 25 mg three times per day. The dose may be increased up 150 mg per day in divided doses, and in rare circumstances, raised to as high as 275 mg per day in divided doses. Effexor has many tolerable side effects such as weight loss, yawning, and dry mouth. Liver function tests and periodic EKG need to be done along with blood level of the medication.

5. **Wellbutrin SR**

The usual dose of Wellbutrin SR is 150 mg two times per day, at times a dose of 200 mg two times per day can be given. Wellbutrin SR has several tolerable side effects, but it is important to monitor liver function tests, EKG, and blood level of Wellbutrin SR.

6. **Ludiomil**

The usual dose of Ludiomil is 75 mg per day. In the elderly, as little as 25 mg per day may be effective. Doses as high as 150 mg to 225 mg may be used with in-patients. Ludiomil has several tolerable side effects, but periodic EKG and liver function tests should be done.

7. **Nopramin**

The usual dose of Nopramin is 100 mg to 200 mg per day. This dose may be increased to as high as 300 mg per day. This medication is not recommended for use in children. Nopramin is not to be used in conjunction with MAO inhibitors. In fact it cannot be used until two weeks after stopping MAO inhibitors. Nopramin has several tolerable side effects. CBC, liver function tests, EKG, and blood thyroid function must be done before starting this medication. These same tests must be done periodically while a patient is on Nopramin.

8. **Pamelor**

The usual dose of Pamelor is 25 mg 3-4 times per day. At times, the dose may be raised up to 150 mg per day. It has several tolerable side effects. While on this medication, EKG, CBC, and liver function tests need to be done along with blood level of Pamelor.

9. **Lithium**

The usual maintenance dose of Lithium is 450 mg, two times per day. Doses as high as 1,350 mg per day have been given. Lithium has several tolerable side effects. Before starting a patient on lithium, CBC, liver function tests, kidney function tests, blood thyroid function tests, and EKG must be done. While on lithium, these same tests must be done and monitored closely. Blood level of lithium must also be monitored. The kidneys are particularly sensitive to the effects of lithium. It must be stopped at the first signs of blood/kidney test abnormalities.

10. **Desyrel**

The usual starting dose of Desyrel is up to 600 mg per day given in divided doses of 150 mg. Desyrel has several tolerable side effects, therefore, an EKG should be done before starting, and periodically thereafter.

11. **Asendin**

The usual dose of Asendin is 200-300 mg per day in divided doses. Asendin has several tolerable side effects. Blood chemistry tests, CBC and EKG should be done while the patient is on Asendin.

12. **Klonopin**

The initial dose of Klonopin is 1.5 mg per day in divided doses. Sometimes the dose can be raised to as high as 20 mg per day. This medication is quite effective in individuals with anxiety reaction associated with depression. It allows the patient to get a good night's sleep. CBC, liver function tests, and EKG should be done before starting and the same tests should be monitored while the patient is on the medication.

13. **Buspar**

The usual dose of Buspar to treat anxiety is 10 mg, two times per day and the dose can be raised up to 30 mg per day in divided doses.

14. **Xanax**

The usual dose of Xanax to treat anxiety is 0.25 mg three times per day. A dose of up to 4 mg per day can be used in divided doses, in certain cases. Xanax has several tolerable side effects, but laboratory tests are not required during the treatment of patient on Xanax.

15. Elavil

The usual dose of Elavil is 75 to 300 mg per day in divided doses. Elavil has several tolerable side effects. EKG, CBC, liver function tests, along with measurements of Elavil in the blood should be done periodically while the patient is on Elavil.

16. Tofranil

The usual dose of Tofranil is 75 mg per day. The dose may be increased up to 150 mg per day. Tofranil has several tolerable side effects. EKG, CBC, and liver function tests along with Tofranil blood level should be done periodically.

17. Anafranil

The usual starting dose of Anafranil is 25 mg per day and the dose may be increased up to 200 mg per day in divided doses. EKG, CBC, and liver function tests, along with Anafranil blood levels should be done periodically while a patient is on Anafranil.

18. Doxepin

The usual starting dose of Doxepin is 75 mg per day. It may be increased up to 300 mg per day. EKG, CBC, blood chemistry tests should be done periodically while the patient is on Doxepin.

19. Parnate

The usual starting dose of Parnate is 30 mg per day in divided doses. The dose may at times be increased to as high as 60 mg per day in divided doses. Frequent monitoring of blood pressure, EKG, CBC, and blood chemistry tests should be done while the patient is on this medication.

Parnate has a long list of medications with which it cannot be used. Further, there are many food products that must be avoided. Among them are: cheeses, foods high in tyramine, sour cream, Chianti wines, sherry, beer, liquors, caviar, anchovies, pickled herring, canned figs, raisins, bananas, avocados, chocolate, soy beans, sauerkraut, yogurt, and yeast extracts.

ECT (Electro-Convulsive Therapy) remains an effective modality of treatment for depression. It is used under a general anesthesia with muscle relaxants, decreasing convulsions, and eliminating the possibility of fractures and other injuries to the patient. ECT is most appropriate for patients who cannot take medications or whose associated illnesses contradict them taking an antidepressant medication.

Also, in certain life threatening situations, when all other anti-depressant medications fail, ECT is the most appropriate and useful.

PSYCHOTHERAPY

Psychotherapy involves counseling and sometimes medication in addition to counseling. The mental health professionals who provide psychotherapy treatments are psychotherapists, psychiatrists, psychologists, and certified social workers. Primary care physicians are well equipped to provide psychotherapy counseling, if they have the time to do it.

The incidence of depression is three to four times more common in women than men. Many women fearing stigmatization refrain from seeking psychiatric treatment for depression, until it's advanced and more difficult to treat.

Working-class black women are often more hesitant than professional and upper-class minority women to seek help. One of the reasons that upper-class minority women are less concerned about going to the psychiatrist is because these women have money and enjoy a high social standing. They don't fear the stigma of mental illness will affect them as harshly as it might be a working-class black woman.

What can be done to lessen the propensity of depression? It is crucial to educate black women. The fact is that 80 percent or more of individuals who suffer from depression can be successfully treated. The best people to seek treatment from for depression are those who have the professional training and expertise in this treatable disease.

But this profession needs more minority therapists who understand the plight of minority patients as well as greater cultural sensitivity on the part of therapeutic professionals overall. Schools for therapists must incorporate more education in cultural diversity of minorities in their training programs, so as to provide these professional men and women with resources to deal with the problems facing minorities and mental health.

Eventually we'll learn to trust one another, making it easier for more black women to be receptive to the care that professionals of any race or gender can provide. For any person seeking help for depression, the following organizations can be contacted:

1. National Institute of Mental Health—00-421-4211
2. American Psychiatric Association—202-682-6220
3. American Psychological Association—202-336-5500
4. National Mental Health Association—800-969-NMHA—Extension 6642
5. National Foundation for Depressive Illness—800-248-4344
6. National Alliance for the Mentally Ill—800-950-NAMI Extension 6264

Alcoholism In African American Women

16

lcohol abuse is one of the most serious medical problems worldwide. Alcohol is sold in liquor stores, bars, restaurants, airport shops, supermarkets—everywhere. Some people start drinking alcohol in their teens; it is not too difficult to see how they start. Parents do it in front of children, so exposure begins very early in life.

Some studies contend that a form of alcoholism is hereditary. Parents transfer an alcoholism gene to their offspring resulting in more alchoholism. The evidence is compelling, and this may indeed be so.

It would appear that whites start drinking at an earlier age than blacks. They have a higher incidence of alcohol abuse than blacks, but blacks suffer more from the physical effects of alcohol abuse.

For example, according to the U.S. Department of Health and Human Services, African American men and women seem to have a greater incidence of cirrhosis of the liver due to alcohol than white men and women. In fact, the death rate from cirrhosis of the liver is two times that of whites.

African American women suffer from health problems as a result of alcohol abuse, as do white women. Diseases such as cancer, hypertension, malnutrition, birth defects, and obstructive pulmonary disease are much more prevalent in alcoholic African American women as compared to alcoholic white women. The risk of fetal alcohol syndrome (FAS) is seven times higher for African American infants than it is for white infants.

Alcoholism is a multisystem disease. The organs most frequently affected by alcohol are:
1. The brain
2. The heart
3. The lungs
4. The liver
5. The pancreas
6. The breasts
7. The gastrointestinal system
8. The blood system
9. The endocrine system
10. The neurological system
11. The psychological system

When a person drinks alcohol, the brain is the first organ to be affected. Alcohol is absorbed from the stomach into the bloodstream and straight to the brain. A woman, who weighs 150 pounds, will reach a blood alcohol concentration of 100 mg per deciliter by drinking four drinks of hard liquor in one hour.

Alcohol is both a stimulant and a neurosuppressor (brain suppressor). The first thing that happens when alcohol reaches the brain is to calm the person who drinks it.

As more alcohol is consumed, a feeling of elation or euphoria ensues. Associated with this level of drinking is a mild form of excitement; the person becomes more talkative and giddy. This is mild social drinking, defined as two or three glasses of wine, one or two drinks of hard liquor, or two or three beers. Further consumption can create a state of drunkenness associated with excitation, rude behavior, and loss of coordination.

Women show impairment from drinking alcohol at a lower blood alcohol concentration, probably 25-30 mg per deciliter. When the blood alcohol concentration reaches between 50-70 mg per deciliter, most drivers are alcohol impaired and are unsuitable to drive. Blood alcohol concentration that is deemed unsafe for driving a car differs from state to state.

WHAT IS ALCOHOLISM?

Alcoholism is a disease. It affects the human mind and body. The psychological dependence on alcohol is real and has devastating consequences on the alcoholic, their family, and society.

Individuals suffer different patterns of alcohol dependency. Some drink in excess every day and have the need to drink every day. A significant percentage of these people are able to go to work and function reasonably well on the job. They usually start drinking at lunchtime. They often consume two or three drinks with lunch, and after work have three or four more. When they get home they will drink again. This is about 10 drinks of hard liquor per day. On weekends that number often quadruples.

These people are called functioning alcoholics. They work to support their families and behave in a reasonably normal manner. Functioning alcoholics are found at all levels of society. They are sometimes just seen as people who can handle their liquor.

There are also working alcoholics, who must drink as soon as they get up in the morning to get going and continue drinking hard liquor throughout the working day. Usually people know that they are alcoholics, but tolerate them because they are often fun, jovial, and productive when sober. The effects of heavy drinking necessitate absenteeism and alcoholics come up with very creative excuse as to why they weren't at work.

A larger group of individuals who drink alcohol in large quantities and on such a regular basis that they become sick too often to keep a job are the hard core, non-functioning alcoholics, entirely preoccupied with alcohol. Individuals in this group are also found in all levels of society.

Alcohol abuse and Peer Pressure

Peer pressure plays a significant role in alcohol abuse in

teenagers. Peer pressure also exists among adults. Alcohol abuse among African American women often starts at an early age, (from adolescence to teenage years). Alcohol is utilized to make it easier to socialize and feel less inhibited.

Use becomes abuse if it increases and turns into solitary drinking on a daily basis. These women become dependent on the alcohol and once that happens they become preoccupied with it, resulting in alcoholism. Frequently, these women grow up in homes where there is either a father or mother who abuses alcohol.

Some of these African American women are heads of household, single parents with children to bring up and the stress of childrearing. Many pressures associated with poverty and racism also lead to heavy alcohol use.

The middle-class African American women who abuse alcohol, do so for reasons similar to those outlined above. The main difference is that this group of women has financial means, which helps them to cover up their alcoholism. As for the small percentage of upper-class African American women, most of them are professionals, businesswomen, athletes, and entertainers and some still abuse alcohol for the same reasons. They are not poor and presumably suffer less racial discrimination because their money, social, and professional status open doors for them. The effects of alcohol on their bodies, however, is the same as that of the poorest women.

Alcoholism affects the human body to the same degree regardless of a person's nutritional state. For example, if a person is undernourished and has an alcohol binge, the fact that the person has low storage of carbohydrates in his or her liver from poor eating over an extending period of time sets them up for hypoglycemia.

Even though African American women start drinking later than their white counterparts, the signs of alcoholism seem to appear earlier in African American women than in white women.

The amount a person must drink on a long-term basis to cause damage to the liver is 80 grams of alcohol per day over seven to fifteen years. A lot of people drink this much beer when they get home from work within the first two or three hours they're home. If one drinks this amount of alcohol on a regular basis, they can develop liver disease as time goes on.

A glass of wine (3.5 fluid ounces) contains 9.6 grams of alcohol. The reason people who drink two or three glasses of wine (20-30 grams) with dinner every night do not develop liver disease is because it takes a minimum of 80 grams of alcohol per day on a regular basis over several years to develop fatty infiltration of the liver. Infiltration lead creates metamorphosis of fat, then necrosis, resulting in alcoholic liver disease with subsequent development of cirrhosis.

The same thing applies to champagne. One glass of champagne has eleven grams of alcohol in it. Some champagnes have thirteen grams, depending on how dry. So it would take a tremendous amount of champagne consumption to add up to 80 grams of alcohol.

Martinis are a different story. Each has 18.5 grams of alcohol. If a person drinks five martinis per day, he or she is already drinking in excess of the minimum amount of alcohol to cause liver disease. Five martinis equal 92 grams of alcohol.

A Manhattan, for instance, has 19.9 grams of alcohol in it. Five Manhattans equals 99.65 grams of alcohol. A gin rickey has 21 grams, so five gin rickey's equal 105 grams of alcohol. Think about it.

A highball has 24 grams of alcohol in it. Five highballs is equal to 120 grams of alcohol. A mint julep has 29.2 grams of alcohol in it. Five mint juleps equals 146 grams of alcohol.

Therefore, it does not take very many of these alcoholic drinks on a daily basis for someone to develop alcoholic liver disease.

The organs most affected by alcohol abuse are:
1. The brain
2. The liver
3. The pancreas
4. The spleen

5. The G.I. system
6. The blood system

Alcohol is very toxic to the brain. The agitated alcoholic state leads to poor physical coordination, which frequently progresses to a state of drunkenness, leading to stupor and at times to coma. When intoxicated, alcoholics are a danger to themselves and a danger to others.

For instance, a person who abuses alcohol risks losing his or her ability to function properly at work. He or she is likely to develop serious psychological problems, or is using alcohol to cover problems up. These problems are at the root of a drinking problem that disrupts his or her family life. The result is too often the breakup of personal relationships and marriages, as well as alienation from children and extended family.

Serious damage to the brain tissues leading to dementia is quite common in chronic alcoholics. Alcohol abuse leads to Karsakoff syndrome as a result of long-term vitamin B deficiencies. It is also known to be associated with episodes of encephalopathy, such as Wernicke's encephalopathy due to thiamine deficiencies.

It's also associated with other neurological abnormalities, such as ataxia (inability to walk in a straight line), altered mood functions with suicidal ideations, and peripheral neuropathy. A chronic alcoholic is prone to develop seizures, either as result of alcohol withdrawal, or of recurrent traumas. The chronic alcoholic is often deficient in folic acid, all the B vitamins, magnesium, protein, and phosphate.

Alcohol affects the liver because it is a direct toxin to the liver tissues. The amount of damage is based on the amount and frequency of consumption, while the length of time an individual abuses alcohol determines its extent.

In some individuals, the damage to the liver occurs quicker than in others, but one thing is certain: as long as a person abuses alcohol, his or her liver will be damaged by it. In some situations, the liver becomes swollen, which can lead to enlargement of the spleen due to elevation of the portal pressure. The consequence is rupture of the spleen, endangering one's life if not diagnosed properly and treated surgically as soon as detected.

CIRRHOSIS OF THE LIVER

Even if lifelong drinkers avoid dramatic physical breakdowns, their drinking is continuously causing tissues within the liver to become inflamed and the recurrent inflammatory reaction in time leads to scarring. The result is cirrhosis of the liver. There is no way to abuse alcohol every day without slowly killing yourself.

Once the liver becomes cirrhotic, a multitude of clinical problems can occur. The liver is needed to synthesize (produce) different proteins, which are needed for good body functions. It makes most of the coagulation factors that prevent bleeding. The liver is needed to store carbohydrates and to break them down into useable sugars to use as fuel in the body.

The liver produces bile, which is needed to break down the fats that humans eat. The largest organ in the body next to the skin and the skeletal system, it contains the largest supply of reticuloendothelial cells, required by the immune system. In addition, the liver helps remove a multitude of byproducts that the human body produces constantly.

So when the liver is sick and unable to produce needed materials for proper body functions, or to help remove waste materials from the body, the person becomes very ill. In other words, when the liver fails, life cannot go on. Alcohol abuse causes the liver to fail—it's a simple equation.

THE PANCREAS

The pancreas is another organ that is quite sensitive to the toxic effects of alcohol. Pancreatitis is a common complication of heavy and chronic alcohol abuse. It is not exactly clear how long a person has to abuse alcohol before his or her pancreas becomes sick, some say it's after seven years of alcohol abuse.

But different individuals have different degrees of resistance and tolerance. Alcohol damages the pancreatic tissues, at first causing inflammation. The inflammation causes marked swelling of the pancreas resulting in acute pancreatitis.

After repeated attacks of acute pancreatitis, over several years, scarring of the pancreatic tissues appears, acute pancreatitis becomes chronic pancreatitis. The constant inflammation and scarring of the pancreatic disease causes destruction of the tissue leaving empty spaces within the pancreas. Pancreatic pseudocysts start to develop. Quite often, these pancreatic pseudocysts become infected, which in turn can lead to abscesses within the pancreas.

Chronic pancreatitis turns into pancreatic failure, meaning the pancreas is so damaged that it is no longer able to produce different enzymes. These enzymes are necessary to aid in the digestive process of ingested fat.

Failure of the pancreas to produce these enzymes, is indicated by greasy diarrhea. To make matters worse, the person with pancreatic failure now becomes diabetic due to the fact that the pancreas has failed, and is not able to produce insulin for sugar metabolism. The person has also been feeling constant and intense left-sided abdominal pain all the while?

THE EFFECTS OF ALCOHOLISM ON THE SPLEEN

Cirrhosis of the liver, due to chronic, heavy alcohol intake, also effects the spleen. When alcohol damages the liver, this damage occludes the blood vessels that run through it. These damaged vessels cause narrowing and obstruction of the circulation inside the liver.

As a result of intraliver obstruction of these vessels over time, the pressure within the liver and the portal system (carries blood to the liver) causes portal hypertension to develop. The portal system is attached to the spleen.

Portal hypertension leads to enlargement of the spleen, resulting in a condition called hypersplenism. The enlarged spleen can become quite bulky resulting in severe and chronic left-sided abdominal pain. The upper gastrointestinal system is involved in this scenario and becomes quite sick because of the effects of cirrhosis of the liver and portal hypertension.

Because of the obstruction and destruction of intrahepatic (intraliver) circulation, the elevation of the portal pressure causes neovascularization (formation of new vessels) to occur, which is the body's way of trying to bypass the obstructed circulation in the intrahepatic system.

The new vessels, however, are superficial. They grow on the surface of the esophagus, resulting in esophageal varices. Because these varices are superficially located on the outer surface of the esophagus, they tend to rupture quite easily and bleed profusely. Esophageal bleeding is a major complication of cirrhosis of the liver with portal hypertension.

GASTRITIS AND ALCOHOL

Another frequent complication of chronic and heavy alcohol abuse is gastritis, with upper gastrointestinal bleeding. Because alcohol is an irritating drug, it damages the superficial lining of the stomach, causing bleeding which at times can be quite severe and copious.

MALLORY-WEISS SYNDROME

Still another problem that may occur in the chronic alcoholic is a condition called Mallory-Weiss syndrome. It is the result of a tear that occurs at the junction of the gastroesophageal area. It happens because of severe vomiting and retching, a common activity among chronic alcoholics.

The force of the retching causes the tear in the upper gastrointestinal tract. It bleeds quite profusely. In all these cases, the bleeding can be severe enough to cause the patient to go into shock.

THE HEMATOPOIETIC SYSTEM (BLOOD SYSTEM)

All of the diseases just discussed end up as blood disease.

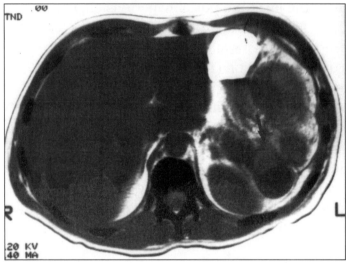

Figure 16.1: CT of acute pancreatitis. CT of the abdomen showing acute pancreatitis with a pseudocyst of the pancreas (Arrow showing swollen pancreas with pseudocyst).

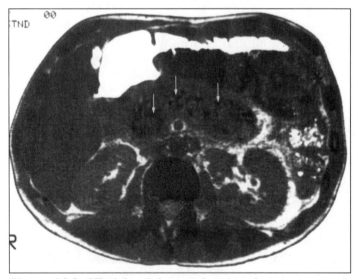

Figure 16.2: CT of the abdomen showing chronic pancreatitis with calcifications. Arrows showing swollen pancreas in a patient who abuses alcohol.

The effects of alcohol on the hematopoietic (blood system) are many. Alcohol can suppress the bone marrow resulting in the lowering of white blood cells, red blood cells, and platelets. Chronic alcoholism can cause anemia as a result of recurrent upper gastrointestinal bleeding or it leads to folic acid deficiency, resulting in a different form of anemia.

Chronic alcohol abuse can result in a condition called hypersplenism, as mentioned above, which causes hemolysis of red blood cells, causing anemia. Hypersplenism can also cause leukopenia (low white blood cells) and thrombocytopenia (low platelet count). These abnormalities in the blood system are the result of the **splenic sequestration**. Because the spleen is enlarged, it soaks up these cells within it.

Chronic alcoholism with liver disease (cirrhosis) causes the white blood cells not to function well, thereby preventing the individual from being able to fight infection properly.

Chronic alcoholic abuse also affects the endocrine system. For instance, the sick alcoholic liver is unable to break down estrogen effectively, which then allows the estrogen to remain in the blood, causing skin changes that are called spider angiomata and break through vaginal bleeding in women. This makes iron deficiency anemia much worse. In men, the elevated estrogen in the blood results in shiny, small testicles and small penises (men do have a small amount of estrogen in their blood).

Reasonable Consumption of Alcohol

Alcohol is a drug and can be quite addictive when used in large quantities over a long period of time. It is potentially toxic to the entire human body. However, literature clearly shows that alcohol in moderate quantities, such as one or two glasses of wine with dinner is helpful in the prevention of coronary artery heart disease.

However, it is prudent that anyone with a propensity toward alcohol abuse refrain from alcohol altogether.

Reasonable consumption of alcohol decreases cholesterol by different mechanisms:

1. It makes platelets less sticky, preventing them from aggregating and in so doing decreases the possibility of clot formation.

2. It increases the level of high-density lipoprotein, the good cholesterol.

Clinical Management of Alcohol Induced Problems

Intoxication causes the intoxicated person to be agitated, unreasonable, sometimes violent, and frequently confused. This group of symptoms and behavior can cause the intoxicated person to get into fights and other altercations which cause problems for their spouses, girlfriends, children, and other members of society with whom they come in contact.

Women who are intoxicated get into fights with their spouses and frequently abuse their children. Men who are intoxicated are generally more abusive; it's hardly a coincidence that more women are beaten on the night of the Super Bowl than any other.

The Emergency Room

These women and men often end up in the emergency room after fights during which they were traumatized, or are brought with upper gastrointestinal bleeding, fever, abdominal pain, and other alcohol-associated problems. Once the intoxicated alcoholic arrives in the emergency room, vital signs, such as blood pressure, pulse, temperature, and respiratory rate must be quickly taken and documented. Then, an intravenous access must be quickly established.

Blood must be drawn and sent for CBC, SMA 20, serum magnesium, serum amylase, blood alcohol concentration. Urine must be sent for drug screening. The urine also must be sent to the laboratory for urinalysis to make sure that there is no blood in it, which can indicate that the patient has had kidney trauma during a fight.

The examining physician will pay particular attention to the examination of the head, looking for signs of trauma. It is important to look for signs of blood coming out of the inner ears. The examination must include a rectal examination looking for signs of blood. If none is found, the stool must be tested for blood using hemoccult.

The neurological examination is extremely important. The doctor is looking for signs of agitation, confusion, hallucinations, stupor, and so on. As soon as the physical examination is completed, the alcoholic must be started on the "alcoholic cocktail." It is composed of:

1. IV glucose (50% in one ampule)
2. Thiamine 100 mg IV or IM
3. Folic acid 1 mg IV or IM or orally if the patient is able.
4. Magnesium sulfate 1-gram IV or IM
5. B complex vitamin IV, IM, or orally

It is absolutely crucial that thiamine is given before the glucose is infused. If the glucose is infused first, it will lead to an acute depletion of whatever trace of thiamine is left in the body. Thiamin depletion will bring on a condition called Wernicke's encephalopathy. Wernicke's encephalopathy causes agitation, confusion, hallucination, and combativeness.

The reason it occurs when fifty percent of glucose is infused in the alcoholic is because the alcoholic is usually deficient in all B complex vitamins such as thiamine, due to poor nutrition. Thiamine is a necessary chemical substance to breakdown sugar, so, its depletion threatens the brain.

Sugar is needed in the acutely intoxicated alcoholic because he or she is likely to be starved, therefore hypoglycemic (low blood sugar). The dangerously ill alcoholic needs folic acid because he or she is always folate deficient; alcohol poisons the folate chemical pathway. All alcoholics are by definition folate deficient.

The sick and intoxicated alcoholic needs magnesium, because all chronic users are magnesium deficient, even though the laboratory may report the blood magnesium level as normal. Alcohol is a diuretic and as such passes large quantities of magnesium in the urine. In fact, the total body magnesium is always low in chronic alcoholics.

Low magnesium can cause low serum calcium. Both low serum calcium and low magnesium in an individual can cause seizures; hypoglycemia (low blood sugar) can as well.

Another deficient substance is phosphate. Phosphate is a by-product of protein breakdown and since the alcoholics are often too preoccupied with alcohol to eat properly, they are deficient. The alcoholic's frequent urination loses large quantities of phosphate in the urine causing **hypophosphatemia** (low serum phosphate).

Low serum phosphate can cause seizures and, if left untreated, hemolytic anemia. Phosphate is needed to provide for a normal level of 2-3 D-PG (2-3 diphosphoglycerate).

The Hospital

If the alcoholic survives the emergency room, the next step is to evaluate him or her for chronic disease. If it is decided that the alcoholic needs to be hospitalized, then all the medications in the alcoholic cocktail must be continued except for the magnesium and the 50 percent dextrose.

The next step in providing care for the alcoholic is observation. The doctor must allow for the possibility of **delirium tremens (DTs)**. Both the blood alcohol concentration level and how the patient looks are important in deciding when to start anti-DT treatment.

Equally important is ascertaining when the patient last drank. Most alcoholics will start showing signs of DTs thirty-six to forty-eight hours after they drank last. It is important to keep in mind the fact that chronic alcoholics can have a blood alcohol concentration of 200-300 mg per deciliter in the blood without appearing drunk.

Delirium tremens is a syndrome which results from the alcohol craving. Different stages of withdrawal bring tremors on, due to lack of alcohol in his or her blood stream.

Five Stages of DTs:

Stage I: The first stage of DTs is manifested by tremors (the shakes), restlessness, increased heart rate, insomnia, diarrhea, and irritability.

Stage II: The second stage is all of the above, plus sweaty palms, and confusion.

Stage III: All the above symptoms, plus sweating, rise in blood pressure, rise in pulse, palpitations, and hallucinations.

Stage IV: All of the above, plus seizures.

Stage V: All of the above, plus coma.

Medications

To prevent DTs from developing, it is recommended that the patient be given Ativan 1-2 mg four times per day by mouth. If the patient can't take medication by mouth, Ativan can be given IM or IV. Alternatively, the patient can be treated with Librium 10 mg, four times per day IM or PO.

Librium is not absorbed well IM and is not a medication to be used if the patient has severe liver disease, because the liver metabolizes it. Ativan is not metabolized in the liver and therefore it can be used even if the liver is severely sick.

Essential to the treatment of DTs are intravenous fluid replacement and intravenous electrolyte management. It is very important to keep the sick alcoholic in an anabolic state. There must always be sugar in the IV fluid. D5 _ normal saline or D5 normal saline is preferred.

If the patient is hypertensive, the IV can be D5 _ normal saline along with specific medication to treat the hypertension. If seizure develops, then the patient must be treated with Dilantin with or without phenobarbital. An EEG and brain CT scan must always be done when the patient is stable.

If the patient comes in with a seizure, a brain CT without contrast must be done as soon possible to be certain that there is no blood collection in the brain as the result of head trauma.

CESSATION

There are medications that can be used to help the patient stop drinking, if they are agreeable. Therein lies the root of the disease. It's really more psychological than anything, after it has progressed to severe alcoholism.

Two such medications are in use today; one is Antabuse (Disulfiram), the other is Naltrexone (ReVia). Both of these medications have side effects and a person who is drinking must not take them. If a person is secretly drinking alcohol and takes Antabuse, he or she can become very ill. In fact it could kill them.

Naltrexone works by decreasing the desire of the alcoholic to drink alcohol. It converts acetaldehyde, which is a byproduct of alcohol, into acetic acid in the liver. That causes an increase in serum acetaldehyde anywhere from five to ten times the normal level.

Because of that, the person can develop flushing of the skin, nausea, vomiting, headaches, hyperventilate, and can develop respiratory distress along with anxiety, palpitations, and sometimes hypertension. That is why it is important that a person does not drink alcohol and take Disulfiram at the same time.

The usual dose of Disulfiram is 250 mg. There is a 500 mg dose that is also made, but frequently the 250 mg dose is sufficient to prevent somebody from craving alcohol. The usual dose for Naltrexone is 50 mg daily for about 12 weeks.

DRUNK DRIVING

Driving while intoxicated remains a major safety problem in the United States and every year many thousands of people die as a result of accidents resulting from drunk driver. Drunk drivers remain a menace to society and every state has laws defining DWI (Driving While Intoxicated). (also see the table on page)

WOMEN AND ALCOHOL

It is said in scientific literature that roughly five to six percent of women in this country have a serious alcohol dependence problem. In the primary care setting, about 25 percent of women patients have serious alcohol problems as defined by the medical profession.

Women who abuse alcohol face a major problem, not only for themselves but also when they are pregnant. Alcohol greatly affects the fetus. Women who drink while pregnant run the risk of their baby developing a condition called **fetal alcohol syndrome (FAS)**.

One in 100 babies born to alcoholic women suffer from the effects of alcohol. Fetal Alcohol Syndrome occurs in ten out of every one thousand babies. The children of alcohol abusers suffer from alcohol related neurodevelopmental disorder (ARND) and fetal alcohol syndrome (FAS).

Alcohol affects two parts of the fetal brain more severely than adults, the hippocampus and the cerebellum. A byproduct of alcohol called acetaldehyde causes the balance of the problem. Acetaldehyde damages the DNA of the developing tissues in the fetal brain.

Women who abuse alcohol while pregnant are doing serious damage to their unborn babies. Many of these babies are born with mental retardation, growth retardation, craniofacial abnormalities, and other brain damage. These babies also suffer ocular anomalies, and hearing disorders such as hearing loss and recurrent serous otitis media (ear problems).

These children often develop speech impairment. They frequently have learning disorders and have to be sent to a special school, which is the *least* of the problems a learning disabled child will have to face.

The abnormalities that these children suffer as a result of fetal alcohol syndrome could basically rob them of a normal life. They are innocent infants who, in effect, may not grow up to become productive members of society or to fulfill their potential as human beings. It's a very sad disease because they did not ask for it and it was *totally preventable*.

It takes a lot of money to care for children born with fetal alcohol syndrome, and society is left to pay the bill. Between 37,000 and 40,000 children are born each year with some form of alcohol related problems. But, even more devastating than the fetal alcohol syndrome is the absence of self respect in mothers who choose to drink and take drugs while pregnant, and the infants they kill as a result.

Infant Mortality

The United States is the richest country on the planet, and yet nineteen of 1,000 babies born to black women die, compared to nine per 1,000 born to white women.

The reason so many babies born to black women die is because alcohol abuse, drug abuse, cigarette smoking, poverty, and lack of prenatal care are prevalent among black women. This is a catastrophe, because these pregnant black women either do not receive or do not seek prenatal care. Whether it's society or the mother who drops the ball, the result is the same—innocent babies are brought into the world unhealthy.

By the time impoverished pregnant women show up in a hospital emergency room to deliver their babies, they usually have serious medical problems. These problems may include gestational diabetes, hypertension, anemia, preeclampsia, eclampsia, syphilis, gonorrhea, chylamydia, genital herpes, HIV infection, and more.

Frequently, both the baby's and the mother's life are at risk in these circumstances. Babies born to mothers affected with these conditions are likely to be born prematurely and are just as likely to develop several serious medical problems. They include mental retardation, congenital heart problems, and a whole host of other permanent medical conditions that guarantee lifelong suffering and dependence on their families (who may not be able to support them), or society for financial support.

PRESCRIPTION DRUGS

Many individuals who abuse alcohol also abuse prescription

drugs, such as Valium, Librium, Ativan, Xanax, and so on. Drinking alcohol and taking these drugs is quite dangerous and can kill without warning.

By stopping alcohol abuse, a woman will have a healthier liver, heart, brain, nervous system, endocrine system, reproductive system, gastrointestinal system, pancreas, blood system, emotional system, and live overall healthier lives.

The following organizations can be called by anyone who needs help for their problems:

1. Alcoholics Anonymous (phone: 212-870-3400)
2. Hazelden (Phone: 800-257-7810)
3. National Clearing House for Alcohol Abuse and Drug Information (Phone: 800-729-6686, Fax: 301-468-6433)
4. National Council on Alcoholism and Drug Dependence, Inc. (Phone: 212-206-6770, Fax: 212-645-1690)
5. Hope Lives (Phone: 800-NCA-CALL)
6. Drug Specific Information (Phone: 800-729-6686)

Drug Addiction In African American Women

17

Illicit drug use is the second most common addictive problem in the United States. According to the National Institute on Drug Abuse, there are about four million drug addicts in the United States. About three million of them are addicted to cocaine. Heroin addiction accounts for about 800,000. Several more millions use and abuse illicit drugs of different types, and they are also considered addicts.

The General Accounting office estimates that in 1998 the Federal Government spent 3.2 billion dollars to pay for treatment of addiction. When cost of prevention of drug-related crimes and time lost from work is added up, more than sixty billion dollars will have been spent. So society and taxpayers spend about 63.2 billion dollars per year on drug addiction and related problems.

ADDICTION

The part of the brain stimulated by drugs resulting in pleasurable feelings is the **dopamine center**, located at the base of the brain. Drugs such as heroin, cocaine, marijuana, opiates, and amphetamines activate dopamine to release neurotransmitter substances, resulting in a pleasurable feeling called a "high." Psychologically, this is what drug addicts crave.

The function of the dopamine center is to experience sensations of joy and pleasure. It's responsible for how we enjoy sex, food, music, art, beauty, and other aesthetic sensations that are pleasing to the senses.

Once an individual becomes addicted to heroin, cocaine, crack cocaine, marijuana, or other drugs they crave these drugs once the level of the drug decreases in the bloodstream. The craving for the drug is quite painful. When the pain becomes physical, you know you're physically addicted.

Drug craving can lead to severe withdrawal symptoms such as sweating, headache, runny nose, abdominal cramps, diarrhea, poor appetite, insomnia, nightmares, and more. Drug addicts—in particular cocaine, heroin, and crack cocaine addicts—will do anything to get money to buy the drugs in order to satisfy the drug craving and to avoid going into drug withdrawal.

Once a person becomes addicted to drugs, it is very difficult to give them up. The addict is dependent on the drugs and spend a great deal of time arranging for the next fix. He or she will spend rent money, food money, mortgage money, and will lie, steal and commit crimes of other types in order to get the money to pay for the drug.

Drug addiction is quite common among blacks, Hispanics, poor whites, Asians, Native Americans, Pacific islanders, and other minorities who live in the inner cities of the United States and of the world. Wherever there is poverty and ghettos, there is a high incidence of illicit drug use. However, for quite some time illicit drug use has gained widespread popularity in the suburbs of the United States. These are middle-class and upper-class whites in one of the richest countries in the world!

WOMEN AND PRESCRIPTION DRUGS

According to the literature, 3.2 million people regularly use illicit drugs and 3.5 million women abuse prescription drugs. Statistically, more white women abuse prescription drugs and more black women and Hispanic women abuse illicit drugs.

The most frequently abused prescription drugs are:

1. Valium
2. Librium
3. Xanax
4. Ativan
5. Tranxene
6. Morphine
7. Hydrocodone
8. Codeine
9. Demerol, etc.

Illicit drug abuse is found in every community in the United States and at all levels of these communities. All professions have people who abuse illicit drugs to one degree or another. Both sexes are involved in illicit drug culture.

African American women and Hispanic women use more heroin and crack cocaine, but white women use more cocaine, marijuana, and amphetamines. Cocaine has, however, moved into the black and Hispanic ghettos because the price of cocaine has gone down to a point where poor minorities can now afford to buy it.

The drug culture is fueled by forces outside of the communities where these drugs are used. People who don't live in these communities are bringing the drugs in. The big question is: who are they and what are their motives?

Some feel that infiltration of illicit drugs into the minority communities is a well-planned conspiracy to destroy a generation of young blacks and other minorities. Whether proof exists to substantiate these allegations is not quite clear. One thing certain is that the illicit drug subculture is highly associated with criminal behavior of different kinds and different degrees. The end result is that communities where illicit drugs are prevalent are also beset with high crime rates.

It might surprise readers to know that per capita, more whites use illegal drugs than blacks. The reason that's surprising is because fewer whites *get arrested* for using drugs and even fewer get sent to jail.

Of all modern societies, the United States has more people in jail at any one time than any other country. According to statistics, an excess of two million people are in jail.

The vast majority of blacks and Hispanics, both men and women, are in jail for drug-related offenses of different degrees. The rate of illegal drug use reported for one year in the United States population, age 12 and older, was 11.9 percent. It breaks down to:

Native Americans	19.8 percent,
Puerto Ricans	13.3 percent,
African American	13.1 percent,
Mexican American	12.7 percent,
Asian Pacific Islanders	6.5 percent,
Caribbean American	7.6 percent,
Central American	5.7 percent and
Cuban-Americans	8.2 percent.

According to the National Center on Addiction and Substance Abuse at Columbia University, 21.5 million women in the United States smoke; 4.5 million are alcoholics; 3.5 million women misuse prescription drugs; and 3.1 million women use drugs. One out of every five pregnant women smokes, drinks alcohol, and/or abuses drugs, totaling more than 800,000 women.

Psychological and Physical Manifestations

The mind set that causes African American women to abuse drugs is no doubt similar to the mindset of other women who abuse drugs. The circumstances of life that are associated with drug abuse are quite different in black women, Hispanic women, and Native American women, than they are in white women.

Most white women who are drug addicts start using marijuana recreationally. They then gradually move on to harder drugs, such as amphetamines, LSD, and other psychedelic drugs. As the addiction deepens, they move on to using cocaine, heroin, and crack cocaine.

Some of these women are financially able to support their addiction because they have good jobs with good pay, which enables them to pay for drugs. Some of these women are in the entertainment world.

Poor white women are often in the same circumstances as minority women in that they don't have money to support their drug habits. A large percentage of women are addicted to prescription drugs. The most frequently abused prescription drugs by women are:

1. Valium
2. Librium
3. Xanax
4. Ativan
5. Tranxene
6. Clonopin
7. Codeine
8. Darvon
9. Demerol
10. Morphine
11. Hydrocodone
12. Ambien
13. Restoril
14. Methadone

Some individuals become addicted to prescription drugs because of chronic pain associated with illness. Sometimes they are no longer able to obtain these prescriptions and resort to illicit drugs to ease their pain, and in this way they become chronic drug addicts.

Drug addiction and all other addictions are psychological illnesses. Women drug addicts, as well as male drug addicts, will do anything to support an addiction that becomes more important than their own self esteem. Some women prostitute themselves in order to pay for the drugs.

Sometimes, a woman will prostitute herself with other addicts for the drug itself. Percentage-wise IV drug addiction is more common among African American women and Hispanic women as compared to white women.

The brain is affected by illicit drug use in many other ways. For example, heavy marijuana use is known to affect the brain in ways that leads to slow and slurred speech and memory loss. Both cocaine and heroin use are associated with seizures. When heroin and cocaine are used intravenously, sepsis and bacterial endocarditits can occur.

Infected emboli can be thrown to the brain from the heart valve resulting in brain abscesses. Most importantly, the brain is affected by drug overdose, and that can kill instantly.

The lungs are affected as well. The most frequent pulmonary problem in drug addicts is pneumonia. Addicts who use cocaine or heroin intravenously develop symptoms of upper airway diseases such as coughing, wheezing, and bronchitis. Pulmonary edema (when the lungs become filled with fluid) can occur as an idiosyncratic reaction from heroin use.

Another complication involving the lungs in heroin and cocaine use is pulmonary embolism (a clot to the lungs). This happens because the addicts use veins in their legs to infuse the drug and sometimes the vessels in the groin and legs get damaged and infected. These conditions can lead to stasis, which in turn can lead to clot formation.

The clots can then migrate through the blood vessels into the lung, causing acute pulmonary embolism. Infected emboli can also be thrown to the lungs from infected vegetation from the heart valves (a condition called bacterial endocarditis).

The incidence of AIDS in African American women is the highest among all women in the United States, specifically because intravenous drug abuse is higher among African American women.

That being the case, black women with AIDS have the most frequent incidence of a lung infection called Pneumocystits carinii (PCP). PCP is a most serious lung infection and frequently is the cause of death of intravenous drug abusers with AIDS.

The incidence of tuberculosis has decreased in the general

population over the last several years, but it has gone up in AIDS patients. Since African American women use more intravenous drugs, they have a high incidence of AIDS. AIDS causes a high incidence of pulmonary tuberculosis.

African American women who are intravenous drug abusers also have a propensity for developing fungus infection of the lung as a result of their depressed immune system, associated with HIV infection.

THE EFFECTS OF DRUG USE ON THE HEART

The heart suffers immensely from illicit drug use. Once in the blood stream, the drugs stimulate the heart causing it to beat too quickly, slowly, or irregularly.

Cocaine use can cause sudden death, acute myocardial infarction (heart attack), myocarditis (inflammation of the heart muscle), cardiomyopathy (enlargement of the heart), and coronary spasm (spasm of the vessel that carries blood around the heart). It is believed that a metabolite of cocaine is responsible for the acute problems affecting the heart.

The heart rate can also be slowed by cocaine. In the middle of cocaine intoxication, the heart can actually rupture abruptly resulting in sudden death. Heroin intoxication can cause the heart to slow down (bradycardia) as well as suppress the respiratory system, which can result in cardiopulmonary failure.

Many things can injure the heart of an intravenous drug abuser, but one of the most serious is a condition called bacterial endocardititis. There are two forms of endocarditis: 1) **acute bacterial endocarditis**, and 2) **subacute bacterial endocarditis**. Endocarditis occurs when bacterial organisms enter the blood stream of the individuals injecting drugs into their veins. Once in the bloodstream, the bacteria multiply, resulting in sepsis. Bacteria then settle on the heart valve causing different types of cardiac decompensations.

In drug addicts, usually the tricuspid valve is affected (54% of the time), followed by aortic (25%), then by the mitral valve about

(20%) and the rest can be mixed right-sided and left-sided endocarditis.

The bacterial organism most frequently found in drug addicts is *Staphylococcus coagulase positive*, followed by *Streptococci* and fungi such as *Candida* and *Aspergillus*. Organisms of different types can also settle on the heart valves. The *Staph coagulase negative* can settle on the heart valve causing bacterial endocarditis. In intravenous drug abusers, when the tricuspid valve is the affected valve, 80% of the time the *Staph coagulase positive* is the organism isolated.

In bacterial endocarditis, the affected person becomes acutely ill with fever, chills, shortness of breath, chest pain, sometimes cardiac arrhythmia, and the development of an acute heart murmur with congestive heart failure.

Other physical findings may include distended neck veins, decreased blood pressure, fast pulse rate, increased respiratory rate, cardiac rub and rales in the lungs (these can be heard). The liver can become enlarged and tender, and a large spleen can be palpated. Acute pain in the lower back is frequently present in an individual who is septic.

Laboratory findings include a high white blood cell count, low red blood cell count, elevated erythrocyte sedimentation rate, low platelet count, positive ANA, and elevated liver function test.

A chest X-ray may show diffuse infiltrates in the lungs. EKG may show either fast rate with regular rhythm or fast rate with irregular rhythm, a slow rate with decreased voltage indicating that the heart is being compromised with fluid around the sac, a condition called cardiac tamponade.

Arterial blood gases may be grossly abnormal. An echocardiogram may show valvular abnormalities such as vegetation, and an enlarged heart may also be seen. A transesophageal echocardiogram may be able to show the presence of vegetation on the heart valves if the technology is available in that particular institution.

The urine may show the presence of protein and red blood cells as a result of emboli to the kidneys. Septic emboli can also affect the skin causing assorted skin lesions. Acute bacterial endocardititis is a severe medical emergency requiring the help of a cardiologist and cardiac surgeon to quickly try to replace the heart valve and save the life. If any delay takes place, the chances of recovery may not be very good in acute bacterial endocarditis. What happens is that the bacteria sits on the valve and literally eats it away and then blood flows back and forth resulting in acute cardiac decompensation with impending death. These individuals frequently have to be intubated if they are in acute congestive heart failure, meaning they can't breathe, and oxygen has to be provided for them.

Blood cultures must be taken and if they are positive, then clinical decisions must be made to provide appropriate treatment. If staph is suspected, which it frequently is, Vancomycin IV is an excellent choice in association with coverage for gram-negative organisms.

If no organism has been identified, a good antibiotic would be Fortaz, which will cover for pseudomonas and other possible gram-negative organisms that the individual may be infected with. Once the organism is identified, then appropriate antibiotic will be provided based on the sensitivity.

The other infection frequently involving the heart is subacute bacterial endocarditis. It can be more insidious in its development so it's difficult to arrive at a diagnosis. Subacute bacterial endocarditis manifests itself as a febrile illness with chills, general malaise, joint pain, low back pain, and headache.

At times a sufferer might present with general weakness, pallor, intermittent low-grade fever, and general feeling of unwellness. The profile of the patient is of major importance, for example, *an intravenous drug abuser who is prone to subacute bacterial endocarditis by virtue of his or her habit and sharing dirty needles with other drug addicts*. Sometimes addicts use water from the toilet bowl to prepare the drug and end up injecting themselves with contaminated materials; this is the sort of thing a physician needs to know while treating them.

The liver is a frequently affected organ in drug addicts. For those who abuse prescription drugs, the liver may get sick from these drugs, in particular when alcohol is combined with them.

285

Intravenous drug abusers livers get sick the most frequently because of Hepatitis B and Hepatitis C. In rare circumstances Hepatitis A can also occur. So can Hepatitis E and G, but those are rarer forms of viral hepatitis. Hepatitis B and C affect the liver of individuals who use intravenous drugs because of sharing of dirty needles through which the hepatitis viruses get transmitted. Hepatitis A can be transmitted intravenously as well.

There are circumstances during which Hepatitis A can cause acute liver disease in intravenous drug abusers. Hepatitis B and C can be sexually transmitted, and many drug addicts when they are high have sexual intercourse with whomever, wherever, and whenever.

Prostitution predisposes drug addicts to sexually transmitted diseases, such as Hepatitis B and C, syphilis, gonorrhea, Chlamydia, genital herpes, and AIDS. Hepatitis B and C, syphilis, gonorrhea, and AIDS can be spread to the liver at different stages of their development. In particular, Hepatitis B and C can cause chronic liver disease such as chronic active hepatitis, chronic persistent hepatitis, and cirrhosis of the liver.

The gastrointestinal tract is affected in drug addicts in several ways. One of the most common gastrointestinal symptoms that drug addicts suffer from is abdominal pain associated with craving for drugs. Secondly, drug addicts suffer frequently from diarrhea. The diarrhea has two bases: 1) anxiety associated with craving for drugs; 2) parasitic infestation, as a result of intercourse involving anal penetration, transmitting organisms such amoebae or Giardia lamblia.

Other gastrointestinal problems occur as a result of cirrhosis of the liver, which comes from Hepatitis B or C, causing portal hypertension with subsequent esophageal varices and upper gastrointestinal bleeding.

The kidneys are infected by intravenous drug addiction in several ways: septic shock causes failure, septic emboli as a result of septic vegetations being thrown from the heart valves to the kidneys, and IV associated nephritic syndrome. This is probably due to antigen-antibody complexes, which form and circulate in the blood stream either as a result of low-grade chronic infection from materials used to cut and mix either cocaine or heroin.

These complexes settle in the tubules of the kidneys resulting in nephritic syndrome. Kidney abscesses can occur in some IV drug addicts.

THE REPRODUCTIVE SYSTEM AND DRUGS

The female reproductive system is quite often affected by IV drug addiction. The most frequent problem that women drug addicts experience is menstrual irregularity, which occurs as a result of endocrine dysfunctions.

When the woman's liver is sick with hepatitis from drug addiction, the sick liver is unable to properly break down estrogen and there is too much estrogen in the blood. This overstimulates the uterus resulting in breakthrough vaginal bleeding.

Many women intravenous drug addicts, as a result of having sexual intercourse with multiple sexual partners, contract cervical cancer. Chlamydia, herpes simplex virus, human papilloma virus, HIV infection, and pelvic inflammatory disease (PID) can be contracted, causing chronic lower abdominal pain with chronic vaginitis.

HIV infection is the most serious and the most deadly infection that afflicts women drug addicts. Once the drugs reach the bloodstream, they get carried to all parts of the body. The blood cells of the body are all affected by drug addiction.

Drug abuse affect suppresses the bone marrow. This leads to anemia, leukopenia, or thrombocytopenia.

The infections associated with IV drug abuse can cause anemia, leukopenia, and thrombocytopenia when the infection is acute. When an IV drug abuser is infected with the AIDS virus, parvovirus B-19 can enter the blood stream resulting in pure red cell aplasia. Hepatitis can cause aplastic anemia, though that is rare. Both Hepatitis C and B have been described in aplastic anemia.

Once in the bloodstream, if doses of drugs are excessive, the result is drug overdose. Too many drugs in the blood can cause confusion, stupor, seizures, coma, or death. Once coma develops, if immediate medical attention is not provided, the patient will die.

The skin is the most frequently abused organ by the intravenous drug addicts. The heroin or cocaine addicts who inject drugs have to go through the skin to get to the veins or arteries to inject drugs. Frequently, the skin becomes infected because of lack of proper cleansing with antiseptics.

Some addicts, when they run out of veins to inject drugs, inject drugs under their skin, a practice called skin-popping. Multiple sores develop over their legs, abdomen, neck, and arms, with very little good skin left. These open sores represent a ready entry point for infection to seed into the bloodstream, resulting in blood infections.

TREATMENT OF DRUG ADDICTS AND DRUG ADDICTION

Drug addiction treatment requires a team effort. The mental aspect of drug addiction requires treatment from mental health professionals and drug counselors, on an outpatient basis and when necessary on an inpatient basis for long term drug rehabilitation treatments.

The medical treatments of drug addicts must be both organ and system directed. One of the key components of intravenous drug abuse treatment is Methadone treatment. Methadone is a synthetic drug that is used to relieve the drug craving of heroin addicts.

Methadone use contributes greatly in reducing HIV infection in IV drug abusers. It helps put people to work and to some degree it helps to decrease the crime rate because these addicts don't have to commit crimes to find money to buy their drugs.

However, according to a published report, only 1.7 million drug addicts can get into a methadone program in the United States. This is about half of the hard core drug users. In New York City about 35,000 of the 200,000 hard-core drug users are able to get into a methadone program. Society at large, and for that matter some people in government, feel that giving addicts methadone is encouraging drug addiction. This is untrue because methadone is a form of medical treatment for heroin addiction.

Drug addicts however, can abuse methadone. Some addicts take the methadone from the clinic and sell on the street. Some lie about the actual dose of methadone and as a result too much methadone is given and they overdose. Some addicts abuse the methadone program and stay on it permanently as a form of work disability.

According to recent reports, whites and people in the middle class, upper middle class and celebrities in the sport and entertainment world use more cocaine, heroine, and crack cocaine than the minorities who live in the ghettos of the United States. The lure of drugs is everywhere.

Drug addiction in African American women and Hispanic women is a major problem that is contributing to the instability of those two communities. It is crucial for those who are in government and in power to get serious and begin to provide the necessary treatments to these women in order that they become free of drug addiction.

Treatments are costly, but they are important. Drug prevention programs, educational programs dealing with the prevention of drugs, and programs to prevent the dissemination of drugs within communities are essential to the survival of African American women.

Drug addiction seminars should begin at the earliest grades in schools across the country so that children can become sensitized to drug addiction's ravages. The facts protect them, when people try to get them involved in drugs. As it is right now, the incidence of drug addiction in schools across the country is high and begins at the earliest age, in elementary school, up through middle school, and high school.

It is crucial that the educational system join forces with the government agencies to try to encourage drug prevention and drug education programs.

Help for individuals addicted to drugs requires money. It also requires the caring of government, educator, clergy, and other members of society. It will take a team to attack this scourge that quietly and daily destroys society.

Afterword

THE ROLE OF RACIAL DISCRIMINATION IN STRESS-INDUCED PREMATURE DEATHS

According to the National Center for Health, white women living in the same country survive black women by four years! This grave disparity is not due to any genetic advantage of white women over black. It is that many white women often enjoy better education, economic situations, social standing, food, employment, and more power in society. They often have fewer children, access to better health care, and if they are not in power, are more likely to marry a white male who is.

According to a recent report by the Center for Disease Control, white women and minority women make up 57 percent of the American work force yet 97 percent of managers are white, and 95 percent are white males in companies that make up the bulk of the power establishment in the United States.

Yet black women go to college and graduate in larger numbers than black men do. There are a lot of highly educated and skilled black women in the United States! Imagine the stress of being in a skilled group consistently passed over for higher-echelon managerial jobs because, quite possibly, of discrimination.

White women, although subject to sexual discrimination, often have advantages that black women don't have. Many are

291

married to the white male power structure. White women can garner a great deal of power, financially, socially, and politically, because their mates occupy these positions.

When they become widows, they inherit the power with all of its privileges. In fact, many white male managers run companies whose majority shares are owned by white women.

At the core of the entire race debate in America is economics. The "haves" do not want the "have-nots" to have. It is camouflaged as racial disharmony. This has been going on for hundreds of years in this, and most modern countries, the world over.

Most white people who choose to discriminate against blacks don't understand this. Some accept racism at face value and maintain the belief until it becomes part of their psyche and eventually their offspring's. It makes them feel good to think that they are better than another person.

What they don't realize is that they are carrying out someone else's agenda—someone that sits in a position of power, who cannot afford to be known as racist. By perpetuating this erroneous concept of racial superiority through ignorant masses they keep their financial security intact.

In order for present day black women to have a chance at improving their lives they must return to the basic concepts and principles of what it means to be a black woman in America. They must lay a new foundation for future black society in this country and rediscover what it means to be a people with a unique and proud culture.

To decrease stress and its negative impact on the cardiovascular system, African American women must understand the dynamics that caused it. To do that they must continue to achieve intellectually, professionally, and economically. With achievements will come social standing.

Black women in this country must set up a more positive standard by which to measure success than only material possessions. It's fine to indulge in luxuries if you have the money to do them but many black women who try to copy the lifestyles of middle and upper class white women drain their own money and energy in pursuit of someone else's ideal. "Luxuries" are very expensive and can be quite distracting and stressful if an individual has to struggle to pay for them.

African American women who are financially successful should remember that many black men are not likely to keep up, because black men generally struggle in America. Because these men are conscious of their own self worth not being reflected in monetary terms, but also conscious that society judges worth by money, they may carry anger at the system that could be misdirected toward successful black women. A black woman concerned with her well-being should be aware of this dynamic. A morally informed black man can be a good boyfriend, a good fiancé, a good husband, and a good father regardless of his earned income. All of these elements in a mate contribute to a fulfilling—in other words, healthy—lifestyle.

Ingredients of a healthy lifestyle include a good education, a good profession, and self-discipline. Achieving one takes planning, patience, high self-esteem, hard work, and the determination to get ahead and stay ahead.

For most poor black people, crying about their poverty is considered a sign of weakness. Perhaps it is in this spirit that black and other minority women allow their diseases to reach advanced stages. But because they ignore their symptoms it is often too late for them to be cured.

To see the decadence and destruction of the human body in the inner city and black ghettos in the United States one would think people are in this country are poor. Don't let America's willingness to sacrifice the ghetto become your willingness to sacrifice your own health.

Epilogue

I was born in Haiti. At age seven, my mother died, by age nine I'd lost my father. I was taken out of a private Catholic school and placed in a public half-time school for poor children. I refused to go. Told I would then be expected to go to work (domestic housework), I rebelled and ran away to my village, Carrefour LaVille.

At about age ten, I began to work as a farmhand for one gourdes (20 cents) per day; working from 7:00 A.M. to 5:00 P.M. To get to the farms, I rose at 4:00 A.M. and walked there barefooted. I had been living on my own and providing for myself since age nine.

After living in Carrefour Laville for many years, I moved to the town of Petite Riviere de L'Artibonite. There I began to learn how to read and write on my own, and taught myself how to speak French, English, and Spanish.

I emigrated to the United States in 1960 and worked in the garment district of New York City, pushing carts loaded with clothes from one factory to another for one dollar an hour. One month after arriving, I enrolled at P.S. 44 in Manhattan for night school, where I received a formal elementary education. Two months after enrolling, I asked to be allowed to take the final exam. I received all As and graduated. My teacher pressed a note into my hand, wished me well and sent me on to Washington Irving Evening High School.

I passed a college entrance exam that allowed me to enroll as a student at Hunter College. While attending high school in the evening, I simultaneously attended Hunter College.

I then enrolled in a medical technology school in mid-Manhattan. I did not yet have a diploma. I decided to be honest with the school's director and explained my predicament, asking to be given a chance to take the entrance examination. The director gave it to me on the spot. I answered every question correctly. She gave me permission to join, and I finished first in the class. I was given my first employment opportunity as a laboratory technician.

I then returned to Hunter College and Washington Irving High School at night while working during the day. I subsequently graduated from Washington Irving High School and went to Queens College of the City University of New York to join its pre-med program, while working in a research laboratory in Brooklyn.

My credentials today are found at the beginning of this book. As you can see, I built my life from very little opportunity, but I did it. You can have every opportunity in America, but as an African American woman, you know it takes a plan.

This book helps you get one. With better health, you will find the other quality you will need to make it in this world—courage. So get out there, be smart, and be the strong black woman you are. I have faith in you.

Source Notes

Introduction

1. Noble, George. "Crisis Looms for Un— Health Care." *The Medical Herald*, V. 6, No. 10, (Nov. 1996): p. 6.

Chapter 1—Hypertension in African American Women

1. "The Sixth Report of the Joint National Committee on Prevention, Detection, Evaluation and Treatment of High Blood Pressure", *Archive of Internal Medicine*, V. 157 Nov. 24 1997

Chapter 2—Stroke in African American Women

1. According to The American Heart Association's 1999 Heart and Stroke Statistical Update.

Chapter 3—High Cholesterol in African American Women

1. According to The American Heart Association's 1999 Heart and Stroke Statistical Update.
2. Fauci, Anthony S. (ed.), *Harrison's Principles of Internal Medicine, 14th Edition*, New York: McGraw Hill, 1997.

Chapter 5—Diabetesin African American Women

1. American Diabetes Association. "Report of the Expert Committee on the Diagnosis and Classification of Diabetes Mellitus." *Diabetes Care* v. 20 #7 July 1997.

2. Burros, Marian. "Despite Awareness of Risks More in US are getting Fat." *The New York Times*. Jul. 17, 1994.

Chapter 6—Heart Disease in African American Women
1. The American Heart Association. *1999 Heart and Stroke Statistical Update.*
2. Fray, John C.S. & Douglas, Janice G., (ed.). *Pathophysiology of Hypertension in Black.* Oxford Univ Press, 19992.
3. Noble, George. "Crisis Looms for Urban Health Care." *The Medical Herald*, Vol. 6, Nov. 1996.

Chapter 12—AIDS in African American Women
1. Center For Disease Control. *HIV/AIDS Surveillance Report*, Dec. 1999, vol. 11.

Chaprter 13—Arthritis in African American Women
1. Wilcox, W.D., MD. "Abnormal Serum Uric Acid levels in Children" *Journal of Pediatrics*, v. 128, #6, June 1996.

Chapter 14—Eye Diseases in African American Women
1. Singh-Hayreh, Sohan, M.D., MS Ph.D., DSC, FRCS. "Retinol Vascular Disorders: Hypertensive Retinopathy" *Opthamology Clinics of North America*, Vol. 11, #4, Dec. 1998.

About The Author

VALIERE ALCENA, M.D., F.A.C.P. has had an amazing medical career. Highlights of his 14 page curriculum vitae include; an appointment as the Chief of General Medicine, St. Agnes Hospital, White Plains, NY; teaching positions such as Associate Clinical Professor of Medicine at the Albert Einstein College of Medicine, Teaching Attending Physician at the Montefiore Hospital, Adjunct Associate Professor, New York Medical College; and the Community Based Excellence in Teaching Award from the American College of Physicians, American Society of Internal Medicine. His writing achievements include being named Reviewer of Manuscripts for the Annals of Internal Medicine, Editor-In-Chief of the *Prestige Medical News*, authoring *The African American Health Book*, as well as numerous other books and articles in medical journals.

In his spare time, Dr. Alcena produces and hosts a television health talk show.